Instilling Ethics

Instilling Ethics

Norma Thompson,
Editor

BJ
101 2
. I67
2000
west

ROWMAN & LITTLEFIELD PUBLISHERS, INC.
Lanham • Boulder • New York • Oxford

ROWMAN & LITTLEFIELD PUBLISHERS, INC.

Published in the United States of America
by Rowman & Littlefield Publishers, Inc.
4720 Boston Way, Lanham, Maryland 20706
http://www.rowmanlittlefield.com

12 Hid's Copse Road
Cumnor Hill, Oxford OX2 9JJ, England

British Library Cataloguing in Publication Information Available

Library of Congress Cataloging-in-Publication Data

Instilling ethics / edited by Norma Thompson.
    p. cm
    Includes bibliographical references and index.
    ISBN 0-8476-9744-4 (alk. paper)—ISBN 0-8476-9745-2 (pbk. : alk. paper)
    1. Ethics. I. Thompson, Norma, 1959–

BJ1012 .I67 2000
170—dc21   99-056842

Printed in the United States of America

⊗™ The paper used in this publication meets the minimum requirements of American
National Standard for Information Sciences—Permanence of Paper for Printed Library
Materials, ANSI/NISO Z.39.48–1992.

Contents

Preface   vii

Acknowledgments   xv

Part One: Sources of Ethical Reflection

1   Aristotle and the Ethics of Natural Questions   3
Stephen G. Salkever

2   War, Peace, and Republican Virtue: Patriotism and the Neglected   17
Legacy of Cicero
Cary J. Nederman

3   Medieval Jewish and Islamic Themes: Ethics and Religion   31
and Philosophical Attitudes toward Ethics
Jeffrey Macy

4   In Defense of the City: Machiavelli's Bludgeoning   39
of the Classical and Christian Traditions
Vickie B. Sullivan

Part Two: Modernity and Problems of Ethical Reflection

5   Rousseau on the Sources of Ethics   63
Clifford Orwin

6   Without Foundation: A New View of Kant   85
Susan Neiman

7   History as Psychology/Morality as Pathology: 97
Nietzsche and the Ethical Tradition
Dwight David Allman

8   Deconstructing Darwin   119
Stephen R. L. Clark

9   Ontology and Ethical "Foundations" in Taylor   141
      Stephen K. White

Part Three: Instilling Ethics Today

10 Are We Living in an Ethical Age?   167
      Louis A. Ruprecht Jr.

11 Ethics Reform: A Study in Failure   179
      Glenn Harlan Reynolds

12 Architecture as Ethical Conduct   195
      Carroll William Westfall

13 The Reality of Information Objects   207
      Michael J. Fischer

14 Full Circle: The Inherent Tension in Ethics from Plato to Plato   215
      Stephanie A. Nelson

Afterword

15 The Importance of "Instilling Ethics"   223
      Walter Nicgorski

Index   229

About the Contributors   237

Preface

This accessible yet deeply scholarly book casts fresh light on a major preoccupation of our time, the confused and ambiguous subject of ethics. Fourteen noted scholars examine the sources, distortions, uses, and future of ethics. The book not only provides a wide variety in style, substance, and angle of view but also uniquely forms a coherent whole. Taken together, these fourteen chapters, with an afterword by a distinguished philosophical scholar, stand as a renewed definition and guide through the thicket of contemporary ethics.

We think about ethics as we do because of Aristotle's *Ethics* and *Politics*. Aristotle's core project, as set out by Stephen Salkever, is to develop a kind of practical rationality. This is not to try to achieve some theoretical certainty but to supply us with a set of questions and standards to use in examining our own characters and the regimes of government in which we act. Indeed, the aim of Aristotle is action rather than knowledge. In this sense we seek the "ignorance" of Socrates, which is really a kind of knowledge of the elusive character of the whole of life. This early chapter helps make clear that what we call *ethics* is grounded in centuries-old effort. Aristotle helps us recognize that discerning the right thing to do in a difficult situation may be very hard to do. Salkever highlights two Aristotelian themes: the absolute necessity of instilling ethical habits in the young, and then the developing of a way of inquiry that enables us to be critically aware of and, as far as possible, in control of our character. What is it that makes us what we are? It is the ability to think through and discuss options and then to act. Although we lack the solace of a foundationalist first premise from which to deduce ethical rules, we can achieve a foundation for ethical conduct in widely diverging contexts.

In a striking example, Salkever cites Aristotle's ethics in mounting a critique of the most widely respected, reputable, and accepted ethos of Athens: the values expressed in Pericles' Funeral Oration, undoubtedly the most praised and famed speech in ancient history. Those values, stated positively as the virtue of manliness in a life of great deeds crowned by honor, can be easily transformed into militarism.

This transformation of values into militarism was exemplified in Roman form. Constant warfare on behalf of the *patria* was the quintessence of republican virtue in Rome. In his chapter on Cicero, the lawyer-politician-philosopher who represents the pinnacle of classical republican experience, Cary Nederman points out that Cicero does *not* conceive of "love of country" in an essentially militaristic fashion. For Cicero, discussion is at the core of civic virtue. Through rational and linguistic capacities, people can govern themselves without recourse to violence: "Nature through reason reconciles man with man by means of speech." In place of militarism Cicero proposes the vexed concept of statesmanship. Nederman defines this in Ciceronian terms as work "for the welfare of the republic, where such welfare is understood in a philosophically informed manner."

The purpose of the Ciceronian republic was *not* to improve the characters of its members but to ensure their submission to wise governors. Jeffrey Macy takes on this theme from a different direction in his commentary on medieval and Islamic philosophers' attitudes on ethics. For the great mass of the population, ethics can be instilled only by the inculcation of habits conducive to a peaceful social order. Ethics for the multitude cannot therefore be true virtue; it is only a means to a desired political and social end.

For the few philosophers inclined and able to take up higher aims, ethics also is a means, Macy says, but a means toward human perfection. An ethical regimen serves to neutralize the passions so that one can concentrate on theoretical-rational virtue. For Maimonides, true human perfection is "acquisition of the rational virtues." Medieval and Islamic philosophers, Macy says, "found the essence of human perfection to be theoretical-rational contemplation, culminating in the attainment of knowledge of first principles based on the attainments of human reason." Fascinatingly, Macy asserts that religions, and the theologians who propound them, stand above and beyond ethics. The acts of suicide bombers seeking martyrdom in the name of God, and those of the sisters of mercy seeking universal salvation, have no need for ethics.

A dramatic turnabout comes with Machiavelli's bludgeoning of the classical and Christian traditions, the subject of Vickie Sullivan's examination. To Machiavelli, ancient Greek philosophers and medieval religious thinkers are contemptible, because their teachings "vitiate any attempt on the part of human beings to defend their homeland." For Machiavelli, what benefits the city (that is, the city-state of Renaissance Italy) is virtue; what harms it is vice. Such great works of the Western tradition as Plato's *Republic* and Augustine's *City of God* are anathema to politics and enfeebling to the body politic. Sullivan describes Machiavelli's works as a revolution in thought so far-reaching that is has profoundly affected politics and philosophy to our day. The state's first interest is the maintenance and acquisition of power, Machiavelli says. Foreign policy takes primacy, becoming high politics and dominating the low politics of domestic policy. The people, in their masses, have vast capacities to provide the means and manpower for the advancement of the state.

Machiavelli provides a powerful, and troubling, interpretation of a major theme of this book and of political philosophy itself. In stark contrast to Aristotle's praise of the *logos* of human beings—the faculty of speech informed by reason—which distinguishes humans from brutes, Machiavelli praises not *logos* but "tongue," or voice, which men share with animals. He gives no regard to the application of reason in political deliberations nor does he side with the people in their claim to rule; they are praiseworthy because they provide the bodies and brawn for the rulers. Leadership consists in extreme acts carried out for the preservation of rule. In the absence of religions or classical principles, the only guide for behavior is expediency. Any deed is justified in the name of the city's defense and glory.

The deeply troubling consequences of loss or rejection of the grounding of life in classic or religious conviction is the pervasive problem of life in the modern age, according to Susan Neiman, in her chapter, "Without Foundation: A New View of Kant." There is much talk of an "age without foundation," she says, but little serious and sustained discussion of it. This is true also of the common perception that Kant, as the principal philosopher of the Enlightenment, sought to put ethics on a firm foundation through his "categorical imperative." But, Neiman says, Kant argues that moral principles are *not* true. His categorical imperative was never intended to function automatically. To Kant, the "ought" has no meaning in nature, and indeterminacy is needed to maintain that freedom that is reason's fundamental characteristic. Every attempt to prove moral law to be true must end in failure. Ethical foundations are impossible.

Taking up, by way of Kant, the central theme of dialogue, Neiman says that reason's function is to derive meaning through its opposition to experience. Only statements of reason carry genuine necessity, and they do so through dialogue that examines cases (examples) of possible moral behavior. Kant's preoccupation with the question of moral education was heightened by his voracious reading of the huge, coming-of-age novel *Emile*, a profound link between the minds of Kant and Rousseau.

Yet if Kant has symbolized the Enlightenment for subsequent generations, Rousseau, Clifford Orwin says, was the founder of the counter-Enlightenment, articulating the discontent with modernity that has dogged it ever since. Rousseau repudiated ethics as the reasoned system envisaged by his predecessors, asserting that humans are not rational. Rousseau instead turned from moral reasoning to moral sentiments. Central to this is Rousseau's perception that education—indeed, all that was regarded as civilized learning in the arts, sciences, and humanities—has occluded the "natural" human being. In contrast to natural man, modern man is bourgeois, denatured, a "floating" creature neither independent nor integrated.

Orwin opens our eyes to Rousseau as the founder of the ethics of the outsider, the first to regard society as a "system" in the modern pejorative sense. And "as for so-called professional ethics," as popularly discussed today, Orwin says "Rousseau would reject it as a contradiction in terms." Rousseau held up a tarnished mirror to society and invited it to view itself from every unflattering angle. His greatest shortcoming, Orwin says, was his failure to foresee the advent of liberal democracy, but in exposing the liberalism he knew, he provides us with a much needed "reality check" on our own.

With the eclipse of reason and the emergence of feeling as the illuminator of life, we find ourselves in the realm of psychology. Dwight Allman's chapter on Nietzsche and the ethical tradition focuses on Nietzsche's insistence on the impossibility of taking up morality without being swept up in psychology. Modern man's attempt to ameliorate the temporal condition of man has produced a profound spiritual crisis. God is dead, done in by man himself, and in his place is a science that "eschews the question of meaning." For Nietzsche, Allman says, the idea of history as the conduit of reason has paralyzed consciousness and generated despair. The only path available, the only place for serious endeavor, is through psychology, which alone in a devastated time can seek out the soul as the distinctive ground of ethical life. Thus Nietzsche rejects all that has emerged from Descartes' *Cogito ergo sum*; reason gives no access to a world beyond the subjective confines of human consciousness. The Western tradition understood in this way has translated ethical thought into a matter of pathology. Moral thought is a record of resentment, of pathologies poisonously flowering from the experience of weakness. Nietzsche, says Allman, "leaves no possibility for an irreducibly spiritual dimension to existence." Allman offers hope only in the possibility that Nietzsche, and what by the end of the twentieth century has been made of him, may be the final expression of a self-consuming modern dynamic. If so, the possibility lies open for a "vigorous resuscitation" of the question of the soul in its traditional way, to go beyond "this all-too-Nietzschean moment."

Stephen Clark points to an immense fault line in currently accepted concepts of contemporary thought. A neo-Darwinian synthesis not only dominates the biological sciences today but also is accepted among leading political, economic, and social thinkers. It demands, Clark says in his "Deconstructing Darwin," that we believe every human action is driven by a struggle for existence and for a share, by proxy, in succeeding generations. The laws of justice and right that moralists preach are, therefore, bogus. Darwinism is the universal acid that leaves no fundamental belief uncorroded or, eventually, undissolved into nothingness. All our beliefs under this law of nature are dictated by "selfish genes" in our DNA and "selfish memes" transmitted in our cultural life through trackless channels. If this is correct, Clark says, the truth is not worth knowing. Yet some among today's most prominent "philosophers" (in quotes because they ostentatiously deny that title) declare both their belief in this all-enveloping Darwinian acid and their self-assured ability to serve as our guides for the most serious choices of societal and individual life.

This varied yet coherent exploration of ethics concludes on a positive note in Stephen White's finding that the dearth of ontological thought in contemporary moral and political theory may be giving way to a renewal of philosophy. White sees a need for fundamental conceptualizations *and* a need to recognize that they are contestable. Stressing the former, White says, produces "strong" ontologies; the latter, a "weak" ontology that recognizes that we live under postmetaphysical conditions. In Charles Taylor's work, White points to a set of existential universals in the form of inescapable questions, insights that fit the modern identity, and interpretations that are best for this "late modern" time. Taylor does not claim to have found metaphysical bedrock, White says. Instead, contemporary identity tends to cluster around one or more of three constellations: the original theistic commitment of the great religions; the objective reason of the Enlightenment project; and the Romanticism of individual creativity and invention, which is unapologetically anthropocentric. The dominant Western conversations admittedly have often been carried on with a falsely universalistic self-understanding, but that does not warrant the thoroughgoing relativism so prevalent today.

Taylor's inclination, White says, is toward the Romanticist constellation, which brings language to center stage. Through reconciliation, expression, and aesthetic sensibility, we gain access to nature and to our fellow creatures. "The moral or spiritual order of things must come to us indexed to a personal vision." White defends Taylor against those who charge him with conventional theism. Taylor is interesting, White says, because he delineates a theism no longer tied to strong ontological claims, for "no one can play strong ontological trump cards with any legitimacy." For Taylor, says White, "only a moral-political vision linked to the articulation of an external moral sense will provide the vivification of finitude and experience of humility necessary for generating an *ethos* in which transformative social projects will not produce monsters." Over all of this looms a threatening Nietzsche, whose vision is linked to such an external sense, but an amoral sense. Taylor, White claims, stands to the Nietzscheans as Taylor's antitheist critics stand to him. To White, the door remains open to the possibility of a successful, weak ontological competitor to Taylor's theism that affirms an external but amoral source.

Few would claim that we live in an ethical age, yet this, undoubtedly, is an Age of Ethics, as Louis Ruprecht points out in chapter 10. Today, not only legal and medical professions but virtually all fields have their committees on ethics. "Ethics centers" proliferate at major universities and service academies. Ethics investigators promulgate extensive regulations on ethics and relentlessly pursue ethical violators in local, state, and federal governmental offices. The intensity of the times has even produced its own profession, that of the ethicist, whose services are retained by businesses that wish not only to act ethically but also to avoid costly litigation on claims of unethical behavior.

Beyond all this has come a new category of ethical perplexity brought about by technological advances coinciding with revolutionary cultural shifts and legal transformations that have spawned a new range of ethical concerns on questions of birth, life, and death. Compelling as these issues are, a more fundamental ethical level is that of the citizen in a democratic society requiring decisions on innumerable issues of governance every day.

Throughout these chapters are signs of innovative efforts to take up these issues, as well as insightful, and helpful, warnings that far more will be required than a return to traditional ways. The complicated mechanisms of modernism have undermined the human condition in ways that cannot be simply shored up with old materials. New structural forms and methods must be developed.

Carrol William Westfall takes up such a project in his "Architecture as Ethical Conduct." He says that our buildings shape us far more than we realize and that a community without an informed involvement with its architectural environment submits itself to an uncertain determinism. The enshrined rubrics of modernism, Westfall says, are as follows: form follows function; form arises from materials; and each epoch has its own architecture. As precepts, all reject tradition. As evidence, Westfall points to what has become of Vitruvius's principles of commodity, firmness, and delight. For contemporary purposes, "commodity" means that the client decides, "firmness" is up to the engineer, and "delight" resides in the individual architect's personal vision. All of these have shattered architecture's connections with the civil activities it continuously works to mold. In response, Westfall reorders and restates the three criteria. What matters, he says, are answers to the questions "What do we see?" and "How do we build?" and "Why do we build?" First comes beauty, for beauty is to architecture, Westfall says, as truth is to the legal system; beauty is the form that ethics take in the buildings of a city. The Vitruvian tradition has been distorted by a modernity that has de-ethicized architecture. Pointing out that the correlation between the practice of architecture and the practice of citizenship has been understood since the Greeks, Westfall calls for an active public discourse on architecture as "a body of knowledge" available to expert and amateur alike.

Across the pages of this book are a variety of recognitions that significant gleanings from tradition were better understood by the Founders of the United States than they are today. Westfall notes that the mathematical proportions of the elements of architecture need to be proportions of *something*, as a column in a church. This traditional understanding made possible a distinctive American architecture in the early republic. Similarly, the works of Cicero, as proposed by Nederman, once were the staples of American education for statecraft. And key perceptions understood since the ancients continue to illuminate current issues, as evidenced by Salkever as he views multiculturalism, deliberative democracy, and liberal education through the Aristotelian lens.

A link between these profound philosophical questions and daily life today is forged by Glenn Harlan Reynolds in his chapter, "Ethics Reform: A Study in Failure," a lively yet troubling description of the Big Bang, the explosion onto the scene some two decades ago of an ethics industry. The decline of moral conviction and of education for character—and the cultural effects of Vietnam and Watergate—produced a proliferation of laws to enforce ethical behavior. The results have been counterproductive: public confusion about what is permitted, cynicism about the politicization of enforcement decisions, and stress caused by awareness that some regulation is being violated by someone at any given time. And, as Reynolds points out, "the moral heat associated with ethical violations has cooled as the volume of behavior encompassed by the ethical universe has grown."

As this introduction has noted, throughout the analyses set forth in this book runs a line of thinking emphasizing the critical role of speech, debate, discussion, and deliberation, of minds engaged intensively upon difficult subjects demanding decisive action.

This context adds a deep dimension to Michael Fischer's work on "The Reality of Information Objects." As human discourse increasingly takes place under the affect of the computer revolution, Fischer points out that our units of communication—digital data grouped into entities—are, as "information objects," diffuse, replicable, modifiable, inherently insecure, and, in many circumstances, virtually incoherent. Fischer goes through the new logic of the computer age to demonstrate how privacy of communication, a fundamental factor for many aspects of intellectual exchange, can never be attained because the complexities of cryptography ultimately will become subject to the very instabilities of the information objects that codes are created to protect, creating novel ethical dilemmas.

Stephanie Nelson's "Full Circle" focuses on perhaps the most consequential issue of our time: the question of individual thought as the critical element in ethics. If ethics depends on individual judgment, how can society form an overall sense of right and wrong? But if society dictates a comprehensive ethical code, individual responsibility is irrelevant and what it means to be human is lost. Nelson points to Plato's *Republic* as a warning that when the "reason" of the state encompasses all, there is nothing for the "reason" of the citizen to do. Yet if Plato poses the challenge, he also offers a way to respond. Citing David Grene's brilliant reading of the *Timaeus*, Nelson argues that there is no ethical vision without a cosmic vision; an ethics based on a vision of the *polis*, a rule-based external morality, needs to be addressed in tension with an ethics that is at once personal and innovative. Nelson's lucid formulations are applicable to propositions and conundrums throughout these chapters and so merit the culminating position in this book.

In the afterword, philosopher-scholar Walter Nicgorski reflects on the volume as a whole and its implications for education and the personal space needed to draw nearer to the truth.

Acknowledgments

This volume grows out of the Olmsted Symposium on Ethics sponsored by Yale University's Program in Ethics, Politics, and Economics in February 1998. As director of that program, Ian Shapiro first encouraged me to bring together this distinctive assemblage. I am grateful for the generous support of the Olmsted Fund as well as for the additional support provided by Yale's Kempf Fund. Special thanks go to all the people who worked with me to make the conference such a success, especially Steven Smith, Rogers Smith, Bruce Ackerman, Gaddis Smith, Vittorio Bufacci, Kelli Farnham, Jennifer Chang, and Patricia Nordeen. For research assistance and suggestions, I thank Susan and David Hennigan an' Colleen Shogan. Romayne Ponleithner, an extraordinary editor, was critical to t' achievement of this volume. And a final thanks to the special invited guests at conference, who prompted such a spirited and fruitful exchange of ideas: F Berkowitz, David Bromwich, Clare Geiman, Victor Gourevitch, David C Karsten Harries, John Hughes, and Barbara Koziak.

Part One

Sources of
Ethical Reflection

Part One

Sources of Ethical Reflection

Chapter One

Aristotle and the Ethics of Natural Questions

Stephen G. Salkever

Aristotle's *Nicomachean Ethics* and *Politics* together constitute a course in ethics and politics, a course intended to be included in the liberal education of young Greeks.[1] The aim of this course, he says in the first book of the *Ethics,* is action (*praxis*) rather than knowledge (*NE* 1, 1095a4–6); he adds in book 2 that the inquiry is undertaken not to acquire theoretical knowledge but in order to become good (*NE* 2, 1103b26–30). But what sort of a work is this? It doesn't correspond to any modern sense of what a philosophical work in ethics and politics looks like. It is not a systematic statement and resolution of central ethical and political issues (as in Thomas Hobbes or John Locke or John Stuart Mill), nor is it an articulation of one specially favored community's deepest insights about such things (as in G. W. F. Hegel or John Dewey or John Rawls). It is not an attempt to supply the theoretical foundation for a set of universally binding ethical principles or rules, nor is it a coolly disinterested *wertfrei* (value-free) account of the place of such principles or rules in human life. What then is the character, what is the rhetorical or pedagogical intent, of these theoretical discourses that aim at *praxis* rather than wisdom but that culminate (in book 10 of the *Nicomachean Ethics* and book 7 of the *Politics)* in the praise of impractical theorizing as the way of life most worthy of choice for human beings?

I believe the work embodies two pedagogical projects, the first more universal than the second, each with important implications for the other, and each of much interest to us today. The first is the attempt to establish the plausibility of a theoretical framework—built around a conception of nature (*phusis*) in general and of the nature of human beings in particular—for criticizing the most widely respected ethical and political beliefs or values (the *endoxa*, the highly esteemed or reputable or generally approved opinions[2]) of any human community. The second is a sustained and subtle critique[3] of the *endoxa* of one such community, the one in which Aristotle teaches, the Greek and especially the Athenian regime, preserved for us in Pericles' Funeral Oration in Thucydides. That community is based on an understanding of virtue as virility or manliness, deeply suspicious of tyranny, vulgarity, effeminacy, and philosophy, and drawn to a life of memorable deeds crowned by honor and greatness of soul. Aristotle's dual project continues the work of his teacher Plato and does so in an indirect and undogmatic style much closer to Plato's than the traditional distinction between Plato's dialogues and Aristotle's "treatises" allows.[4]

I want to say a word about how this works in the *Nicomachean Ethics* and the *Politics* and follow with some comments about how thinking along with Aristotle can help us make sense of three present-day aspirations: multiculturalism, deliberative democracy, and liberal education. My central contentions here are that, for Aristotle, the core project of prephilosophic moral education or character (*ethos*) development is not to instill duty or responsibility[5] (though these are necessary conditions for good character) but to develop a certain kind of practical rationality; and that the business of moral and political philosophy is not to anchor character in theoretical certainty[6] but to supply us with a set of questions and standards for examining our own characters and regimes and those of others.

Thus Aristotle's practical philosophy, like Plato's, is zetetic rather than dogmatic—a preparation for self-critical inquiry rather than a defense or explication of a principle. But this is not to say that it is merely skeptical or agnostic. Just as Socratic knowledge of ignorance is not simply ignorance but, in Leo Strauss's phrase,[7] knowledge of the elusive character of the whole, Aristotle's stress on questions itself reflects a definite sense of what human nature and human excellence or virtue is—a particular collection of tasks and abilities that, properly understood, suggests what I want to call natural questions rather than natural laws or principles. These natural questions have to do with the extent to which the customs and habits that form our characters promote the capacity for thinking and speaking in a distinctively and specifically human way, the hard-to-translate quality that Aristotle calls *prohairesis*—hard to translate because it combines two qualities, independence and reflectiveness, in a way that is unfamiliar to us, and not only to us but to Aristotle's contemporaries as well. *Prohairesis* is probably not a term taken from ordinary language,[8] but an artful combination of *hairesis*, choice, and *pro-* (before).

Thus Aristotle does not intend to puzzle or to encourage inquiry without advancing substantive positions of his own. Two Aristotelian propositions, both in book 6 of the *Nicomachean Ethics*, express his bedrock understanding of the good human life, of practical reason or *phronesis*, and of political science or philosophy. The first delineates the relationship between two intellectual virtues: "Political science (*politike*) and *phronesis* are the same *hexis* [capacity], but their being (*to einai*) is not the same" (1141b23–24). That is, in context, you cannot be fully one without also being the other—though political science is directed toward universals, and *phronesis* toward particular actions. For Aristotle, moral education and the development of *phronesis* call for the study of *politike*. *Politike* is not a sufficient condition for *phronesis*, but it comes close to being necessary.[9] To be good and to act well, we need as clear a sense as possible of who we are as human beings. To be sure, Aristotle's ethical and political theory culminates, in book 10 of the *Nicomachean Ethics* and book 7 of the *Politics*, *not* in a series of basic principles or natural laws, but in difficult and practically unresolved questions (that is, with respect to the actions we will undertake after considering them) about our relationship to beings superior to us, to Aristotle's gods.[10]

The second is Aristotle's teleological definition of humanity mentioned above, his account of what it is among all the things we do and suffer that makes us who we are, a definition that gives chief place to *prohairesis*, not merely "choice" or "intentional choice," and certainly not "free will," but the ability and the inclination to think through the options available to us and then to act on the basis of those deliberations. "*Prohairesis* is either understanding combined with desire or desire combined with thought; and what originates [movement] in this way is a human being (*anthropos*)" (*NE* 1139b4–5).[11] This *prohairesis* is the quality that makes a human being a human being, for better or worse: "It is by prohairesing (*toi prohairesthai*) that we are such as we are, and not by opining" (*NE* 1112a1–3).[12] Having a virtuous character is difficult, not because one needs a strong will or excellent genes to overcome pleasurable temptations but because discerning the right thing to do in a particular situation, finding the mean, in Aristotle's typical metaphor, is very hard to do (*NE* 1109a24–32).

To be sure, we also are shaped in a preliminary way by our inborn biological potential for character of a certain kind, and even more so by the habits we develop as children before we become capable of extensive deliberation (*NE* 1103b23–25). We become just and moderate, and so on, by performing just and moderate actions. Thus political people and others interested in character education and instilling ethics must pay careful attention to the habits we acquire as children, especially to the kinds of songs and stories children become accustomed to (*Politics* 8). But primarily we are individuated as human beings not by our habits, our actions, our desires, or our beliefs, but by the way we think.[13]

Aristotle's philosophical ethics is thus separate from, though continuous with, the instillation of ethics ordinarily understood. Both aim at forming better human beings, but in different ways. The latter habituates young people to respond in approved ways to emotions and circumstances; the former assumes such habituation and teaches a way of questioning and inquiry that lets us be critically aware of and, as far as possible, in control of our character.[14] Those questions have to do with the relationship between the habits and institutions we experience and a conception of natural problems and standards. It is not hard to state what Aristotle wants his audience, his students, to learn to do: We are to learn to treat ethical practices not simply as the *endoxa* they are, but as if they were criticizable solutions to problems posed by our inherited biological nature under various distinct circumstances, problems concerning how the prohairetic life can best be realized.

But teaching a way of questioning requires a different pedagogy from teaching a set of lawlike rules. For one thing, Aristotle's pedagogy in the *Nicomachean Ethics* and the *Politics* acknowledges the particular beliefs, the *endoxa*, that form the moral horizons of its audience—just as Plato's Socrates (or the Eleatic or Athenian Strangers) of the dialogues must speak to the particular situation of the souls of each of his interlocutors. Aristotle's lectures are of necessity (because of their relatively impersonal lecture format) less subtle in this respect than Plato's dialogues are, but it seems clear that he assumes a Periclean culture of the kind described above and adapts his speech accordingly. One of the key problems of reading Aristotle (or Plato) well now is to imagine how the texts might read if the audience and its habits were not, as we are not, shaped by the virilist *endoxa* of the classical *polis*—even if we assume, as I think we can, that Aristotle's conception of the structure of potentiality and actuality that distinguishes human nature is in general outline perfectly believable.[15]

The second pedagogical difference required by this philosophical ethics of natural questions is that it must be indirect. Aristotle, no more than Plato, thinks he can present a substantive morality that can supplant the *endoxa*. In Aristotle's terminology it is important that, as far as possible, "the phenomena" or the appearances of ethical and political philosophy, that is, the *endoxa*, be preserved by his analysis. Thus, to succeed, Aristotle must both preserve the prevailing ethics and call them into question before the bar of human nature, teleologically understood. If his hearers are simply confirmed in their commitment to the virtues of the *polis*, or if they decide to turn their backs on the *endoxa* entirely in favor of a new idea of law, Aristotle will have failed. His techniques for avoiding these extremes are well worth observing. They cannot be adequately described in a short space, but the following is a general picture of what I think happens in the *Nicomachean Ethics* and the *Politics*.

Aristotle begins the *Ethics* by problematizing human happiness (*eudaimonia*), by proposing an *aporia* (perplexity) about the best life he is unwilling to undo. The first book is doubly aporetic. Aristotle says that the content of the human life most worthy of choice is political praxis, yet he says this may be challenged by a philosophical life, which he mentions but immediately sets aside for later discussion. He further says that virtue is the constitutive condition of human flourishing. At the same time he says that we can never be sure of whether a life has been happy, because its quality depends not only on the actor but on fortune during his life and on the lives of friends and descendants after death. He then proposes, as a method for gaining clarity, a discussion of human nature and of the human soul centering on the place of habit and *prohairesis* in developing virtues. He then discusses particular virtues, beginning with manliness (*andreia*), seeming only to describe or catalogue them but at the same time indicating conceptual and practical instabilities in these virtues, something that becomes particularly clear in the case of greatness of soul, the way of life that single-mindedly pursues honor but despises those who give it.

The *Nicomachean Ethics* describes an ascent from less to more stable virtues or ways of life, starting with those which, from manliness to magnanimity, exist within the horizon of honor as the highest good. This is superseded, after a sort of new beginning, by a pair of virtues—justice and decency or equity (*epieikeia*) —that revolve around law (*nomos*) rather than honor. The description of these virtues is followed by an exploration of practical reason and friendship, virtues and activities that exist within the horizon supplied by the specifically human good, *prohairesis*, and not by honor or the *nomoi*. Last, after yet another new beginning, is the theoretical or contemplative life that aspires beyond humanity to the condition of continuously actualized thought thinking itself, to which Aristotle gives the name of *immortality* or *divinity*. Such naming is utterly opposed to the way gods are thought of by the *endoxa*—something Aristotle calls attention to in the *Metaphysics* but passes over in the *Ethics* and the *Politics*.[16]

But this theoretical life is not the end of the story. No way of life, no *answer* to the natural questions, is such an end, since it demands more of us than we can deliver. In this respect it is perhaps a mirror image of magnanimity, which demands more of others than it thinks they can possibly deliver, though they are surely superior to it. We cannot escape from the emotions and occasions that make up the rest of life; hence, we need to return to the political questions and proceed to the *Politics*. Here again there is a movement from the politics of ruling and virility to the politics of justice and a further move to a restatement of the theme of the contemplative life. The teaching is again that the happy or actualized human life is a prohairetic one (*Politics* 3, 1280a33–34), but also that what such a life involves cannot be stated theoretically or universally. What theory provides is a conviction of the need to ask the question and some of the resources for asking it in a variety of contexts. Philosophical ethics and politics thus provide a transcontextual foundation for ethics but not a foundationalist first premise from which ethical rules can be deduced. It is instead a guide to spotting[17] the key problems and possibilities that define situations to which we can make a variety of responses.

What then is the consequence of this Aristotelian foundation for the ethical life? How are we different for adopting it? General answers rarely get beyond the level of cliché, but I want to suggest that thinking through an Aristotelian perspective may help place in a new light three contemporary ethical problems: the question of deliberative democracy as a standard for political life, the question of the value of multiculturalism, and the question of the nature of liberal education. In a nutshell, I want to argue for these three insights into these problems. The deliberative model is effective only if it contains a better theoretical account of the kind of rationality it wants to promote; the value of multiculturalism depends on its capacity to stimulate the prohairetic life; contemporary liberal education lacks a sense of purpose that might be supplied by critical philosophizing on the Aristotelian model.

The contemporary proponents of deliberative democracy[18] are for the most part, though not entirely, the successors of the defenders of participatory democracy. Participatory democrats have held that democracy needed to be rescued from the subtly linked evils of liberal constitutionalism and capitalism—Marx's *Jewish Question* and a Beardian reading of Madison's *Federalist* 10 are key texts—and that idealized images of Athenian democracy and of modern revolutionary movements provided a sense of a workable alternative to the liberal democratic model. Participatory democracy loses its appeal as recognition dawns that democratic decisions can be both highly participatory and grossly unjust.

What might be required is something that sounds quite Aristotelian—a project of making democracy more deliberative by making democratic citizens more deliberative in our habits of judging. But this conclusion is resisted by proponents of deliberative democracy on grounds that the virtues of individual citizens are less crucial than the structure of society—democracy will be deliberative insofar as structural obstacles (such as social and economic inequalities or technological determinisms) to deliberation are removed. Unless, however, the proponents of deliberative democracy are willing to examine seriously the ways in which individuals can become better deliberators (including the institutions and practices within which this political education occurs)—by learning to listen to others as well as to speak and think with more understanding—the structural solutions seem abstract, merely theoretical, and narrowly academic, beside the point. But to consider the question of citizen education leaves these democrats vulnerable to a charge of "elitism" they are unwilling to risk. Why promote abilities that all citizens may not be able to possess equally? Why not simply trust the implicit rightness of purified democratic judgment? To consider that question adequately requires bracketing, in an Aristotelian way, our *endoxa* affirming that democracy and equality are ends in themselves—not dropping them, not replacing them with some "elitist" or oligarchic alternatives, but bracketing these action-guiding *endoxa* for the sake of returning to them with a clearer sense of how democracy might better promote prohairetic lives.

A caveat is in order here: I don't want to claim that Aristotle is an early adherent of deliberative democracy. Aristotle sees deliberation as a virtue of human individuals rather than a characteristic of a regime as a whole.[19] The neo-Kantian notion of a "public reason" linked with "moral" freedom, so crucial to the current deliberative model as expounded by Habermas and Rawls, has no Aristotelian equivalent, and Aristotle would probably deny that the most deliberative democracy is generally the best democracy,[20] although he might well agree that some form of democracy is the best possible regime today, as in his own time. On the other hand, I do not claim that an appreciation of Aristotle proves the worthlessness of deliberative democracy theory. We need metaphors and models that suit the times, and Aristotle cannot supply them for us. The deliberative model is in several respects a clear improvement over other prominent contemporary models of democracy. Besides calling attention in a promising way to the question of the quality of the speech and thought that inform contemporary politics, it suggests the need to reconsider ways of thought that are built into the increasingly global economy and our nearly worldwide commitment to modern technology. As an alternative to the contract model[21] and liberal "rights talk," the deliberative models gives us a way to avoid the communitarian's exaggeration of the idea of the reality of "culture," both as a motive power in the world and as a central human need. The deliberative model seems truer to the insight[22] that the modern world is a place of unstable and complex identities, replete with both opportunities and threats for those serious about living well. The model also allows us to question, without simply endorsing existing liberal democracy, the mysticizing valorization of "activism" and "the political" or "the people" or "democracy" all too typical of friends of the participatory model of democracy.[23] The model's strength lies in its valorization of a certain kind of reason in politics, but the critical power of the model is severely limited by the modelers' reluctance to take seriously the problem of giving a justificatory account of the conception of reason that defines their model.[24]

Concerning multiculturalism, it seems clear that the central question here should be about the extent to which reading works from various cultures can help us see what I've called the *natural questions*. Too often the debate is framed in terms of demands for our unquestioning allegiance to some *endoxa*—either those celebrating the Western tradition or others rejecting it. Both are beside the point. I've written about this with my colleague Michael Nylan; similar arguments have been made by K. Anthony Appiah and Martha Nussbaum.[25] From an Aristotelian point of view, the real danger is not multiculturalism as such but the commitment of many multiculturalists to an unthinking relativism or social constructionism that makes raising the natural questions as impossible as the narrowest monoculturalism.[26]

Perhaps a deeper issue is one that emerges from the multiculturalism debate, that of the danger, from the point of view of the prohairetic life, stemming from the almost universal habit of treating "culture" as an autonomous agentlike reality. David Bromwich is sharply critical of the belief he calls "culturalism": "the thesis that there is a universal human need to belong to a culture . . . to a self-conscious group with a known history." [27] Bromwich argues that this idea is either trivially true or illiberally false. The anthropologist Paul Rabinow says something quite similar about the harm that indiscriminate use of "culture" as an agent can do in his *Essays on the Anthropology of Reason*.[28] Part of the current appeal of culturalism is that the only alternative to it in the contemporary *endoxa* is the sort of individual rational agent strikingly rendered by Hobbes and sustained by modern economics and rational choice theory. I think that attending to Aristotle's manner of ethical and political philosophizing can give objections to "culturalism" a certain depth and power they might otherwise lack by anchoring them in a teleological though nonfoundationalist account of human nature that provides us with an alternative to neo-Kantian as well as neo-Hobbesian visions of human agency and reason.[29]

Students of ethics and politics have had much to say about liberal education in recent years. Generalizations have rarely avoided banality,[30] and the liveliest and most helpful discussions pay attention to the details of how this education is conducted in particular places. What a general consideration of the ethics of natural questions might add to this discussion is this: The study of moral and political philosophy can justify itself *only* as liberal education, as college teaching, and not as a separate scientific specialty or *Wissenschaft* within a research university. Aristotle's and Plato's writings on these subjects are undergraduate courses. We cannot simply repeat (or try to repeat) what Plato and Aristotle did without violating one of the central tenets of the ethics of natural questions—as the *endoxa* change, pedagogy must change as well. Our job is to find a way to achieve a similar effect through very different means.[31]

The first step in this direction is to oppose as strongly as we can the impetus to adopt *Wissenschaft* as a vocation. The second step would be to insist that our pedagogy not, as so often happens, accept sloppiness as a necessary consequence of rejecting professionalism or disciplinarity. The whole point of American liberal education as a distinctive enterprise is to develop a strong sense of how to distinguish natural questions from less important ones and to develop the skills and habits of mind to continue doing this after leaving college. It is an education in books, rather than in *the* book—and we should choose books on the basis of their ability to lead students to what we take to be the natural questions we face in our time.

What can be done? Students need to resist being flattered and also to resist the thought that what they need from their education is a set of useful skills or pre-professional knowledge. This isn't easy; it is hard to acknowledge that you need help in learning to read and write and think about natural questions. One well-spoken and successful Bryn Mawr student, who spoke at a Bryn Mawr faculty meeting about a newly instituted requirement that all students during their first two years take two seminars designed to evoke and address natural questions in the sense outlined here, expressed her doubts whether students need to be taught how to think about such questions at all. What we need from these required courses, she said, is instruction in writing skills—and in an ancillary way, experience in getting along well in our new environment. Students have enough questions, thank you very much; what they need now is answers. Let's leave the questions until the upper-level courses in the major, when we have acquired the discipline-specific tools for analyzing them and solving them.

However discouraging and typical this student response may be, the blame for failing to see the importance of raising natural questions does not rest with students. Not unlike the original listeners to Aristotle's lectures on ethics and politics, the students are just coming into adulthood and are therefore especially sensitive to what their society seems to expect of them. In our society, a highly competitive commercial republic, students are not unreasonable in being anxious about finding a good place in it. They are "careerists" because our "reputable opinion" about what matters most in life assigns a very high place to financial success. The problem is less with the students than with the *endoxa*. The responsibility for stressing the importance of education in the natural questions rests entirely with faculty and administrators: We should be the ones clamoring for it, because it is precisely the work of setting the *endoxa* in a critical context that justifies what we do. Too often, the prime obstacle is our own exaggerated careerism, our identification with a disciplinary specialty rather than with the project of liberal education itself.

Reforming the excessive disciplinarity of American higher education will be difficult, but not impossible. The difficulty lies in finding incentives for more administrators and faculty to seek changes than is now the case. It is not easy for administrators to formulate a rationale for new programs that are neither of evident practical value nor follow existing disciplinary lines. Part of the difficulty is our unwillingness to confront the possibility that education in the humanities cannot be organized in the same way as education in the natural sciences. Overcoming institutional inertia will require more than words, but the project of liberal education would be seriously advanced by what we do in terms of a language of an ethics of natural questions. Adopting this approach could even lead faculty to develop new standards for publication, standards that acknowledge that undergraduate education, both literally and more extensively, is the major purpose of scholarship and writing in the humanities, and that, therefore, papers submitted for publication and dissertations should be evaluated in part on the extent to which they contribute to enriching the discussion that goes on in undergraduate classrooms. Finding ways to articulate and measure the significance and quality of those discussions should be our first priority.[32]

NOTES

1. And perhaps also those not so young, if we believe Carnes Lord's attractive conjecture that the *Politics* was the basis for a program of adult education (in the introduction to Lord's translation of the *Politics* [Chicago: University of Chicago Press, 1984], 10–11). On the audience of the *Ethics* and *Politics*, historical and implied, see also Aristide Tessitore, *Reading Aristotle's* Ethics: *Virtue, Rhetoric, and Political Philosophy* (Albany: State University of New York Press, 1996); Richard Bodéüs and Thomas Smith, *Political Dimensions of Aristotle's* Ethics (Albany: State University of New York Press, 1993); Gordon Clark and T. V. Smith, *Readings in Ethics* (New York: F. S. Crofts, 1931). In this chapter the *Nicomachean Ethics* is cited in the text as *NE*.

2. "The *endoxa* are opinions about how things seem that are held by all or by the many or by the wise—that is, by all the wise, or by the many among them, or by the most notable (*gnorimoi*) and endoxic (*endoxoi*, most famous) of them." (*Topics* 100b21ff.) Aristotle's critical distance from the *endoxa*, like Plato's, is signaled by the fact that each avoids using words like *gnorimos* and *kalosk'agathos* as terms of genuine praise, preferring instead the less familiar *spoudaios* (serious) and *epieikes* (equitable, decent).

3. For discussion of the critical character of Aristotle's political writing, see Gerald Mara, "The Near Made Far Away," *Political Theory* 23 (1995): 280–303.

4. There are substantive differences between Plato and Aristotle, but they are not ethical and political ones. Leo Strauss sees a key difference in a letter to Alexandre Kojève:

"[T]he difference between Plato and Aristotle is that Aristotle believes that biology, as a mediation between knowledge of the inanimate and knowledge of man is available, or Aristotle believes in the availability of universal teleology, if not of the simplistic kind sketched in *Phaedo* 96." Leo Strauss, *On Tyranny*, eds. Victor Gourevitch and M. S. Roth (New York: Free Press, 1991), 279.

5. Unlike the Rousseau of the *Social Contract*.

6. Unlike Immanuel Kant.

7. Leo Strauss, *What Is Political Philosophy? And Other Studies* (Glencoe, Ill.: Free Press, 1959), 9–55.

8. The word is first used in several places by Plato and occasionally by Xenophon. Aristotle uses it more extensively and prominently than either Plato or Xenophon and explicitly distinguishes it from *hairesis* (choice).

9. Although experience is sometimes enough (*NE* 6, 1143b11–14).

10. But Aristotle's *politike* does tell us that human beings are far from the best, most fully actual, or switched-on beings in the *kosmos*, and that it would therefore be absurd to think that either *politike* or *phronesis* is the most excellent or serious (*spoudaiotate*) intellectual virtue.

11. The meaning of *prohairesis* is perhaps most revealingly indicated in the *Eudemian Ethics* (*EE* 2, 1227a3–5), where he speaks of it as more than the sum of wish plus belief: "As for *prohairesis*, it is neither simply wish nor simply opinion, but opinion and desire (*orexis*) when these follow as a conclusion of deliberation." For discussion, see Nancy Sherman, *The Fabric of Character: Aristotle's Theory of Virtue* (Oxford: Clarendon Press, 1989), 67.

12. Terence Irwin's translation of this passage is: "It is our decisions to do what is good or bad, not our beliefs, that make the characters we have." *Nicomachean Ethics* (Indianapolis: Hackett, 1985), 61.

13. For Aristotle, the virtuous person is a self-lover who possesses a certain kind of integrity: "The *spoudaios* [serious man] is in agreement with himself, and desires the same things according to his whole *psuche*. . . . He wishes himself to live and to be preserved, especially that by which he thinks (*phronei*). For being is good to the *spoudaios*, and each person wishes good things for himself" (*NE* 9, 1166a13–20). That is to say, people are identical with their practical reason, their *phronesis*.

14. The nearest Platonic analogue to this Aristotelian distinction is the two kinds of moral education described by the Eleatic Stranger in the *Sophist* (229e–31b): The paternal way of direct exhortation and admonition and the Socratic way of the practitioners of the "well-born" type of the sophistic art, who take pupils who think they know and through *elenchos* perform a sort of *katharsis*, making their student-patients dissatisfied with themselves rather than with others.

15. At any rate, considerably more plausible than Hegel's History or Kant's Reason. See Iris Murdoch, *The Sovereignty of Good* (London: Ark Paperbacks, 1970, 1985), 47: "Kant believed in Reason and Hegel believed in History, and for both this was a form of a belief in an external reality. Modern thinkers who believe in neither, but who remain within the tradition, are left with a denuded self whose only virtues are freedom, or at best sincerity, or, in the case of the British philosophers, an everyday reasonableness."

16. *Metaphysics* 12, 1074b.

17. "Spotting" is Richard Sorabji's helpful suggestion about how best to translate the verb *noein*, an activity Aristotle distinguishes from deductive reasoning and uses to characterize both practical reason, whose horizon is the human good, and theoretical wisdom,

whose horizon is the good of the most fully actual of all the beings. See Richard Sorabji, *Animal Minds and Human Morals: The Origins of the Western Debate* (Ithaca: Cornell University Press, 1993).

18. I am thinking here of the remarkable convergence around the notion of deliberative democracy that now includes such past critics as Jurgen Habermas and Michael Sandel, as well as staunch liberal theorists such as John Rawls. For a good range of perspectives on the model, see the essays in *Democracy and Difference: Contesting the Boundaries of the Political*, ed. Seyla Benhabib (Princeton: Princeton University Press, 1996).

19. But see Susan Bickford's excellent discussion of the way Aristotle's *Rhetoric* provides an outline for thinking about deliberation as a public practice in ways that go beyond the modern deliberative model in *The Dissonance of Democracy: Listening, Conflict, and Citizenship* (Ithaca: Cornell University Press, 1996), 41–53.

20. In *Politics* 2, 1268b–69a, in his discussion of Hippodamus the great innovator, Aristotle argues that laws, traditions, and habits should often be treated as more authoritative than reason. Moreover, the best democracy, according to *Politics* 6, 1318b, is one in which the *demos* votes for officials and audits their conduct, as well as judging in the law courts, but does not always rule directly by deliberation. Similarly, he praises farming democracies because the *demos* composed of farmers often prefers to let the old laws stand. Much deliberation over many topics by many people is not the mark of the healthiest Aristotelian democracy.

21. For an interesting argument that the deliberative model provides a better guide to practice than the contract model in one particular case, see Simone Chambers, "Contract or Conversation? Theoretical Lessons from the Canadian Constitutional Crisis," *Politics & Society* 26 (March 1998): 143–72.

22. I'm thinking here primarily of Appiah's critique ("The Multiculturalist Misunderstanding," *New York Review of Books*, 9 October 1997) of Charles Taylor's communitarianism and of varieties of multiculturalism that are unreasonable because they are identity constraining.

23. Interestingly, one unique feature of the modern world that deliberative democracy seems wholly unable to grasp is the rise in the importance of religion in people's lives in the last half of the twentieth century. Neither Rawls nor Habermas is of much help in sorting through the complex relation between religions on the one hand and the deliberative ideal on the other. This deficiency might flow from the "neo" in their neo-Kantianism.

24. One excellent study that raises these questions in a fascinating political context is Jeffrey Abramson's *We, the Jury: The Jury System and the Ideal of Democracy* (New York: Basic Books, 1994). Abramson considers the history of the jury and current proposals for jury reform in America (dealing with the unanimity requirement and with the representative jury, among other matters) in the light of a quite Aristotelian idea of deliberation.

25. Stephen G. Salkever and Michael Nylan, "Comparative Political Philosophy and Liberal Education, 'Looking for Friends in History,'" *PS: Political Science and Politics* 27 (1994): 238–47; K. Anthony Appiah, "The Multiculturalist Misunderstanding," *New York Review of Books*, 9 October 1997, 30–36; Martha Nussbaum, *Cultivating Humanity: A Classical Defense of Reform in Liberal Education* (Cambridge: Harvard University Press, 1997).

26. For defenses of a version of multiculturalism from a natural questions perspective (though the authors do not identify themselves in this way), see the essays by Anne Norton and Lorraine Pangle in *Multiculturalism and American Democracy*, eds. A. Melzer, J. Weinberger, and R. Zinman (Lawrence: University Press of Kansas, 1998).

27. David Bromwich, "Culturalism, the Euthanasia of Liberalism," *Dissent* 42 (Winter 1995): 89–102, followed by defensive responses from Charles Taylor and Michael Walzer. For a similar critique of what Bromwich calls "culturalism," see George Kateb, *The Inner Ocean* (Ithaca: Cornell University Press, 1992), 36–56.

28. Paul Rabinow, *Essays on the Anthropology of Reason* (Princeton: Princeton University Press, 1996).

29. This account is nicely elaborated in Nussbaum's discussion of what she calls Aristotle's "thick but vague conception of the good." "Aristotelian Social Democracy," in *Liberalism and the Good*, eds. R. Bruce Douglass, Gerald Mara, and Henry Richardson (New York: Routledge, 1990), 203–52.

30. Anything written by Eva Brann is, in my view, an exception to this general rule. She explores the history and develops a justification of liberal education in *Paradoxes of Education in a Republic* (Chicago: University of Chicago Press, 1979); defends the Great Books approach in "The Canon Defended," *Philosophy and Literature* 17 (1993): 193–218; and criticizes Allan Bloom's views on American liberal education in "The Spirit Lives in the Sticks," in *Essays on* The Closing of the American Mind, ed. Robert L. Stone (Chicago: Chicago Review Press, 1989), 181–90.

31. I think that Leo Strauss provides a wonderful beginning for anyone who wants to follow this path: "Liberal education consists in listening to the conversation among the greatest minds. But here we are confronted with the overwhelming difficulty that this conversation does not take place without our help—that in fact we must bring about that conversation. The greatest minds utter monologues. We must transform their monologues into a dialogue, their 'side by side' into a 'together.' . . . We must then do something which the greatest minds were unable to do. Let us face this difficulty—a difficulty so great that it seems to condemn liberal education as an absurdity. Since the greatest minds contradict one another regarding the most important matters, they compel us to judge of their monologues; we cannot take on trust what any one of them says. On the other hand, we cannot but notice that we are not competent to be judges. . . . Each of us here is compelled to find his bearings by his own powers, however defective they may be." "What Is Liberal Education?" in Leo Strauss, *Liberalism Ancient and Modern* (New York: Basic Books, 1968), 7–8. Timothy Fuller presents a good discussion of Strauss on education in "Reflections on Leo Strauss and American Education," in *Hannah Arendt and Leo Strauss*, ed. Peter Kielmansegg (Cambridge: Cambridge University Press, 1995), 61–80.

32. A good place to start is Ruth Grant, "The Ethics of Talk: Classroom Conversation and Democratic Politics," *Teachers College Record* 97 (1996): 470–82.

WORKS CITED

Translations from Aristotle are my own, guided by Irwin's *Nicomachean Ethics* and Lord's *Politics*.

Abramson, Jeffrey. *We, the Jury: The Jury System and the Ideal of Democracy*. New York: Basic Books, 1994.

Appiah, K. Anthony. "The Multicultural Misunderstanding." *New York Review of Books,* vol. 44, no. 15 (9 October 1997): 30–36.

Appiah, K. Anthony. "Identity, Authenticity, Survival: Multicultural Societies and Social Reproduction." In *Multiculturalism: Examining the Politics of Recognition*, ed. Amy Gutmann. Princeton: Princeton University Press, 1994. Pp. 149–63.

Benhabib, Seyla, ed. *Democracy and Difference: Contesting the Boundaries of the Political*. Princeton: Princeton University Press, 1996.

Bickford, Susan. *The Dissonance of Democracy: Listening, Conflict, and Citizenship*. Ithaca: Cornell University Press, 1996.

Bodéüs, Richard, and Thomas Smith. *The Political Dimensions of Aristotle's "Ethics"*, tr. Jan Edward Garrett. Albany: State University of New York Press, 1993.

Brann, Eva. *Paradoxes of Education in a Republic*. Chicago: University of Chicago Press, 1979.

Brann, Eva. "The Spirit Lives in the Sticks." In *Essays on* The Closing of the American Mind, ed. Robert L. Stone. Chicago: Chicago Review Press, 1989. Pp. 181–90.

Brann, Eva. "The Canon Defended." *Philosophy and Literature* 17 (1993): 193–218.

Bromwich, David. "Culturalism, the Euthanasia of Liberalism." *Dissent* 42 (Winter 1995): 89–102.

Chambers, Simone. "Contract or Conversation? Theoretical Lessons from the Canadian Constitutional Crisis." *Politics & Society* 26 (March 1998): 143–72.

Fuller, Timothy. "Reflections on Leo Strauss and American Education." In *Hannah Arendt and Leo Strauss*, ed. Peter Kielmansegg et al. Cambridge: Cambridge University Press, 1995. Pp. 61–80.

Grant, Ruth W. "The Ethics of Talk: Classroom Conversation and Democratic Politics." *Teachers College Record* 97 (1996): 470–82.

Irwin, Terence, trans. *Aristotle: Nicomachean Ethics*. Indianapolis: Hackett, 1985.

Kateb, George. *The Inner Ocean: Individualism and Democratic Culture*. Ithaca: Cornell University Press, 1992.

Lord, Carnes, trans. *The Politics of Aristotle*. Chicago: University of Chicago Press, 1984.

Mara, Gerald. "The Near Made Far Away: The Role of Cultural Criticism in Aristotle's Political Theory." *Political Theory* 23 (1995): 280–303.

Melzer, Arthur, Jerry Weinberger, and Richard Zinman, eds. *Multiculturalism and American Democracy*. Lawrence: University Press of Kansas, 1998.

Murdoch, Iris. *The Sovereignty of Good*. London: Ark Paperbacks, [1970] 1985.

Nicgorski, Walter. "Leo Strauss and Liberal Education." *Interpretation* 13 (1985): 233–50.

Nussbaum, Martha. *Cultivating Humanity: A Classical Defense of Reform in Liberal Education*. Cambridge: Harvard University Press, 1997.

Nussbaum, Martha. "Aristotelian Social Democracy." In *Liberalism and the Good*, ed. R. Bruce Douglass, Gerald Mara, and Henry Richardson. New York: Routledge, 1990. Pp. 203–52.

O'Connor, David K. "The Aetiology of Justice." In *Essays on the Foundations of Aristotelian Political Science*, ed. Carnes Lord and David K. O'Connor. Berkeley: University of California Press, 1991. Pp. 136–64.

Rabinow, Paul. *Essays on the Anthropology of Reason*. Princeton: Princeton University Press, 1996.

Salkever, Stephen G., and Michael Nylan. "Comparative Political Philosophy and Liberal Education: 'Looking for Friends in History.'" *PS: Political Science and Politics* 27 (1994): 238–47.

Sherman, Nancy. *The Fabric of Character: Aristotle's Theory of Virtue*. Oxford: Clarendon Press, 1989.

Smith, Thomas G. "The Audience of the *Nicomachean Ethics*." *Journal of Politics* (forthcoming).

Sorabji, Richard. *Animal Minds and Human Morals: The Origins of the Western Debate*. Ithaca: Cornell University Press, 1993.

Strauss, Leo. Letter to Alexandre Kojève, 28 May 1957. In *Leo Strauss on Tyranny*, rev. ed., ed. Victor Gourevitch and Michael S. Roth. New York: Free Press, 1991. Pp. 276–80.

Strauss, Leo. "What Is Liberal Education?" In *Liberalism Ancient and Modern*. New York: Basic Books, 1968. Pp. 3–8.

Strauss, Leo. "What Is Political Philosophy?" In *What Is Political Philosophy? And Other Studies*. Glencoe, Ill.: Free Press, 1959. Pp. 9–55.

Tessitore, Aristide. *Reading Aristotle's "Ethics": Virtue, Rhetoric, and Political Philosophy*. Albany: State University of New York Press, 1996.

Turner, Stephen P. *The Social Theory of Practices: Tradition, Tacit Knowledge and Presuppositions*. Chicago: University of Chicago Press, 1994.

Chapter Two

War, Peace, and Republican Virtue: Patriotism and the Neglected Legacy of Cicero

Cary J. Nederman

One of the lingering fascinations among recent critics of liberalism has been the historical tradition of civic republicanism. Political and intellectual historians, such as John Pocock and Gordon Wood, no less than social and moral philosophers, such as Charles Taylor and Alasdair MacIntyre, have turned to classical and early modern versions of the republican thesis (primarily represented by Aristotle and Niccolò Machiavelli) to bolster their contention that liberal theory and practice yield an impoverished and distorted conception of human community and public life.[1] Broadly speaking, republicanism is viewed as a remedy for liberalism's perceived inability to redress the absence of moral cohesion, public-spiritedness, and participatory practice so apparent in current democratic societies.

The reliance upon republican thought has by no means gone unchallenged by proponents of liberalism. Don Herzog, for instance, is troubled by the nature of the historical precedents that latter-day republicans propound. Not only has contemporary republicanism "advanced a remarkably hazy doctrine," he contends, but its quest to identify "shared commitments" seems likely to demand "religious and political indoctrination" on a scale inappropriate to modern democratic society and perhaps uncomfortable even to a devoted communitarian.[2] In a similar vein, Amy Gutmann observes that republicans have been lax in defending a "communitarian politics directly," and they seem to embrace the view that "when members of a society have settled roots and established traditions, they will tolerate the speech, religion, sexual, and associational preferences of minorities," historical precedent to the contrary.[3] To these liberals, in sum, the contemporary variant of the republican thesis appears naive at best, culturally conservative (perhaps authoritarian) at worst.

In an effort to elucidate their doctrine in the face of such liberal misgivings, republicans have sought to provide concrete evidence of the resonance of public virtue in political life. This had led, almost inexorably, to the identification of the "virtue" of patriotism as a paradigm of how republican values continue to be realized today. The persistence of "virtuous" patriotism, according to MacIntyre, signals the personal attachments that arise from communal identities and public narratives, particular "ways of life."

> Detached from my community, I will be apt to lose my hold upon all genuine standards of judgment. . . . A central contention of the morality of patriotism is that I will obliterate and lose a central dimension of the moral life if I do not understand the enacted narrative of my own individual life as embedded in the history of my country.[4]

Patriotism derives from a person's well-defined sense of self mediated through his or her community. As a consequence, one is prepared to sacrifice one's immediate self-interest at times for the good of the society. As Taylor remarks, "The bond of solidarity with my compatriots in a functioning republic is based on a sense of shared fate, where the sharing itself is of value."[5] Patriotism reflects "strong citizen identification around a sense of common good."[6] One's particular patriotic ties to one's fellow citizens thus pick out a good that is separate and distinct from such atomistic goods as rights, personal freedom, and privacy, which are promoted by liberalism. Patriotism points toward the existence, in Taylor's sense, of a holistic good.[7]

THE MILITARISTIC PARADIGM

For both MacIntyre and Taylor, the paradigmatic example of the republican virtue of patriotism is warfare, the readiness of citizens to fight and die for their country. MacIntyre asserts that

> [P]atriotism entails a willingness to go to war on one's community's behalf. . . . My allegiance to the community and what it requires of me—even to the point of requiring me to die to sustain its life—could not meaningfully be contrasted with or contraposed to what morality required of me.[8]

Likewise, Taylor upholds "national defense" as "the foremost example" of the republican thesis in practice: "A republican regime will generally call on its citizens to fight for their own freedom. . . . People who live in and cherish a free regime will be motivated to fight for themselves."[9] The sacrifices entailed by citizen participation in military affairs (either directly, by fighting, or indirectly, by surrendering one's property or personal freedom) demonstrate a depth of commitment to communal associations that cannot be adequately explained in liberal terms (such as enlightened self-interest). This connection between warfare and civic self-awareness is by no means new. Hegel long ago pointed out that "war is the state of affairs which deals in earnest with the vanity of temporal goods and concerns," since through it citizens acknowledge the centrality of shared communal life ("the substance of the state") in comparison with their mere personal interests.[10]

To identify warfare as the highest expression of patriotism and the quintessence of republican virtue—what I shall call the "militaristic paradigm"—is surely troubling on several counts. Most obviously, it upholds war as not just a necessity, but even a worthy goal, for every "virtuous" nation. Indeed, republican militarism implicitly attributes the greatest virtue to those countries that most often and efficiently mobilize their citizens in the pursuit of armed conflict. (Certainly, this is part of the logic of Machiavelli's advocacy of republicanism: republics are better equipped than other sorts of regimes for the imperialist conquest of new territories.[11]) Since "national defense" is such an elastic concept—as anyone who has studied recent global events must admit—it seems evident that the militaristic paradigm can easily license and glorify acts of the most brazen aggression. Republican militarism rests, moreover, on the assumption of a permanent dichotomy: in order for there to be an "us," there must be a "them," an "other" who represents a direct threat to "our" way of life. Even in circumstances where actual warfare rarely occurs, the militaristic paradigm promotes a cold war mentality: "we" must be in a state of constant military preparedness, lest "they" attack us and catch us unawares.

It is certainly true that, historically speaking, many of the precedents of republican thought as well as practice are imbued with such militaristic overtones—a fact that helps to explain the lingering militarism among the current crop of republicans. Is the link between warfare and republican patriotism a necessary one? I wish to propose a negative answer by examining a different historical precedent, offered by the Roman philosopher and politician Marcus Tullius Cicero. Without question, Cicero deserves to be counted among the most important classical republican theorists. Yet his writings have been strangely neglected in the recent revival of interest in republicanism.[12] For Cicero, the pursuit of peace, rather than war, and statesmanship, rather than military command, are the prime tokens of patriotism and the exemplars of republican virtue. I shall argue that Cicero affords us an alternative plan for constructing republicanism, a blueprint that avoids many of the pitfalls of the militaristic paradigm.

PRINCIPLES OF REPUBLICAN PATRIOTISM

It is perhaps not too great an exaggeration to say that Cicero was the most influential republican thinker of the ancient world. Although many other classical authors contributed significantly to the understanding of the theory and practice of the republic—Polybius, Sallust, and Livy come immediately to mind—Cicero enjoyed the widest audience and most loyal following, both in antiquity and in later times. Drawing on Hellenic and Hellenistic philosophies, as well as his knowledge of Roman history and his personal experiences with the practical requirements of republican rule, Cicero in many ways represented the pinnacle of classical republican experience.[13]

Cicero clearly framed his devotion to the Roman Republic in patriotic terms. As he enumerates the various forms of human association in *De officiis*, moving from a general bond of common humanity to intimate relations among kin and friends, he reserves priority for the republic. "There is no social relation," he says, "more close, none more dear than that which links each one of us with our republic." Cicero reasons that, in comparison with other human attachments, "a country [*patria*] embraces all of the affections of all of us. What good man would hesitate to confront death for her, if it would render her a service?"[14] In the ordering of moral duties, therefore, "country is foremost" (along with our parents), since "we are obliged to them for the greatest benefits."[15] Cicero insists that this demands sacrificing "not only money, but also life for the country"; indeed, the true patriot must be prepared to surrender even "personal glory and honor" to secure the advantage of the nation.[16] Similar expressions of patriotic fervor are to be found throughout Cicero's writings. In *De legibus*, for instance, he proclaims that "that one [*patria*] must stand first in our affection in which the name of 'republic' signifies the common citizenship; for her it is our duty to die, to give ourselves entirely, to place upon her altar and almost consecrate all that we have."[17] It is hardly an exaggeration to observe that Cicero's own political career was a testament to the depth of his patriotic belief in the Roman way of life.

Although he regards the citizen's readiness to sacrifice his life as a feature of patriotism, Cicero does not conceive of "love of country" in an essentially militaristic fashion. Quite to the contrary, *De officiis* denounces the view, held by "most people," that "the achievements of war are more important than those of peace."[18] In Cicero's view, the glorification of armed conflict amounts to a denigration of characteristically human qualities in favor of a bestial nature: "There are two ways of settling a dispute: the one, by discussion, the other, by force; and since the former is proper to human beings, the latter to the brute, we may resort to force only when discussion is not possible."[19] In other words, warfare is inconsistent with distinctively human nature; it reflects the animalistic side of our existence. Hence, peace is the true natural condition of humanity, according to Cicero: if we draw upon our rational and linguistic capacities—those characteristics with which we are born and which we share with the gods[20]—we will be able to settle all disputes and govern ourselves without recourse to violence. "The only rationale for going to war, therefore, is that we may live in peace [*pax*] uninjured," he remarks.[21] Cicero believes that Rome, at least as long as it was under "temperate" republican rule, followed policies consonant with this principle: armed conflict was pursued only as a last resort, when negotiations had proven ineffective at settling disputes, and vanquished enemies were not generally enslaved or slaughtered but were (like Cicero's own ancestors) extended Roman citizenship and permitted to exercise political rights within the republic.[22] It is only by adopting such policies, Cicero believes, that the goal of peace may be achieved.

Cicero's condemnation of violence and praise for peace are, therefore, clearly rooted in his fundamental philosophical precepts. The Ciceronian position depends upon a conception of human nature conceived in terms of the native powers of reason and speech: "Nature through reason reconciles man with man by means of speech."[23] The primacy accorded to reason and speech reflects the fact that these powers stimulate "the processes of teaching and learning, of communicating, discussing and reasoning [that] associate men together and unite them into a sort of natural fraternity."[24]

In Cicero's view, intellect and language may be regarded as nature's method of endowing the human species with the capacity it needs to survive,[25] for from social contact emerges the full range of political and economic relationships through which men sustain and support themselves:

> Without the association of men, cities could not have been built or peopled. In consequence of city life, laws and customs were established, and then came the equitable distribution of private rights and a definite social system. Upon these institutions follows a more humane spirit and consideration for others, with the result that life was better supplied with all it requires, and by giving and receiving, by mutual exchange of commodities and conveniences, we succeed in meeting all our wants.[26]

In effect, the result of natural human sociability is the preservation and protection of the species. The powers of speech and reason alone render possible all the advantages of political and economic association. Yet it is not strictly to satisfy their physical needs, but because of their native linguistic and rational faculties, that human beings seek out fellowship with one another and congregate into communities.

The rational and linguistic features of human nature thus explain the origins of social organization. Cicero postulates people in a primordial condition where they lead a scattered, brutish existence devoid of intellect, religion, family, and law.[27] But these primitive creatures also harbor the powers of speech and reason that naturally impel them to be sociable.[28] Speech, in particular, is crucial to human association, insofar as "it does not seem possible that a mute and voiceless wisdom could have turned human beings suddenly from their habits and introduced them to different patterns of life."[29] The realization of humanity's social sentiments required, however, the guidance of a wise and eloquent man, by whose instruction others discovered and improved their own rational and discursive capabilities. Through the persuasion of this especially skilled individual,[30] his fellow creatures exchanged their solitary existence for a social one. At his behest, they learned useful and honorable occupations, assembled into cities, obeyed voluntarily the commands of others, and observed law; in sum, "he transformed them from wild savages into a gentle and kind folk."[31] All of these developments Cicero emphatically premises on the natural ability of speech coupled with reason: not merely does rational discourse separate man from lesser animals, but it renders possible the mutual understanding through which the sacrifices and burdens of human association may be explained and justified. In the absence of reason combined with eloquence, none of the blessings of social and political community could be acquired.

It is worthy of note that violence and force play no role in the process of social formation depicted by Cicero—indeed, coercion seems antithetical to his account. Political order rests on the rational agreement of the masses to the eloquent persuasion of their leaders, not on intimidation and threats of injury. Otherwise, no social order could be just, since justice itself requires for Cicero the absence of harm.[32] Cicero underscores the incompatibility of violence and mature human civilization in *Pro Sestio*. He begins by repeating the familiar formula of social origination:

> There was a period of evolution . . . when man led a solitary and nomadic existence, and his possessions were what he could grasp for himself by brute force, murder, and violence, and keep if he was able. It was due entirely to some early men of genius and wisdom, who realized the extent of humanity's capacity to learn, that these scattered creatures were persuaded to congregate and were thereby brought from a state of savagery to the rule of justice and civilization.[33]

Having described the transformation of human existence from disorder to order—the process of the creation of republican rule—Cicero concludes, "Now the chief distinguishing feature between that early crude existence and this later civilized life that I have described lies in the difference between the rule of law and that of force. If you will not have the one, you must have the other."[34] When people live according to law and respect the determinations of courts and magistrates, they are living in a manner most consistent with true human nature. When they live in a violent manner, beyond and outside the law, they are in effect living not as human beings but as beasts, in denial of their capacities for reason and speech, as well as of all the benefits of peaceful community that flow therefrom.

In sum, the use of physical force may on occasion remain a necessity for civilized human beings, but it can never really be a virtue, according to Cicero. The successful prosecution of war does not confer any special glory upon the republic if the result is something less than the restoration of peace and the advancement of civilized order. Hence, patriotism cannot find its fullest and highest expression in militarism, since violence stands starkly opposed to the foundations of the republic derived from human nature itself.[35] If we realize most completely our natural humanity when we demur from physical force, then virtue itself (which Cicero defines as "reason perfected, which is certainly in accord with nature"[36]) may never be said to partake of that which is unnatural.

STATESMANSHIP, COURAGE, AND *OTIUM*

If Cicero utterly rejects the militaristic paradigm for patriotism, in what does republican virtue consist for him? How does one's love of country find its fulfillment? The answer seems to lie in the realm of public affairs, through the exercise of statesmanship. Admittedly, Cicero's concept of the statesman is vexed and has formed a subject of wide scholarly dispute.[37] At times, the Ciceronian statesman appears to be the magistrate or officeholder, at other times the orator, and in still other contexts the public-spirited citizen. Regardless of whom Cicero may have had in mind, statesmanship clearly denotes for him a patriotic duty to set aside one's personal safety and comfort to perform what is required for the welfare of the republic, where such welfare is understood in a philosophically informed manner. Thus, the true statesman must be entirely devoid of personal ambition and completely courageous in the face of opposition.

Cicero makes it evident in *De officiis* that he regards the life of such a statesman to be superior to that of either philosophical detachment from public affairs or military command. He admits that retirement from politics with the leisure to contemplate the great questions of philosophy has its attractions, especially in light of the dangers and corruption of political life. Nonetheless, if the statesman conducts himself with a philosophical bearing and genuinely applies himself to the common benefit of the republic, his station is loftier and more worthwhile than that of the philosopher.[38]

By comparison, Cicero has no qualms about the precedence of statesmanship over military affairs. He suspects that those who are inclined toward martial arts have a propensity to disturb the peace by finding excuses to engage in armed conflict. This contributes only to their own glory but does little or nothing for the republic even when they are successful. "If we wish to judge truly," Cicero remarks, "there have been many civic achievements greater and more famous than achievements of war."[39] He compares favorably the numerous accomplishments of great Greek and Roman statesmen with the victories of their military counterparts: Solon with Themistocles, Lycurgus with Lysander and Pausanius, Publius Nasica with Scipio Africanus, and so on.[40] He concludes that the work of statesmen makes possible the victories of generals, both by creating institutions that encourage self-sacrificing civic virtue and by providing the domestic assistance and counsel that support the legions in the field.

Cicero somewhat immodestly cites his own suppression of Catiline's conspiracy while consul in 63 B.C.E. as a salient example of how statesmanship alone, with no army to support it, conquered illegal violence against the republic.

> Did not some yield to the toga, when I was at the helm of the state? Never was the republic in more serious peril, and never was there greater repose [*otium*]. Thus as the result of my counsels and my vigilance, the weapons slipped suddenly from the hands of the most audacious citizens and fell to the ground. What deed done in war, then, was ever so great? What triumph compares?[41]

Had not prudent statesmanship proved superior to physical force, Cicero boasts, the great Pompey himself would have never again gained a military triumph, since "he would not have had a place to celebrate it except through my services to the republic."[42] Bragging this may be, but it clearly illuminates the paragon of

Ciceronian patriotism: one who protects the republic by fearlessly opposing those using violence to grab the reins of political power.

De officiis's comparison of statesmanship with military command comes in the midst of its discussion of the virtue of courage, illustrating Cicero's challenge to the facile equivalence of fortitude with acts of physical bravery, especially on the field of battle. Although, in the common mind, that greatness of spirit that gives rise to courageous acts is almost always associated with deeds of military valor,[43] Cicero believes that such apparent virtue is in fact generally vicious, because it is not constrained by justice: "If the lofty spirit that is manifest in times of danger and toil is devoid of justice, if it fights not for the common welfare but for itself, it is a vice; for not only is it not a virtue, but it is rather a savagery that repels all things human."[44]

Justice requires that we refrain from committing injuries and that we see to it that others are not injured as well.[45] But military conflict often results in harm to combatants and even noncombatants, whether its occurrence is a calculated cruelty or it is committed accidentally in the heat of battle. Martial courage thus readily succumbs to vice, Cicero contends, in a way that what we might call "civic courage" does not.

The person of preeminent civic courage is, of course, the statesman: "Courageousness in domestic affairs is by no means inferior to military courage; indeed, the former demands even greater effort and exertion than the latter."[46] True greatness of spirit expresses itself in the ability to refrain from the use of physical force except when entirely necessary. The really courageous person is one who is cautious and guided by reason, who seeks the public benefit and places peace above whatever glory can be achieved from warfare:

> The civilians who are in charge of the republic are no less beneficial than those persons who conduct its wars. And thus by their counsels wars are often avoided or concluded. . . . We must therefore value the reason which makes decisions above the courage which makes battle; yet we must be careful to do that not for the sake of avoiding war but because we have reasoned about what is useful. War, then, should be undertaken in such a way that nothing else than peace is seen to be the aim.[47]

For Cicero the courage of the patriot stems from prudent judgment about the propriety of warfare and from a love of peace rather than from a desire for battle and conquest. "To charge rashly into battle and engage the enemy hand to hand is monstrous and beastlike," he declares.[48] Admittedly, Cicero is no pacifist. Every citizen of the republic must be prepared, if need be, to fight when no other option is available. But the courageous patriot resists the blandishments of those "who put war before civil affairs" and "to whom dangerous and hot-headed counsels appear greater and better than calm and thoughtful ones."[49] This amounts to a nearly complete rejection of received wisdom about courage as the archetypical martial virtue and underscores Cicero's insistence that the measure of patriotism is one's contribution to civic deliberation, instead of one's prowess on the battlefield. For Cicero, the statesman is far more likely to evince the qualities of the genuine patriot than of the general or the soldier.

Cicero's preference for peace over war, and thus for public affairs over military leadership, seems to mirror accurately the philosophy of life that is often regarded to be quintessentially Ciceronian: *otium cum dignitate*.[50] This phrase has been subjected to many different interpretations.[51] However we understand these watchwords, they suggest that no true virtue is ever to be found in violence or combat. If *otium* (alternatively translated as "repose," "leisure," or "peace") is the proper condition of human existence, then people in their natural state must abjure the fury of armed conflict; the latter is antithetical to the good order and harmony implied by *otium*. By contrast, *otium* is perfectly consistent with statesmanship, since the role of the civic leader is to keep and guarantee the peace in a manner consonant with justice. The goal of the statesman is precisely *otium cum dignitate*; the phrase encapsulates the rightful end of the republic as a whole, as well as of its individual citizens. Although the statesman must involve himself in verbal duels and complex plots, these have but one purpose: to strengthen the public welfare of the community itself. It follows, therefore, that physical force has no place in politics, and that armies ought to be strictly subordinated to civilian leaders and to the entire citizen body. (Indeed, Cicero regards the disintegration of republican rule in Rome during his own time to be largely the result of a failure of politicians to observe those two principles.[52]) The convergence of patriotism, republican virtue, and statesmanship is, then, summarized by the maxim *otium cum dignitate*. This precept conveys a worthy alternative to the militaristic paradigm that has attracted other republicans, classical as well as contemporary.

CONCLUSION: REVALUING CICERO

It is certainly curious that civic republicanism has declined to learn from a figure such as Cicero, who was a consummate practitioner of republican virtue as well as one of its stellar theorists. Yet Cicero's nonmilitaristic account of patriotism reminds us of an important, but sometimes overlooked, dimension of republican thought: that a truly civic politics is built not merely upon the rare occurrence or the grand gesture, but on the recognition that communities are sustained and developed in the mundane daily activities of, and relations between, their citizens and leaders.

A Machiavellian would have us confound republicanism with the quest for collective glory, the achievement of exceeding fame and honor for one's country (and incidentally for one's self) through military skill and victory. Cicero admits that this has been one common understanding of classical republican virtue, but he shows us how it is faulty and how it invariably leads to the decay and destruction of republican institutions and values. The politics of the common good, which forms the heart of the cause of republican liberty, is most adequately realized in the exercise of everyday virtues within the public sphere, not in the performance of acts of uncommon valor on the battlefield. The decline of a republic is bound to occur when generals believe that their military prowess is all that is necessary for effective and virtuous statesmanship.

This lesson should be chastening to current republicans drawn to the militaristic paradigm, an antidote to their sometimes uncritical enthusiasm for Machiavellian *virtù*. If a republic can retain its vitality only by going to war, or at any rate by maintaining itself in a state of constant armed preparedness, then we may rightly wish to question why and whether it is worth fighting for in the first place. More appealing perhaps is the Ciceronian vision of civilian public service as the highest calling of the republican citizen: good laws (and their careful enforcement) claiming precedence over good arms. The difficulty, of course, is how to instill a sense of duty, a character, in citizens that will lead them to value the virtues of the statesman and to aspire to participate in public life (as an intelligent follower, if not as a leader). In other words, a Ciceronian republican politics must recapitulate, or at least echo, the process by which society was formed in the first place—the collective act, stimulated by rational eloquence, of setting aside wholly individual pursuits in the name of a great social harmony.

Is this a "hazy" or untenable doctrine? I do not think so. Unlike, say, Aristotle, for whom public virtue required the rigorous moral education of all citizens, Cicero's requirements for the citizen body at large are relatively undemanding. Aristotle had insisted that citizenship could exist only among moral equals capable of ruling and being ruled in turn, and he thus counted the inculcation of the full range of human virtues as the highest and most honorable purpose of the *polis*. Perhaps because they tend to follow this Aristotelian model, many recent civic republicans have come to view the primary goal of government as instilling in citizens the sort of character that would assure virtuous action. As a result, current republicans have been confronted with a number of uncomfortable questions about both their strategies for education and the content of their proposed lessons.[53]

By contrast, Cicero appears to view the moral education of the populace at large as at best a secondary aim of law and government. Perhaps because he tied virtue so closely to the effective maintenance of peaceful association, he was concerned primarily with perpetuating the outward manifestations of social cooperation—such as private property—implied by justice.[54] Laws were not designed and enforced to make human beings good according to some overarching moral scheme, but to uphold the bonds of communal solidarity dictated by reason but only imperfectly realized by individuals left to their own devices. Education was thus primarily required of the prospective statesman, and Cicero was not shy about stipulating the curriculum, which included not only philosophical studies but also acquisition of the techniques of rhetoric and oratory necessary to communicate with the republic's ordinary citizens. Cicero, of course, held to a strict division between the best sorts (the *optimates*), who form the pool from which statesmen are drawn, and the vast mass of citizens, who are in need of wise guidance rather than demagogic popular leaders.[55]

The purpose of the Ciceronian republic, then, was not to induce or improve the characters of all of its members, but to ensure their submission to wise governors whose goal is the establishment and maintenance of peaceful coexistence. As Cicero asserts in *De republica*, the statesman must direct the community by example and persuasion, "improving and examining himself continuously, urging others to imitate him, and furnishing in himself, as it were, a mirror to his fellow citizens by reason of the supreme excellence of his life and character." The statesman who accomplishes his task is like a musical conductor: he produces a melodious harmony, a state of concord among the dissonant elements within the republic; hence, he assures the bonds of peace.[56] The citizens do not all come to possess identical characters or qualities; instead their inevitable and irreconcilable differences are negotiated so as to produce "agreement among dissimilar elements."

Therefore, it seems most plausible to characterize Cicero as a sort of intellectual intermediary between the teachings of recent republicans and the precepts of liberalism. He was unwilling to sever entirely some connection between political community and personal virtue. Governance was still to be vested in those whose minds and souls qualified them to frame wise laws and policies. Yet it seems evident that Cicero diminished the standards of public virtue in line with his belief in the primary social good of peace. The promulgation and enforcement of law existed to facilitate human concord rather than to inculcate moral character in citizens. The peaceful and ordered bonds of society required the rule of wise and virtuous people, but creation of such individuals was not a primary aim of government.

NOTES

A version of this chapter was presented to the political science department at Texas A&M University. I wish to thank Ed Portis and other members of that department for their insightful criticisms. I also wish to credit Walter Nicgorski for his encouraging observations about some of my earlier work on Cicero.

1. See, for instance, J. G. A. Pocock, *The Machiavellian Moment* (Princeton: Princeton University Press, 1975); Gordon S. Wood, *The Creation of the American Republic* (Chapel Hill: University of North Carolina Press, 1969); Alasdair MacIntyre, *After Virtue*, 2nd ed. (London: Duckworth, 1981); Charles Taylor, "Cross-Purposes: The Liberal-Communitarian Debate," in *Liberalism and the Moral Life*, ed. Nancy Rosemblum (Cambridge: Harvard University Press, 1989), 159–82.

2. Don Herzog, "Some Questions for Republicans," *Political Theory* 14 (August 1986): 473, 484–88.

3. Amy Gutmann, "Communitarian Critics of Liberalism," in *Communitarianism and Individualism*, ed. Shlomo Avineri and Avner de-Shalit (Oxford: Oxford University Press, 1992), 131–32.

4. Alasdair MacIntyre, "Is Patriotism a Virtue?" in *Communitarianism: A New Public Ethics*, ed. Markate Daly (Belmont, Calif.: Wadsworth, 1994), 312, 316.

5. Taylor, "Cross-Purposes," 170.

6. Ibid., 173.

7. Ibid., 166–67.

8. MacIntyre, "Is Patriotism a Virtue?" 310, 312.

9. Taylor, "Cross-Purposes," 171. Even Maurizio Viroli (*For Love of Country: An Essay on Patriotism and Nationalism* [Oxford: Clarendon Press], 183–86), who struggles mightily to resist the militaristic overtures of patriotism, cannot, in the end, avoid generating a definition that involves "resistance" and "struggle" against "enemies of liberty."

10. G. W. F. Hegel, *Philosophy of Right*, tr. T. M. Knox (Oxford: Oxford University Press, 1967), 209–10. See Cary J. Nederman, "Sovereignty, War and the Corporation: Hegel on the Medieval Foundations of the Modern State," *Journal of Politics* 49 (1987): 507–9.

11. Niccolò Machiavelli, *Discourses*, II.2, in *Machiavelli: The Chief Writings and Others*, ed. Alan Gilbert (Durham: Duke University Press, 1965), 329.

12. Viroli, *For Love of Country*, 170–71, acknowledges the Roman roots of republicanism but expends no significant effort examining Cicero's thought. For a corrective, see D. Burchell, "Civic Personae: MacIntyre, Cicero, and Moral Personality," *History of Political Thought* 19 (Spring 1998): 101–17.

13. For an overview of Cicero's career and thought, see Neal Wood, *Cicero's Social and Political Thought* (Berkeley: University of California Press, 1988).

14. Cicero, *De officiis*, ed. Walter Miller (Cambridge: Harvard University Press, 1913), I.57. I have often departed from Miller's translations, sometimes in consultation with the fine rendering by M. T. Griffin and E. M. Aktins, *Cicero: On Duties* (Cambridge: Cambridge University Press, 1991).

15. Cicero, *De officiis*, I.58.

16. Ibid., I.83–84.

17. Cicero, *De legibus*, ed. C. W. Keyes (Cambridge: Harvard University Press, 1928), II.5.

18. Cicero, *De officiis*, I.74.

19. Ibid., I.34.

20. Ibid., I.22–27.

21. Ibid., I.35.

22. Ibid., I.35–38.

23. Ibid., I.12.

24. Ibid., I.50.

25. Ibid., I.11.

26. Ibid., I.15.

27. Cicero, *De inventione*, ed. H. M. Hubbell (Cambridge: Harvard University Press, 1949), I.2.

28. Cicero, *De oratore*, ed. E. W. Sutton and H. Rackham (Cambridge: Harvard University Press, 1942), I.32–33.

29. Cicero, *De inventione*, I.3.

30. Cicero, *De oratore*, I.31.

31. Cicero, *De inventione*, I.2.

32. Cicero, *De officiis*, I.20.

33. Cicero, *Pro Sestio*, ed. R. Gardner (Cambridge: Harvard University Press, 1958), 91.

34. Ibid., 92.

35. The connection between human nature and republican rule has been stressed by Robert Denoon Cumming, *Human Nature and History*, 2 vols. (Chicago: University of Chicago Press, 1969), I, 245.

36. *De legibus*, I.45.

37. A recent survey of the controversies is offered by Walter Nicgorski, "Cicero's Focus: From the Best Regime to the Model Statesman," *Political Theory* 19 (May 1991): 230–51.

38. Cicero, *De officiis,* I.69–73.
39. Ibid., I.74.
40. Ibid., I.75–76.
41. Ibid., I.77.
42. Ibid., I.78.
43. Ibid., I.61.
44. Ibid., I.62.
45. Ibid., I.23.
46. Ibid., I.79.
47. Ibid., I.79–80.
48. Ibid., I.81.
49. Ibid., I.82.
50. The phrase is coined by Cicero in *Pro Sestio,* 98.
51. See Cumming, *Human Nature and History,* 254, 276–77; Wood, *Cicero's Social and Political Thought,* 197–99.
52. See *De officiis,* I.25–26, I.34, I.57.
53. For example, Herzog, "Some Questions for Republicans," 484–87.
54. *De officiis,* II.73, II.78–79. See Hadley Arkes, "That 'Natural Herself Has Placed in Our Ears a Power of Judging': Some Reflections on the 'Naturalism' of Cicero," in *Natural Law Theory: Contemporary Essays,* ed. Robert P. George (Oxford: Oxford University Press, 1992), 245–77.
55. Cicero, *Pro Sestio,* 96–101.
56. Cicero, *De republica,* ed. C. W. Keyes (Cambridge: Harvard University Press, 1928), II.69.

Chapter Three

Medieval Jewish and Islamic Themes: Ethics and Religion and Philosophical Attitudes toward Ethics

Jeffrey Macy

In this chapter, I would like to address two issues: the place of ethics in medieval Jewish and Islamic philosophy and, to a lesser extent, the general issue of the relationship between ethics and religion. I would like to highlight the following points:

(1) The medieval Jewish and Islamic philosophers, who were greatly influenced by Aristotle's *Nicomachean Ethics*, discuss two different types of ethics, not unlike the description we have heard in Stephen Salkever's chapter on Aristotle.[1] In the writings of medieval Jewish and Islamic philosophers such as al-Farabi, ibn Rushd (Averroës), and Maimonides, there are ethics for the masses and ethics as they relate to the philosophic individual. Ethics for the masses can be instilled in one of two ways: either in what might be called the bulk method, by promoting habits through law (usually religious law, but as invented or interpreted by the philosophers), or by a more individual treatment (compared to the way in which the physician chooses and administers the proper selection of medication to an individual who is sick). On the other hand, philosophic ethics are developed through education and teaching an individual to regulate himself or herself rather than submitting to an externally imposed regimen.

(2) In addition, the philosophers always see ethics as no more than a means. In the case of the masses, ethics is an important political tool to regulate the masses and promote peace and order in society. It is difficult to say that this type of ethics leads to true virtue, because true virtue requires knowledge. This type of ethics usually is grounded in habit, and it is reinforced by external persuasion, either through words or through fear of punishment. While the character of philosophic ethics differs from that of ethics for the masses, it, too, is no more than a means. Philosophic ethics is no more than a means on the way to true human perfection, which is attained in the theoretical-rational rather than the practical-rational faculty of the soul. Although it is true that moral virtue has importance, it *is not* and

31

cannot be the ultimate human end. Philosophic ethics is directed toward the neutralization of the passions in order to allow an individual to concentrate on the development of theoretical-rational virtue.

(3) In relation to the foregoing point, there are two senses in which ethical behavior is evaluated: ethics for the masses should lead to the proper harmony in society, to a great extent by restraining an individual's passions or self-interested and base desires. This will decrease conflict in the political association. This type of moral virtue or ethical behavior is evaluated primarily on the basis of its political efficacy. On the other hand, in the case of philosophic ethics, the most important aspect of ethical behavior is individual, not political. It is concerned with the individual who is acting in accordance with moral virtue more than it is concerned with the object of the moral action. Thus, what is important is how moral virtue affects the soul of the doer and his or her ability to attain intellectual perfection. In this case, little or no emphasis is placed on the impact of these ethical activities on others.

(4) Fourth, and most striking, the philosophers emphasize, through the use of supposedly historical examples, that human perfection and happiness can be attained even when the law is violated, and it can be attained by individuals whose actions depart from conventional standards of ethics or morality. Indeed, the medieval Jewish and Islamic philosophers sometimes downplay the importance of ethical virtue altogether, once an individual has reached a level of intellectual perfection. In this regard, it is interesting to note that the preeminent medieval Jewish philosopher, Maimonides, claims there was no concern with ethics or politics in the ideal first stage of the Garden of Eden, before the eating of the fruit of the tree of the knowledge of good and evil. According to Maimonides, prior to this stage Adam and, perhaps, Eve were concerned only with matters of true and false, or theoretical-rational virtue.[2] Ethics and politics became important only afterward, as a result of a lowering of the human horizon.

(5) The connection between religion and ethics is a topic worthy of a symposium in its own right. By personal interest, I will use medieval Jewish and Islamic theology as my jumping-off point for some brief reflections, although beyond the medieval context of these comments, I believe there is contemporary and more general relevance.

In the Middle Ages, traditional Judaism and Islam presented their own systems of following the right path—what we would be tempted to call morality and ethics. Yet is the right path, or the standard for good actions, really synonymous with what *we* would normally call ethics? Because the demands of religions that are thought to be divinely revealed often depart from human-centered or rational standards for action, actions that are thought to be good may even appear to contradict what the medieval philosophers would call moral or ethical actions (let alone what we would call moral or ethical actions). It is true that different theological trends present their positions on the possible rationality of religious law in different fashion: while some theologians attempt to point to the so-called rationality and humanly understandable standards of justice that can be found in the religious law, other groups of theologians are less concerned about justifying as ethical or moral the actions their religions require.

Yet the claims of theologians must be examined—and the examination of these claims raises doubts about the very character of what can be defined as ethical and moral. For example, we should note that there may be a problem classifying as ethical and moral religiously enjoined commandments, such as the injunction to wage war against the infidel (who is a nonbeliever), the defense of radical inequality in the treatment of the nonbeliever, or religious commands to the believer that cause him or her to depart from moderation. Indeed, consider a modern variation on a medieval theme: is the suicide bomber who kills the enemies of God, together with himself, a morally virtuous individual? He may well have been assured that such activity would make him a righteous individual worthy of otherworldly reward. Are the children sent to explode minefields by racing through them, with the promise of immediate entry into heaven for any who die in this way, acting in a way that promotes moral virtue? Is such action the high point of happiness or the high point of folly? Further, are those religious authorities who sanction the activity of the suicide bomber or who distribute keys to the "heavenly gardens" to the children who are sent across minefields acting in a way that is moral, even if they believe that such activity truly is supported by religious law?

We need to discuss in more detail the defining character of morality and ethical actions, if, in fact, they have a defining character, before we can truly evaluate the relation between religion and ethics; our discussions thus far do not appear to have provided us with an overview of this issue. What, if anything, can be presented as a minimal guideline or standard for ethical or moral action? Only after we clarify the possibility of the existence of such a standard or standards can we evaluate all claims to ethical and moral action—including those raised by religious fundamentalists who have been assured by their religious mentors of the sanctity and goodness of their missions.

Having summarized my chief points, I would like to illustrate some of the points I have attributed to the medieval Jewish and Islamic philosophers by referring to two passages in Maimonides' *Guide of the Perplexed*.[3] What makes these passages particularly striking is Maimonides' generally accepted reputation as one of the great teachers of ethics in Judaism. In the final chapter of his *Guide of the Perplexed*, after describing "perfection of the moral virtues," Maimonides goes on to discuss what he calls the highest type of human perfection.

> [True human perfection] consists in the acquisition of the rational virtues—I refer to the conception of the intelligibles. . . . This is in true reality the ultimate end, this is what gives the individual true perfection, a perfection belonging to him alone; and it gives him permanent perdurance; through it man is man. If you consider each of the three perfections mentioned before [perfection of possessions, perfection of bodily constitution and shape, and perfection of the moral virtues], you will find that they pertain to others than you, not to you, even though, according to the generally

accepted opinion, they obtain both to you and to others. This ultimate perfection, however, pertains to you alone, no one else being associated in it with you in any way. . . . Therefore you ought to desire to achieve this thing, which will remain permanently with you, and not weary and trouble yourself for the sake of others, O you who neglect your own soul so that its whiteness has turned into blackness through the corporeal faculties having gained dominion over it. . . . Neither the perfection of possession nor the perfection of health nor the perfection of moral habits is a perfection of which one should be proud or that one should desire. . . .[4]

The secondary character of moral virtue, the ultimate emphasis on individual perfection rather than concern for the object of moral action, and the difference between morality for the masses and the aims of the philosopher are stated boldly here. The following passage, with its striking characterization and critique of the masses, reinforces the distinction between the masses and the philosopher and emphasizes the ultimately solitary character of the philosopher's perfection and the "transmoral" basis for his concern with most people.

In the *Guide of the Perplexed*, book 2, chapter 36, Maimonides writes:

He [the perfect individual] should rather regard all people according to their various states with respect to which they are indubitably either like domestic animals or like beasts of prey. If the perfect man who lives in solitude thinks of them at all, he does so only with a view to saving himself from the harm that may be caused by those among them who are harmful if he happens to associate with them, or to obtaining an advantage that may be obtained from them if he is forced to it by some of his needs.[5]

Medieval Moslem philosophers speak in more than one voice, but for all of them, issues of ethics and justice are matters that concern the practical intellect, which is not the locus for attaining human perfection. While his position is somewhat extreme, the twelfth-century Islamic philosopher and physician Ibn Tufayl[6] goes so far as to suggest that ultimate human perfection can be attained only by a self-trained philosophic individual living on a desert island, far from society and the common run of human beings. If ethics exists in the world of Ibn Tufayl's philosophic hero, Hayy ibn Yaqzan, it is inward-looking and designed primarily to create the proper balance in his soul. For the unphilosophic multitude of men, however, the importance of ethics is related most directly to the social and political necessity to insure order in society by regulating the actions of the masses. In addition, unlike the philosopher, the masses of humans are in need of organized religion. Because the masses will never reach the level of intellectual perfection, they need some sort of framework and rules to guide them. Religion and ethics provide that framework.

It should not be surprising that Moslem and Jewish philosophers acknowledge that there will be times when the intellectually perfect leader will transgress both religious law and accepted standards of morality to attain a lofty end—either when this is necessary to protect his political regime or to achieve something that is necessary for his own individual perfection.

Time restraints prevent me from presenting the positions of the medieval philosophers or, for that matter, the medieval theologians in greater detail. However, before concluding, I would like to make a number of additional general comments.

It is true that there are many points of difference between the thought of medieval Jewish and Islamic philosophers and medieval Jewish and Islamic theologians. To oversimplify a bit for the sake of comparison, medieval Jewish and Islamic philosophers found the essence of human perfection to be theoretical-rational contemplation, culminating in the attainment of knowledge of first principles based on the attainments of human reason. In contrast, medieval Jewish and Islamic theologians looked to divine revelation and authentic tradition for their guidance. In addition, the medieval philosophers perceived the ultimate happiness and perfection that could be attained in this world by humans as fundamentally individual, rather than communal.[7] Again, in contrast, almost all of the medieval Jewish and Islamic theologians who were not mystics conceived of a collective-communal aspect to human perfection that required participation in group activities, including ritual actions and the fulfillment of religiously enjoined commandments/rules. In Jewish religious thought, the idea that all Jews are guarantors for the proper actions of all other Jews[8] compels the observant Jew to be involved in his community or remain imperfect and culpable himself. He or she is not allowed to say—as Maimonides does in the *Guide of the Perplexed*—that one "should not weary and trouble [oneself] for the sake of others."[9]

From these remarks, one would think that the philosophers and theologians would have had markedly different approaches to ethics. We have already seen that, to a great extent, that assumption is correct. However, philosophers and theologians share an important common point of perspective regarding the role of ethics. They both see ethics as no more than a means to an end that transcends this-worldly communal life. We have already heard Maimonides' words on this subject.

Moslem and Jewish theologians place much more primacy on following the commandments of the law—for it is a revealed divine law—than on acting in accordance with ethical or moral standards per se. In addition, it is a matter of great debate whether God is limited by humanly intelligible standards of justice and morality. Thus, according to fundamentalist Islamic thinkers such as al-Ashari, at least when predicated about God, standards of justice and ethics have no meaning. God is, as it were, beyond good and evil. The following passage from al-Ashari's *Kitab al-Luma'* (*Book of the Highlights of the Polemic against Deviators and Innovators*) illustrates this point:

Q. Is God free to inflict pain on infants in the next life?
A. God is free to do that, and in doing it He would be just. Likewise, whenever He inflicts an infinite punishment for a finite sin, and subordinates some living beings to others, and is gracious to some and not to others, and creates men knowing well that they will disbelieve—all that is justice on His part. And it would not be evil on the part of God to create them in the painful punishment and to make it perpetual.

The proof that He is free to do whatever He does is that He is the Supreme Monarch, subject to no one, with no superior over Him who can permit, or command or chide or forbid or prescribe what He shall do and fix bounds for Him. This being so, nothing can be evil on the part of God. For a thing is evil on our part only because we transgress the limit and bound set for us and do what we have no right to do. But since the Creator is subject to no one and bound by no command, nothing can be evil on His part.[10]

If God's standard bears no relation to humanly understandable or humanly acceptable standards of justice and ethics, one would be incorrect in assuming a convergence between following God's law and acting in accordance with rationally derived or universally applicable ethical standards. For example, it would be hard for us[11] to affirm the morality of inflicting bodily harm on someone for not following God's will as expressed in a particular interpretation of the religious law, but this would not be a problem for some fundamentalist theologians and many of their believing followers. To give but one contemporary example, there are countries in the Middle East today where the primacy of (divinely revealed) religious law is upheld, as well as other countries where fundamentalist groups are engaged in political and military struggles to make the state's laws subordinate to their interpretation of the divinely revealed religious laws.

Indeed, if we abstract from the Jewish and Islamic context of this discussion and turn to positions that have been put forward by the militant, and perhaps extreme, religious right in pluralistic America—or for that matter consider the history of religious wars and persecutions—it would appear that religion and morality are far less synonymous than appellations such as "the Moral Majority" would seem to suggest. On the other hand, the issue of the relationship between religion and ethics is far more complex than I can do justice to in these brief remarks. There is no doubt that religion can be a vehicle for instilling ethics, just as it can incite action that does not seem to conform to traditional definitions of morality. Nevertheless, giving the final word in this chapter to the medieval Jewish and Islamic philosophers, they would contend, in the spirit of Plato, that religion is too serious a matter to be left to priests, poets, and the pious.

NOTES

I gratefully acknowledge the assistance provided by the Levi Eshkol Institute for Economic, Social and Political Research at the Hebrew University of Jerusalem, which aided me in the preparation of this article.

1. See Stephen G. Salkever's "Aristotle and the Ethics of Natural Questions," the first chapter in this volume.

2. Moses Maimonides, *Guide of the Perplexed*, translated with an introduction and notes by Shlomo Pines and an introductory essay by Leo Strauss (Chicago: University of Chicago Press, 1963), book 1, chap. 2.

3. Maimonides is the preeminent medieval Jewish philosopher and one of Judaism's outstanding legal codifiers. He was born in Córdoba, Spain in 1135 or 1138 and died in Egypt in 1204.

4. Maimonides, *Guide,* book 3, chap. 54, 635–36.

5. Maimonides, *Guide,* book 2, chap. 36, 372.

6. See Ibn Tufayl's philosophic novel, *Hayy ibn Yaqzan.* A good modern English translation of this work can be found in Lenn Evan Goodman, *Ibn Tufayl: Hayy ibn Yaqzan* (New York: Twayne, 1972).

7. This generalization is true for all the medieval Jewish and Islamic philosophers, even though the ultimate perfection of the individual often is said to cause him to transcend himself and become part of a more universal "world-of-being" or "world-of-knowledge." This universal framework is not communal in the political sense, and, indeed, may be nothing more than a symbolic sphere. Regarding this point, most of the medieval Jewish and Islamic philosophers (with the notable exception of Ibn Sina [Avicenna]) wrote, at least metaphorically, of a "world-to-come" where there would be an ultimate uniting of separate (intellectual) souls. In this philosophically described "world-to-come," the separate noncorporeal souls of similarly perfected philosophers would be united into something like a world-soul, based on these souls' theoretical-rational attainments. (Ibn Sina maintains that individuality can be preserved even after death and the separation of the soul from the body.)

8. כל ישראל ערבין זה בזה *Babylonian Talmud, Shevu'ot,* 39a.

9. See note 4.

10. English translation from Richard J. McCarthy, *Theology of Al-Ashari* (Beyruth: Imprimerie Catholique, 1953), 99.

11. By "us" I mean those of us who do not feel obligated to accept and follow the commandments of a religious law that dictates that such belief and action are obligatory.

Chapter Four

In Defense of the City: Machiavelli's Bludgeoning of the Classical and Christian Traditions

Vickie B. Sullivan

In his long disquisition on the history of republican Rome in his *Discourses on the First Ten Books of Titus Livy,* Niccolò Machiavelli recounts how the Roman commander Camillus gained the allegiance of the foreign city he was besieging without a bloody last assault or a long siege intended to starve his quarry into submission. In achieving this city's goodwill, Camillus had a great deal of help in the form of "a schoolmaster of the noblest children of that city, [who], thinking to gratify Camillus and the Roman people, went out of the town with them under color of exercise, led them all to the camp before Camillus, and presented them, saying that through them the town would give itself into his hands." Camillus, however, rejected in spectacular fashion this officious overture of the schoolmaster. Having stripped and bound the master, Camillus gave to each one of those children a rod

> so that the pupils could beat their teacher along the length of the path that led them back to their city. When that affair was learned of by the citizens, the humanity and integrity of Camillus pleased them so much that, without wishing to defend themselves more, they decided to give [the Romans] the town. (*D* 3.20.1)[1]

Admittedly, Machiavelli's retelling of this story seems far removed from any purported revolution that he effected in ethics. Nevertheless, upon consideration it replicates his most damning charge against the philosophic lessons derived from such venerable teachers as Plato and Aristotle, as well as against the Christian dictates intoned by such masters as St. Augustine and St. Thomas Aquinas. These philosophic and religious teachings, Machiavelli alleges, vitiate any attempt on the part of human beings to defend their homeland. As different as the classical and Christian traditions are, Machiavelli views them as being united in devaluing, and hence in harming, the city. In teaching people to cultivate their souls, they enjoin people to look beyond the needs and the rewards of their earthly cities for their happiness or salvation. Hence, they weaken people's resolve to commit the deeds that, in Machiavelli's view, healthy cities demand. For Machiavelli, in contrast, the city is all. Nothing exists above and beyond the requirements of the city. What benefits the city is virtue; what harms it is vice.[2] These old masters, in effect, take their charges outside the confines of the city, and, in so doing, they turn the city over to its enemies.

Moreover, Machiavelli's retelling of this story offers a characterization of his own technique in countering the harm that such philosophic and religious lessons inflict. It is to be expected, of course, that the citizens of the city against which the schoolmaster plotted would find his humiliation gratifying. What is surprising, however, is Machiavelli's own enthusiasm for the spectacle. He calls Camillus's beating of the schoolmaster "a humane act full of charity" (*D* 3.20.1). Machiavelli, I believe, so praises Camillus's humanity and charity in having the noble youth administer that beating because it is precisely the type of beating he would like to see administered to the masters of the old and venerable traditions for their crime of attempting to lead similar youth outside of their cities. Machiavelli is, then, akin to Camillus. Like Camillus, Machiavelli will return the youth to the city; like Camillus, Machiavelli will have that beating administered by youth, the youth whose "spirits" he claims in the *Discourses* to wish to move to action (*D* Preface 2.3). Machiavelli believes this bludgeoning of the old masters is a "humane act full of charity" because they are traitors to the cause of the city.

In rare instances, Machiavelli is remarkably forthright in his criticism of the teachings of the classical and Christian traditions. One such instance occurs in *The Prince*, when he declares that he diverges from what others have taught regarding what "the modes and government of a prince should be with subjects and friends." In treating the topic, he baldly announces that he "depart[s] from the orders of others" because he will go to the "effectual truth of the thing." He notes that this procedure differs from those who "have imagined republics and principalities that have never been seen or known to exist in truth; for it is so far from how one lives to how one should live that he who lets go of what is done for what should be done learns his ruin rather than his preservation" (*P* 15.61).[3] Plato's imaginary republic or Augustine's city of God is anathema to politics in Machiavelli's view. The builders of such imaginary states may strive to teach goodness, but their constructions result in political enfeeblement.[4]

This bold declaration of war on his adversaries represents a divergence from Machiavelli's normal method of procedure. Most often he maintains a stony silence with regard to the venerable traditions he opposes, as he wishes to consign their teachings to oblivion.[5] Moreover, he advocates his own view with such urgency and belligerency that he allows his readers little breath, let alone opportunity for reflection.

I will examine the character of the revolution that Machiavelli effects in ethics as a result of his attempt to defend the city against the masters of old, whom he claims undermine the city. I will observe Machiavelli's defense by considering how his view of the necessity and desirability of war, his praise of the capacities of human beings as soldiers, and his rejection of leisure put him at odds with the thought of one old master in particular—Aristotle. After having illustrated how Machiavelli rejects the education that Aristotle offers, I will consider the character of the education Machiavelli offers in its stead.

THE NECESSITY OF WAR

Machiavelli relishes war and lauds the characteristics of the warrior. Quite obviously, his embrace of war brings him into conflict with the Christian tradition, which terms the Savior the Prince of Peace. He reveals his dissatisfaction with the results of Christian teaching when he complains that "[o]ur religion has glorified humble and contemplative more than active men." Rather than following paganism in declaring that humanity's "highest good" is to be found "in greatness of spirit, strength of body, and all other things capable of making men very strong," Christianity finds that good "in humility, abjectness, and contempt of things human" (*D* 2.2.2). Machiavelli identifies the devastating effect this transvaluation of values has had on politics when he complains that modern leaders, such as King Louis XII of France, will go to the extreme of parceling out portions of their conquests to avoid further war (*P* 3.15).

Thus, in this manner, Machiavelli calls attention to his opposition to the Christian teaching regarding war. Nevertheless, one should not overlook the fact that he also contradicts Aristotle's reflections on the proper relation between war and peace. That contradiction comes to view when one compares Aristotle's reflections on the Spartan regime with those of Machiavelli. Each finds Sparta deficient, but for strikingly different reasons. According to Aristotle, the Spartans were too focused on warlike virtue; according to Machiavelli, the Spartans were not correctly organized for dealing with their military conquests. Thus, in Machiavelli's view, the Spartans, although warlike, were deficient because they were incapable of sustaining that posture. Examination of Aristotle's and Machiavelli's opposing views of Sparta highlights their divergent notions regarding the purpose of politics.

In examining the Spartan regime, Aristotle finds that, although commendable in some regards, it is organized with too great a view toward war. He commends Sparta's founder, Lycurgus, who organized the laws with a view to inculcating virtue in the citizens: "only in Sparta, or in a few other cities as well, does the legislator seem to have attended to upbringing and practices."[6] In Aristotle's view, however, Sparta's legislator misunderstood the character of virtue, because he aimed at instilling only a part of virtue—that of warlike virtue—in the Spartans.

As a result, when the Spartans had been successful in their wars and had subdued their foes, they did not know how to handle themselves in peace. "Yet while they preserved themselves as long as they were at war, they came to ruin when they were ruling [an empire] through not knowing how to be at leisure, and because there is no training among them that has more authority than the training for war."[7] In Aristotle's view, then, the Spartans were too little concerned with their internal affairs and too concerned with dominating other cities. Aristotle's discussion of Sparta concludes that war is not an end in itself; rather, war should be fought for the sake of peace, in which condition a more complete notion of virtue can be inculcated.[8]

In contrast, Machiavelli concludes that war must be the end of any state. A state must not only embrace war but also be prepared to face the consequences of waging it successfully. He reaches these conclusions early in the *Discourses*. Before he will focus in that work on Rome as the republic most worthy of imitation, Machiavelli scrutinizes the other possible claimants to the designation of exemplary republic. He contrasts Rome with the aristocratic republics of ancient Sparta and modern Venice. Sparta receives the designation "aristocratic" because it kept its ruling class small and prohibited foreigners from becoming citizens; Venice, because it did not use the members of its lower class as its soldiers. He favors Rome, which used its people as its soldiers in the prosecution of its wars, and which, as a result, found it necessary to give them a prominent place in the republic in the form of the institution of the tribunes. This institution gave voice to the concerns of the people. Because of the people's critical role as Rome's soldiers, and because of their continual efforts to claim the highest political offices of the city as their own, Rome offers a stark contrast to Sparta and Venice. Whereas domestic tranquillity characterizes these other republics, Rome is famous for its tumults. Machiavelli, in fact, has to concede that the events that occurred there—"the people together crying out against the Senate, the Senate against the people, running tumultuously through the streets, closing shops, the whole plebs leaving Rome"—can "frighten whoever does no other than read of them" (*D* 1.4.1).

Having drawn this distinction between Rome on the one hand and Sparta and Venice on the other, Machiavelli initially protests his impartiality on the issue of whether a popular or an aristocratic republic is to be preferred:

> In the end, he who subtly examines the whole will draw this conclusion from it: you are reasoning either about a republic that wishes to make an empire, such as Rome, or about one for whom it is enough to maintain itself. In the first case, it is necessary for it to do everything as did Rome; in the second, it can imitate Venice and Sparta, for the causes that will be told in the following chapter. (1.5.3)

When he turns in the following chapter to the issue of how to implement either of these two types of constitutional arrangements, he shows instead how the Roman alternative is, in fact, the only alternative. His rejection of domestic tranquillity as the goal for the city derives from the prominence of foreign relations in his analysis.

Machiavelli's analysis in the following chapter at first appears to fulfill his promise to describe how both types of republics can be ordered. He specifies that "[i]f someone wished . . . to order a republic anew, he would have to examine whether he wished it to expand like Rome in dominion and in power or truly to remain within narrow limits" (*D* 1.6.4). If this would-be orderer chooses the way of conquest, then he must "make a place for tumults and universal dissensions." If, however, the orderer chooses domestic tranquillity, "he . . . should, in all the modes he can, prohibit [the republic] from acquiring, because such acquisitions, founded on a weak republic, are its ruin altogether."

In this manner, Machiavelli has broached the decisive factor—that of foreign relations—that will impel him to jettison the alternative for political life that Sparta and Venice represent. Before he takes this drastic step, however, he still entertains the possibility that the nonaggressive state can manage foreign relations so as to assure its stability. The orderer must situate his state "in a strong place of such power that nobody would believe he could crush it at once." Nevertheless, that place should not be of such power that it would "be formidable to its neighbors" (*D* 1.6.4). Situated in such a location, the state would encourage neither offensive forays nor preemptive strikes. It would be strong enough to assure that no neighbor would be foolhardy enough to believe that it could win an easy conquest, and it would not be so powerful as to be intimidating. As a result, the city located in such a desirable location could cultivate its internal life without concern for war.

Machiavelli quickly reveals, however, that this "middle way" is a dream not to be realized in truth, an imaginary republic whose pursuit will surely eventuate in a republic's ruin rather than in its preservation. The dream of a nonaggressive republic evaporates with the recognition that "since all things of men are in motion and cannot stay steady, they must either rise or fall; and to many things that reason does not bring you, necessity brings you" (*D* 1.6.4).

Although reason seems to favor, then, the middle way of a republic that renounces an offensive posture and arms itself merely for defense, a glance at necessity demands that that way be rejected. Necessity intrudes in the form of other states, which will not be deterred by the state's defensive posture and which will seek to conquer it. If the state is fortunate enough to survive these attacks, then it will have dependent territory to administer. The organization of Sparta and Venice is simply inadequate to the task of holding conquered territory: "So when a republic that has been ordered so as to be capable of maintaining itself does not expand, and necessity leads it to expand, this would come to take away its foundations and make it come to ruin sooner" (*D* 1.6.4). Indeed, both Sparta and Venice succumbed to this necessity; he reveals that they came to ruin when they lacked the strength to withstand the rebellions of the territories they held (*D* 1.6.4).

To hold such acquisitions, a state must permit its foreign relations to determine its domestic relations. It cannot foster domestic tranquillity; it cannot prohibit foreigners from becoming citizens, as did Sparta, or prohibit the plebs from being the city's soldiers, as did Venice. Because it must seek power, it must arm all comers so that it can use them in its wars. As a result, it will be a boisterous and tumultuous place. Although he began by offering a choice between domestic tranquillity and chaos, Machiavelli ends his investigation by denying the existence of a choice: "I believe that it is necessary to follow the Roman order and not that of the other republics—for I do not believe one can find a mode between the one and the other" (*D* 1.6.4).

The contrast with Aristotle could not be clearer. The Spartans, according to Aristotle, were too warlike, whereas for Machiavelli they were not warlike enough because they were insufficiently organized to deal with the inevitable effects of their military adventures. If only the Spartans had better prepared for dominating their neighbors, laments Machiavelli. The compromise that, in Machiavelli's view, the Spartans attempted to effect was insufficient. When speaking of the "middle way," which represents the possibility that a city could defend itself while not encouraging incursions from hostile neighbors, he comments: "Without doubt I believe that if the thing could be held balanced in this mode, it would be the true political way of life and the true quiet of a city" (*D* 1.6.4). It is as if Machiavelli acknowledges the type of aspirations for political life that Aristotle's highly qualified endorsement of the Spartan legislator's pursuit of virtue expresses, but replies that the human condition does not permit that pursuit.[9] The quest for such a "true political life" will bring only ruin and not preservation.

MACHIAVELLI'S PRAISE OF THE PEOPLE'S CAPACITIES

Machiavelli makes much of the fact that he endorses the democratic republic of Rome over its aristocratic competitors. Indeed, it is on this basis that he attempts to assume the mantle of true democrat and defender of the people, announcing that this role distinguishes him from all previous writers. Despite his ingratiating gestures, however, he loves the people not for themselves but as a means to an end: the people can, just as they did in republican Rome, provide the manpower for the acquisitions of their cities. Nevertheless, this basis for his regard for the people still distinguishes him from both the Christian and classical traditions. In positing the soldier as the model to which human beings should aspire, he wishes to displace the current models. Both the Christian saint and the classical gentleman endeavor to cultivate their souls. Few can attain the summits that these models represent, and the very attempt distracts human beings from what should be their most pressing concerns—the defense and aggrandizement of their earthly homelands. These goals of Machiavelli require not the cultivation of the soul but the deployment of brawn and muscle. Machiavelli is, indeed, a democrat because he opposes the old masters, whom he believes set a standard for the cultivation of capacities that few possess and who hence disparage the capacities of the majority of human beings.

On this basis, Machiavelli views himself as the defender of humanity as a whole against those whom he deems its critics.

Aristotle is one whom Machiavelli would regard as a critic of the people. Aristotle praises the *logos* of human beings—the faculty of speech informed by reason—and declares that that faculty distinguishes human beings from brutes. A well-known passage of Aristotle's *Politics* runs:

> That man is much more a political animal than any kind of bee or any herd animal is clear. For, as we assert, nature does nothing in vain; and man alone among the animals has speech [*logon*]. The voice indeed indicates the painful or pleasant, and hence is present in other animals as well; for their nature has come this far, that they have a perception of the painful and pleasant and indicate these things to each other. But speech [*logos*] serves to reveal the advantageous and the harmful, and hence, also the just and unjust. For it is peculiar to man as compared to the other animals that he alone has a perception of good and bad and just and unjust and other things [of this sort].[10]

The faculty of reason that Aristotle praises is not possessed by all in its fully developed form; not all human beings will be either rulers or philosophers.

Machiavelli expresses both his divergence from "certain moral philosophers" and his deep gratitude for the capacities of human beings in general in a chapter in the *Discourses* devoted to necessity. He says by way of introduction to the topic: "As it has been written by certain moral philosophers, the hands and the tongue of men—two very noble instruments for ennobling him—would not have worked perfectly nor led human works to the height they are seen to be led to had they not been driven by necessity" (*D* 3.12). Although he appears to join with moral philosophers in praising necessity, reflection on his teaching in this chapter shows his very deep divergence from his predecessors on the issue of the capabilities of human beings generally.

Machiavelli praises not the *logos* of human beings, but their "tongue." Whereas for the Greek, one word denominates both speech and reason, for the Italian, two words are necessary. Machiavelli chooses to use only one word, that being the voice, a faculty that human beings share with animals, according to Aristotle's analysis. Machiavelli, of course, would not deny that human beings possess the ability to reason, but he seems not to regard it as most worthy of praise. Moreover, by ignoring the faculty of reason in this discussion, he obscures the ends to which Aristotle points "the application of reason in political deliberation concerning the just and unjust and in philosophical contemplation.[11] In this way, Machiavelli jettisons Aristotle's elitism. In this place, he distinguishes himself from the tradition in wishing to glorify the many, rather than the few.

The deep significance for Machiavelli of his defense of the people becomes evident when he announces a break not only with his historian, Livy, but also with "all the writers." Machiavelli makes his pathbreaking announcement in the chapter title of *Discourses* 1.58: "The multitude is wiser and more constant than a prince," and in the body of the chapter he notes that he disagrees with the assessment of Livy, who affirms that "nothing is more vain and inconstant than the multitude." Just below he emphasizes the uniqueness of his position in defending the people when he notes that he "wish[es] to defend a thing that, as I said, has been accused by all the writers." In this manner, he acknowledges that he is opposing himself to the tradition as a whole. Machiavelli chooses to announce his break with the tradition in the context of its disparagement of the people (*D* 1.58.1).

Machiavelli's chapter title suggests that the people are fit to rule on account of their wisdom and constancy, but Machiavelli's chapter does not, in fact, fulfill the promise that appears to be contained in the chapter's title. Instead, he praises the people for their dedication to their homeland: "Whoever considers the Roman people will see it to have been hostile for four hundred years to the kingly name and a lover of the glory and common good of its fatherland" (*D* 1.58.3). This is still praise, surely, but it does not champion the ruling capacities of the people on the basis of their wisdom and constancy. The Roman people, as he depicts them, never achieved the position of the highest rulers of their republic.

Machiavelli's depiction of the Roman republic and the place of the people within it is consistent with—indeed illustrative of—one of his central political teachings: the fundamental distinction between princes and peoples. When Machiavelli uses the term *prince*, he refers not only to a sole ruler of a principality but also to a leading man in a republic, who, in contending with other princes of the republic such as himself, is not alone in rule. As a result, he can refer to the leaders of the Roman republic as "princes of the city" (e.g., *D* 1.12.1). Princes are distinguished from the people on the basis of their passions; whereas princes covet honor and glory above all, the people value their lives and the security of their property (*D* 1.5 and 1.16; *P* 9). Although when discussing Rome he uses the terms *patricians* and *plebeians* to distinguish these types, he does not believe that birth is the decisive factor in determining an individual's membership in either party.[12]

In adhering to this distinction between peoples and princes, Machiavelli insists that the people, taken as a class, do not rule. For instance, in describing the basis for the contention between the plebeians and patricians in Rome, he reports that the plebeians wished to hold the highest offices in the city. They made their claim to the consulate on the basis of the facts that the plebeian class "had more part in the city, because it carried more danger in wars, because it was that which with its limbs [*le braccia*] kept Rome free and made it powerful" (1.47.1).[13] Although he reports in this way the arguments of the plebeians, he never sides with the people in their attempt to rule. In fact, in this place he commends the people for recognizing their unsuitability for those offices. Elsewhere, he commends the trickery that the patricians employed to keep the plebeians from dominating the ruling positions of the city, reporting with unconcealed glee how the patricians played on the superstitious nature of the plebeians and took advantage of their gullibility to circumvent the election of plebeians (*D* 1.13 and 1.48).

Machiavelli cannot, in fact, ultimately support the people's claim to rule if he wishes to cultivate war. The plebeians believed that Rome's wars arose not so much from the ambition of its neighbors as from the ambition of the city's nobles (*D* 1.39.2). Wishing to preserve their lives and enjoy their possessions free from the dangers of war, the plebeians repeatedly threatened to defect from the Roman cause (e.g., *D* 1.13). If they had been in a position to act on their dissatisfaction, then Rome would have been a very different city, a city that would not merit Machiavelli's endorsement. As we know, the plebeians were not able to act on their inclinations, however, because the patricians' tricks kept the people's representatives from the highest offices. Thus, in showing how Rome's princes were able to dupe its people in order to maintain the people's allegiance to the city, its leaders, and its wars, Machiavelli also suggests a distinction in acumen between the people and their princes.

Although his defense of the people does not ultimately support a claim for their holding the highest offices of the city, Machiavelli does intend in a very serious way to defend them. His defense, however, occupies different ground from that which he originally appeared to claim. He praises them for using their bodies in establishing Rome's martial superiority. He says later in *Discourses* 1.58 that "one sees that cities in which peoples are princes make exceeding increases in a very brief time, and much greater than those that have always been made under a prince, as did Rome after the expulsion of the kings" (1.58.3). In this chapter, devoted to the defense of the people, he grants more power to the people than his discussion of Rome elsewhere in the work reveals. The people were princes only in the sense that the city was a republic, but, as we have seen, the people as a whole could not be said to have been princes in Machiavelli's depiction of the events in that city. Nevertheless, he acknowledges here, as he does elsewhere, that Rome achieved its greatness by giving the people a prominent place in the republic as its soldiers. He defends the people precisely because their bodies made Rome free and powerful.

Pernicious Leisure

In assessing the qualities of human beings generally, Machiavelli values not their wisdom but their brawn. He finds, however, that he cannot merely ignore what he does not value. Reason in its role as minister to the pursuit of wisdom is so pernicious and so insidious that Machiavelli finds that it demands his active engagement. Indeed, so dangerous does he find philosophy that he endeavors to expel from the city the leisure that nurtures it.

Far from condemning leisure, as does Machiavelli, Aristotle praises it. In the *Ethics* he states: "Happiness seems to be found in leisure, since we accept trouble so that we can be at leisure, and fight wars so that we can be at peace."[14] Moreover, in praising leisure, he is praising philosophy. Indeed, the above-quoted praise of leisure appears in his discussion of the life dedicated to the pursuit of knowledge. That discussion clearly points to a life more gratifying than the one devoted to politics. Aristotle recognizes that the political life can without doubt give rise to actions that are "fine and great." Nevertheless, such actions "require trouble, aim at some [further] end, and are choice-worthy for something other than themselves."[15] In contrast, the life given over to study is the most gratifying human life because it utilizes reason, "the supreme element in us," and is the most pleasant and self-sufficient activity.[16] Further, in the *Politics* he recommends to those who seek "pleasures unaccompanied by pains" that they "not seek a remedy except in connection with philosophy."[17]

Machiavelli's rejection of leisure comes to sight in the continuation of his discussion of the choices available to the orderer of a republic in 1.6 of the *Discourses*. After having insisted on the necessity of war, he reflects: "So, on the other hand, if heaven were so kind that it did not have to make war, from that would arise the idleness to make it either effeminate or divided; these two things together, or each by itself, would be the cause of its ruin" (*D* 1.6.4). Even if ideal conditions could be found, even if a state could find in those conditions respite from the world's chaos, the state would meet its collapse in such conditions just as assuredly as if it were ill-armed among hostile neighbors. Ironically, then, in such a case heaven's kindness in permitting peace would eventuate in heaven's cruelty in the form of the city's collapse. Such potential cruelty on nature's part would arise, in Machiavelli's view, as a result of the fact that idleness is pernicious in the highest degree, so much so that one must foster war in order to expel it from the city.

Idleness, *ozio* in the Italian, can also be translated as "leisure." In the *Florentine Histories*, Machiavelli comments on a philosophic type of leisure:

> it has been observed by the prudent that letters come after arms and that, in provinces and cities, captains arise before philosophers. For as good and ordered armies give birth to victories and victories to quiet, the strength of well-armed spirits cannot be corrupted by a more honorable leisure [*onesto ozio*] than that of letters, nor can leisure enter into well-instituted cities with a greater and more dangerous deceit than this one. (*FH* 5.1)

He continues that Cato understood the danger of the threat when young men took to following around the philosophers who had recently arrived in Rome from Athens. Cato had the philosophers expelled from the city, an action that Machiavelli wholly applauds. Thus, Machiavelli castigates not merely the "contemplative" Christian men of his own times (*D* 2.2.2), but also the contemplative men of antiquity.

Just as in the *Discourses*, Machiavelli claims that leisure leads to downfall. In the discussion from the *Discourses* it causes either effeminacy or division. Effeminacy, apparently, will lead to ruin either when other states perceive that the city is no longer prepared for war or from internal division that the lack of the necessity to fight encourages. While philosophic leisure is not the only type of leisure,[18] it is surely just as virulent in this form: it leads to the corruption of the city. When Machiavelli condemns leisure, he is also condemning philosophy.[19]

Therefore, whereas Aristotle declares that war is fought for the sake of peace and that peace may have the benefit of giving rise to philosophy, Machiavelli insists that war is for the sake of war and that war will have the benefit of preventing philosophy from gaining a foothold in the city. In Machiavelli's view, it is necessary to arm one's people, to relish their martial prowess, and to fight wars. Does he insist on these necessities because of the inevitability of war, given the rapacious nature of human beings, or merely because war is an effective measure against philosophy? Given his view of the human condition, war is more likely than not to occur, so preparation is essential. Nevertheless, preparation for and prosecution of war has a decidedly positive benefit in expelling from the city both leisure and the pursuits to which it gives rise.

ENFEEBLED POLITICAL ACTORS

Machiavelli's condemnation in the *Florentine Histories* of the "honest leisure" of philosophy acknowledges at least a portion of Aristotle's treatment of the theoretical life. After all, Machiavelli relates that the young men of Rome took to following the philosophers around town; in this manner, he grants the attractiveness of the activity. Nevertheless, he condemns its attractiveness precisely because it leads the young from war and politics to peaceful pursuits. As a result of this depletion of talent, the state becomes enfeebled.

Machiavelli's condemnation of philosophy, however, goes far beyond this rather simple point that the positing of a life more satisfying than the one dedicated to war and politics depletes the resources of the city when its youth, in pursuit of that life, undergo conversion from warriors to sages. The young men need not pursue the life of philosophy to the exclusion of politics to harm their homelands and themselves. Harm results from the teachings of philosophy, even when the young continue to engage in politics.

In *The Prince*, Machiavelli reveals the negative impact that the writer Xenophon, a student of Socrates, had on the young Roman commander Scipio. Xenophon induced the young Roman general to adhere to his portrayal in the *Education of Cyrus* of an ancient conqueror whose exploits Xenophon did not actually witness. So faithfully did Scipio follow Xenophon's depiction that "whoever reads the life of Cyrus written by Xenophon will then recognize in the life of Scipio how much glory that imitation brought him, how much in chastity, affability, humanity, and liberality Scipio conformed to what had been written of Cyrus by Xenophon," Machiavelli insists (*P* 14.60). At this point, Machiavelli seems satisfied with the results of Xenophon's tutelage; Scipio learned virtue from the writings of Xenophon, and those virtues brought him glory.

Only three chapters later, however, Machiavelli looks disapprovingly on the influence that writers, such as Xenophon, exert on political men. The ethics they inculcate lead to ruin rather than preservation. Noting with approval the "inhuman cruelty" of the Carthaginian general Hannibal, Machiavelli declares that without that cruelty, "his other virtues would not have sufficed to bring about this effect." Despite what he believes to be the truth of his statement, Machiavelli notes that those who write on such matters have not adequately promulgated it: "And the writers, having considered little in this, on the one hand admire this action of his but on the other condemn the principal cause of it" (*P* 17.67). He then returns to the subject of Scipio's virtues and offers a stinging criticism of them. To prove that virtue would not have brought Hannibal the same results as did his cruelty, Machiavelli adduces the example of Scipio: "to see that it is true that [Hannibal's] other virtues would not have been enough, one can consider Scipio." As a result of Scipio's "excessive mercy, which had allowed his soldiers more license than is fitting for military discipline," his armies in Spain rebelled against him (*P* 17.68). Scipio apparently learned too well Xenophon's lessons in "affability, humanity, and liberality" (cf. *P* 14). His troops did not fear him, and his authority was thereby vitiated. Machiavelli claims that if Scipio had not been ruled by the Senate, these faults would have effaced his glory—the very glory his virtues had won him.

Against Xenophon, Machiavelli maintains that the writers who praise the virtues do not consider how they conflict with the practice of politics. The virtues that Scipio cultivated constrained him, hindering him from ruling effectively. Xenophon's depiction of Cyrus is another example of a principality that has never been seen nor known to exist in truth. After all, Scipio studied not the historical Cyrus, but Xenophon's depiction of him. Thus, Xenophon's tutelage of Scipio is tantamount to the old master's taking the young Roman outside the walls of his city in an attempt to turn him over to his enemies. As a result of the youth's captivity to philosophy within the political sphere, the youth measures his behavior by an ethical standard that discounts political success. Similarly, when Aristotle asks whether the virtue of a good ruler is the same as that of a good man, Aristotle peers over the walls of the city to descry the qualities that human beings should cultivate.[20] For Machiavelli, this is an act treasonous to the city. To suggest that human beings should judge behavior by a standard above or beyond the demands of politics is to defect from one's homeland.

MACHIAVELLI'S EDUCATION FOR RULE: EXTREME ACTS

If rulers are not to use the writings of Xenophon or Aristotle as their guide for behavior, what then is to be their lodestar? Machiavelli has a simple answer: their earthly good. The primary concern for a ruler should be the preservation of rule. This goal demands extreme acts—acts that the old masters neither highlight nor gleefully endorse.

Much of his political writings are devoted to decrying the leaders who recoil from the extreme acts that would preserve their rule. The extent of the problem comes to view when Machiavelli discusses how to deal with a subject city that is divided by faction. He announces that the ruling city has three options: to kill the leaders of both factions; to exile the leaders from the city; or to make peace by forcing each side to come to an agreement. The Romans, so successful in dealing with their conquests, consistently chose the first expedient, but to the shame of modern politics, such resolve is no longer in evidence.

> Because such executions have in them something of the great and the generous, how-ever, a weak republic does not know how to do them. . . . But the weakness of men at present, caused by their weak education and their slight knowledge of things, makes them judge ancient judgments in part inhuman, in part impossible. (*D* 3.27.2)

Machiavelli blames the absence of such executions on modern education. Christianity implants a reluctance to follow the Roman example. It enjoins human beings to seek peace. As a result of following this Christian dictate, the ruling city does not spill blood by eliminating the leaders of each faction but rather enjoins the disputants to resolve their differences peacefully. Machiavelli insists, however, that such an injunction is not effective; the chaos that results from the factions will persist. The Romans, unsullied either by the philosophical teachings of the Greeks or the religious teachings of the Christians, summarily quashed the discord.

Apparently, Machiavelli can be so bold as to claim that such executions are generous because they serve to prevent the remainder of the population from suf-fering from the chaos caused by the feuding factions. He states this conclusion more pointedly in a different context when he commends Cesare Borgia for administering a conquered territory in a harsh manner. After Cesare acquired the Romagna, he eliminated the "lords" there "who had been readier to despoil their subjects than to correct them, and had given their subjects matter for disunion, not for union" (*P* 7.29). Although Machiavelli's point is that the ultimate happiness of the province results from harsh measures, or in other words that one has to be cruel to be kind (*P* 17), the recognition that a prince or republic will rule more securely if the generality of the population is satisfied is no small inducement to princes and republics to follow Machiavelli's advice. By blaming the conduct of his contemporaries, he is teaching his readers to eschew it.

Similarly, Machiavelli offers for its educational value the example of the hap-less Piero Soderini, who could not fortify himself for brutal acts that would have preserved both his rule and the Florentine republic itself. In 1502 Soderini was elected *gonfalonier* of the Florentine republic, for which Machiavelli served as a secretary from 1498 until its collapse in 1512. The leaders of the Medici family, which had ruled Florence as princes from 1434 until their expulsion in 1494, sought a way to restore their place as rulers of the city. In hindsight, Machiavelli offers blunt advice to his former boss: Soderini should have killed the partisans of the Medici in Florence. He declares that "whoever makes a free state and does not kill the sons of Brutus, maintains himself for little time." In speaking of the sons of Brutus, he refers to the Roman Brutus, who helped to found the republic, and who, as consul, sentenced his own sons to death for conspiring to overthrow the fledgling republic by bringing the rule of kings back to the city. Rather than taking this harsh step, Soderini "believed he would overcome with his patience and goodness the appetite that was in the sons of Brutus for returning to another government, and who deceived himself" (*D* 3.3.1). Later in the *Discourses* Machiavelli relates Soderini's hope that "with time, with goodness, with his fortune, with benefiting someone, he would eliminate this envy; seeing himself very young of age, and with so much new support that the mode of his proceeding brought him, he believed he could overcome as many as were opposed to him through envy without any scandal, violence, and tumult." Machiavelli adds, however, that Soderini "did not know that one cannot wait for the time, goodness is not enough, fortune varies, and malignity does not find a gift that appeases it" (*D* 3.30.1). As a result of Soderini's defective knowledge, the Medici returned, expelled Soderini from office, and overturned the republic.

So pervasive is the problem in the modern world that criminals, who seem unmoved by either classical ethics or Christian morality, recoil from the extreme acts that would secure their rule. Giovampagolo Baglioni, tyrant of Perugia, provides a salient example. This fellow was notorious for having killed his cousins and nephews to acquire his rule and for having committed incest with his sister. Despite his crimes, when Pope Julius II undertook to expel him from his city, Baglioni capitulated without the slightest struggle. Machiavelli relates that "the cowardice of Giovampagolo [was] noted by the prudent men who were with the pope, and they were unable to guess whence it came that he did not, to his perpetual fame, crush his enemy at a stroke and enrich himself with booty, since with the pope were all the cardinals with all their delights" (*D* 1.27.1).

Because in the past he had not suffered from the pangs of conscience, Baglioni seemed to be the perfect candidate to rid Italy of its scourge—the clergy who lived and ruled as a corrupt court (*D* 1.12 and 55).

> So Giovampagolo, who did not mind being incestuous and a public parricide, did not know how—or, to say better, did not dare, when he had just the opportunity for it—to engage in an enterprise in which everyone would have admired his spirit and that would have left an eternal memory of himself as being the first who had demonstrated to the prelates how little is to be esteemed whoever lives and reigns as they do; and he would have done a thing whose greatness would have surpassed all infamy, every danger, that could have proceeded from it. (*D* 1.27.2)

The Christian conscience appears at the damndest times to thwart what Machiavelli regards as desirable political ends.

In an attempt to overcome this feebleness, Machiavelli emphasizes the extreme acts that the highest type—his great founders—commits. He names Moses, Romulus, Cyrus, and Theseus as the great founders of all time, who should be admired and, if possible, imitated (*P* 6). It must be assumed, of course, that the

Cyrus whom he praises here is not the Cyrus of Xenophon's rendition. We already know that Machiavelli accuses writers of offering misleading depictions of their heroes. Indeed, when discussing Romulus and Moses in his *Discourse,* he emphasizes and praises what the "writers" would most certainly call their crimes. In speaking of Moses in the *Discourse,* he notes approvingly, "whoever reads the Bible judiciously will see that since he wished his laws and his orders to go forward, Moses was forced to kill infinite men who, moved by nothing other than envy, were opposed to his plans" (*D* 3.30.1). Because the Bible does not highlight Moses' extreme acts, one must read it judiciously to comprehend the true character of Moses' leadership.[21] In contrast, Machiavelli's work, far from failing to highlight extreme acts, advocates them.

In the case of Romulus, however, Machiavelli does not so much emphasize his crimes as he invents them. This invention on Machiavelli's part serves as an educational tool intended to illustrate what he demands of a founder. He uses Romulus to illustrate the truth of his declaration contained in a chapter title that "it is necessary to be alone if one wishes to order a republic anew or to reform it altogether outside its ancient orders" (*D* 1.9). Because of this necessity, he exonerates Romulus for those acts that assured his sole rule: the murder of his brother Remus and of the Sabine, Titus Tatius, with whom Romulus shared rule of their two peoples. Legend, of course, has it that Romulus slew Remus in a dispute over who would rule the new city, and Livy dutifully reports the incident in his history. Livy does not report, however, that Romulus killed his colleague in rule. Livy says that Tatius was killed by a group of Laurentians in revenge for Tatius's failure to punish his kinsmen who had mistreated a group of Laurentian envoys. The only guilt that Livy imputes to Romulus with regard to the whole incident derives from his feeling "less distress at [Tatius's] death than was strictly proper."[22] Conversely, Machiavelli does not even mention those who committed the murder, saying only that Romulus "deserves excuse in the deaths of his brother and of his partner," thus implying that Romulus was fully responsible for both (*D* 1.9.2). Machiavelli's Romulus must be excused for even greater crimes than those contained in the legend for Machiavelli to teach what he thinks is required of a founder.

Machiavelli offers those excuses with alacrity, an alacrity based on his eagerness to teach the lesson that Xenophon and even Livy do not teach effectively—that great men must take the most extreme actions. Perhaps if Soderini had imbibed the correct lessons from the examples of Brutus, Moses, and Romulus, he would not have hesitated to be alone and to extinguish envy. A defective education, then, was the cause not only of Scipio's troubles but also of the failures of Machiavelli's contemporaries—Soderini, Baglioni, and those who hold subject cities.

Machiavelli's Education for Rule: The Greatest Glory

Security in politics demands a hard heart. Protect your rule at all costs, exhorts Machiavelli. He also promises that other goods will come from such resolution.

The depredations of warring factions will cease, for example, or Italy will be rid of a rapacious class of clergy. There are even greater benefits, however, to be derived from the successful implementation of Machiavelli's education in rule. To those princes with the greatest of ambitions, he holds out the greatest of goods: perpetual fame as a result of the founding of a long-lived state. A republic best serves as the vehicle for such glory, owing to its resilience and acquisitive power.

The existence of that greatest reward comes dimly to sight in *The Prince* when Machiavelli offers additional encouragement to political men to satisfy their desires. He says there that "truly it is a very natural and ordinary thing to desire to acquire, and always, when men do it who can, they will be praised or not blamed" (*P* 3.14). He offers a familiar refrain: "do not worry about the means; worry about attaining the results." What appears in this statement to be a mere afterthought on Machiavelli's part, the insertion of the phrase "or not blamed," is actually quite important. Only the right type of acquisition assures praise, rather than merely an avoidance of blame. Machiavelli conveys this idea much more clearly in the *Discourses*.

The right type of acquisition is the acquisition of sole authority in the name of reforming a corrupt state. "And truly, if a prince seeks the glory of the world, he ought to desire to possess a corrupt city—not to spoil it entirely as did Caesar but to reorder it as did Romulus. And truly the heavens cannot give to men a greater opportunity for glory, nor can men desire any greater," affirms Machiavelli (*D* 1.10.6). But Romulus did not so much reorder Rome as found it.

Machiavelli's linking of Romulus with the task of refounding is justified because he is looking for a latter-day Romulus to undertake the difficult task of refounding in the modern world. Machiavelli holds up Romulus as a model to be emulated not only because he was capable of committing crimes that maintained his sole authority, but also because he used that authority to allow others to rule after him.

> That Romulus . . . deserves excuse in the deaths of his brother and of his partner, and
> that what he did was for the common good and not for his own ambition, is demon-
> strated by his having at once ordered a Senate with which he took counsel and by
> whose opinion he decided. (*D* 1.9.2)

Romulus's crimes were done for the sake of the common good. He killed so that he could have sole authority, but he used that sole authority to establish the institution of the Senate, which played a central role not only in the kingship but in the republic.

Machiavelli is asking quite a lot of his orderer. This orderer must be hard-hearted enough to kill if necessary to put his plans into place, but once they are in place he must step aside, allowing others to rule. He knows precisely how demanding his requirement is; he knows he requires this unlikely combination of a bad and a good man. He confirms the necessity of that unlikely combination when he discusses how to overcome corruption so widespread that it is evident to all. In such a case "it is necessary to go to the extraordinary [modes], such as vio-lence and arms, and before everything else become prince of that city, able to dis-pose it in one's own mode" (*D* 1.18.4). Once one has become prince in this way, a true founder should use his newfound power for good rather than bad ends.

> Because the reordering of a city for a political way of life presupposes a good man, and becoming prince of a republic by violence presupposes a bad man, one will find that it very rarely happens that someone good wishes to become prince by bad ways, even though his end be good, and that someone wicked, having become prince, wishes to work well, and that it will ever occur to his mind to use well the authority that he has acquired badly. (*D* 1.18.4)

This is quite a bind indeed.

Nevertheless, Machiavelli has a solution, and his solution is further education. The potential founder must be educated to the fact that Machiavelli's conception of a republic will be the best way to assure the founder's fame. The component of allowing others to rule after the founding or reordering is critical to the founder's or restorer's ultimate success, according to Machiavelli: "if one indi-vidual is capable of ordering, the thing itself is ordered to last long not if it remains on the shoulders of one individual but rather if it remains in the care of many and its maintenance stays with many" (*D* 1.9.2). In addition, in 1.58 of the *Discourses*, the chapter in which he offers his defense of the people, he declares "[i]f princes are superior to peoples in ordering laws, forming civil lives, and ordering new statutes and orders, peoples are so much superior in maintaining things ordered that without doubt they attain the glory of those who order them" (*D* 1.58.3). The founder's long-term interest, then, demands that he relinquish some of his power.

Even more specifically, the founder will acquire glory if he founds an acquisi-tive republic. To do this, he must have a Machiavellian appreciation of the capac-ity of the people to be soldiers. He must also understand the capacities of those of the princely type to acquire glory for themselves that will, in turn, redound to the founder's memory. A republic, well stocked with "infinite most virtuous princes who are successors to one another," will be able to do more than just acquire the world (*D* 1.20.1).

His bestowal of praise and blame works to educate men to embrace bad means for good ends. Thus Machiavelli excoriates those men who have a good end in mind, but who stumble before the prospect of the bad means that their end requires. Soderini is, of course, a case in point. Machiavelli, however, blames him not only for failing to kill the partisans of the Medici, but also for failing to take sole power. Soderini recognized "that if he wished to strike his opponents vigor-ously and to beat down his adversaries, he would have needed to take up extraor-dinary authority and break up civil equality together with the laws." He did not take the steps that would have given him sole power because he feared that it would discourage the people of Florence from ever again making a *gonfalonier* for life, the office that he would have used to acquire that sole power. Machiavelli concedes that Soderini's hesitancy "was wise and good." Soderini was, after all, a good man. That fact, however, does not prevent Machiavelli from ridiculing him: "nonetheless he should never allow an evil to run loose out of respect for a good, when that good could easily be crushed by that evil" (*D* 3.3.1). The good that Soderini pursued was the preservation of republican rule, but in attempting to preserve it by upholding a good example, he allowed it to be overthrown. Because his means were ineffectual, the end he cherished crumbled.

This, then, is Machiavelli's education for rule. In short, one must not look for one's honor or glory outside of the political realm. There is no goodness apart from the political good, and that good, such as it is, is incomplete. He declares that "prudence consists in knowing how to recognize the qualities of inconveniences, and in picking the less bad as good." Because he insists that one must choose the less bad, he implies that there is no good as such. Indeed, Machiavelli insists that "in the order of things it is found that one never seeks to avoid one inconvenience without running into another" (*P* 21.91). The only good for human beings is the hope of the acquisition of property, of glory, or of both. The acquisition of either necessitates the acquisition of more (*D* 1.37). There is no rest. For Machiavelli, politics is all, and Machiavelli's politics is ridden with strife.

CONCLUSION

Machiavelli offers an education that he believes will counter the harmful effects of the education offered by humanity's previous teachers. His new education rejects the notions of goodness that the classics and the Christians posited. To mitigate the shock and revulsion that that rejection is sure to induce, Machiavelli contends that his attack on the previous traditions is actually evidence of his humanity and charity, just as Camillus's beating of the old teacher was evidence of Camillus's humanity and charity. Having taught the youth to beat their teachers, he hopes that, like Camillus, he will gain the city for himself. If he accomplishes this feat, then Machiavelli is the savior of the city, offering salvation from the political chaos that the other traditions fostered. No longer will the interests of the city be sacrificed to the attainment of a virtue that demotes, rejects, or denounces those actions that an effective politics demands.

Despite Machiavelli's claim that he offers his teaching in service to humanity, humanity must pay a very high price for adhering to it. First, human beings must be willing to accept the consequences of his demand that politics is all. He severely circumscribes the extent to which any citizen can escape from the demands of his notion of politics. The people must heed at all times the call that they be soldiers in service to a city that seeks continual expansion. In addition, the city's princes cannot find respite from politics in philosophy or in any other "idle" activity. The individuals who inhabit Machiavelli's new world must offer their complete dedication to politics. Second, humanity must accept the consequences that flow from his teachings that offer justification for any deed whatsoever done in the name of the city's defense and glory. The ability to justify such deeds cannot help but eventuate in the type of Machiavellianism to which this defender of humanity gave his name.

The ramifications of Machiavelli's teachings become clearer when we compare him with a thinker who followed him in seeking an earthly salvation for humanity. Thomas Hobbes attempts to find such salvation in a Machiavellian world in which one is forced to choose among inconveniences. Hobbes declares that this new understanding of the world repudiates the claims of the ancients: "there is no such *Finis ultimus* [utmost *ayme*], nor *Summum Bonum* [greatest Good], as is spoken of in the Books of the old Moral Philosophers."[23] Like Machiavelli's, Hobbes's quest induces him to berate the teachers of old. His castigation of Aristotle is, in fact, quite pointed: "I believe that scarce any thing can be more absurdly said in naturall Philosophy, than that which now is called *Aristotles Metaphysics*; not more repugnant to Government, than much of that hee hath said in his *Politiques*; nor more ignorantly, than a great part of his *Ethiques*."[24] With respect to political matters, Hobbes objects in particular to Aristotle's distinction between good and deviant regimes because this distinction fosters disrespect for law and hence encourages disputes in the realm of politics. People tend to chafe under any authority, but Aristotle's distinction between regimes lends authority to their complaints. Rather than admitting their dissatisfaction with any rule whatsoever, they can appeal to Aristotle's distinction, calling their ruler or rulers unjust. In contrast, Hobbes denies that there is a standard beyond what the laws decree by which a citizen or subject can render a decision regarding a regime's goodness or badness.

Although Machiavelli does not emphasize obedience to law, as does Hobbes, at base his position on the relation between morality and politics is identical to that of Hobbes: there shall be no appeal beyond the city. The difference between them — and it is a critical one — lies in the fact that Hobbes intends to foster peace. There shall be no contention over just and unjust laws, and, hence, civil harmony will reign. Indeed, Hobbes takes peace as his guide: "Reason declaring Peace to be good, it follows the same reason, that all the necessary means to Peace be good also, and therefore, that *Modesty, Equity, Trust, Humanity, Mercy* (which we have demonstrated to be necessary to Peace), are *good Manners*, or habits, (that is) *Vertues*. The *Law* therefore, in the means to Peace, commands also *Good Manners*, or the practice of *Vertue*: And therefore it is call'd *Moral*."[25]

Rather than the good residing in military exploits that bring acquisition, Hobbes finds the good in peace. Peace determines what is virtuous, what is lawful, what is moral. With the promise of "commodious living" to those who adhere to his notion of morality, Hobbes hopes that peace and the arts and sciences it promotes can bring the acquisition that hitherto had come only as a spoil of war.[26] Because Hobbes does not recognize the necessity of war, he can offer the people the private life that, even according to Machiavelli's analysis, they always sought. As a result, Hobbes is more a friend of the people than is Machiavelli, despite the latter's loud protestations that he is the people's defender.

Hobbes's bestowal of a private life distances him from Machiavelli and moves him decidedly closer to the liberalism under which we live. Nevertheless, the two are united in demanding that whatever benefits the city, according to the prescription of the good that each offers, is praiseworthy and moral.

NOTES

1. Quotations from Machiavelli's *Discourses on Livy* will be cited in the text and indicated by the abbreviation *D*, followed by the book, chapter, and paragraph number. I use the translation by Harvey C. Mansfield and Nathan Tarcov (Chicago: University of Chicago Press, 1996). Quotations from *The Prince* will be indicated by a *P* in the text, followed by the chapter and page number, and are derived from *The Prince*, tr. Harvey C. Mansfield (Chicago: University of Chicago Press, 1995). The *Florentine Histories*, tr. Laura Banfield and Harvey C. Mansfield (Princeton: Princeton University Press, 1988) will be cited in the text with the abbreviation *FH*, followed by the book and chapter number.

2. Clifford Orwin convincingly identifies this formulation of virtue and vice as Machiavelli's innovation ("Machiavelli's Unchristian Charity," *American Political Science Review* 72 (1978): 1218–19.

3. Isaiah Berlin takes seriously Machiavelli's claim that "his path has never before been trodden by any man" and finds that he ignores the "concepts and categories" that thinkers of his day used to "express themselves." In examining Machiavelli's originality, Berlin finds Machiavelli's silence regarding natural law more surprising than that regarding Christian concepts such as sin and salvation. Ultimately, however, Berlin finds that Machiavelli rejects Christian morality in favor of an older morality—pagan morality that seeks to aggrandize men and states ("The Originality of Machiavelli," in Isaiah Berlin, *Against the Current* [New York: Viking Press, 1980], 36–37 and 54–55). I argue that Machiavelli did not seek an unmitigated return to pagan morality because Christianity's victory reveals paganism's defects. To overcome Christianity, Machiavelli proposes to use Christianity's insights against it (Vickie Sullivan, *Machiavelli's Three Romes: Religion, Human Liberty, and Politics Reformed* [DeKalb: Northern Illinois University Press, 1996]).

4. Leo Strauss's *Thoughts on Machiavelli* (Chicago: University of Chicago Press, 1958) offers the most comprehensive treatment of Machiavelli's opposition to both the Christian and classical traditions.

5. In the *Discourses,* Machiavelli examines the political utility of oblivion: it allows founders to create a new epoch without reference to the former epoch (*D* 2.5). He often overlooks ancient Greece, as if he wished its memory could be obliterated. For example, in the preface to the second book of the *Discourses*, he describes how virtue has migrated throughout the world and fails to mention Greece as a venue for virtue.

6. Aristotle, *Nichomachean Ethics* 1180a25–26. I quote from Terence Irwin's translation (Indianapolis: Hackett, 1985), 294. See also *Politics* 1271b1–2.

7. Aristotle, *Politics* 1271b2–6. I quote from Carnes Lord's translation (Chicago: University of Chicago Press, 1984), 78.

8. See Aristotle, *Politics* 1333a30–3, 1334a4–5 and 15.

9. In discussing how Machiavelli's notion of virtue differs from Aristotle's, Harvey Mansfield states: "Machiavelli's notion of virtue . . . replaces confidence in the kindness of nature or God with a more secure base in necessity. It is necessary for humans to trust in necessity" (*Machiavelli's Virtue* [Chicago: University of Chicago Press, 1996], 15). Machiavelli's concern with necessity is surely evident in his discussion of war, and that concern impels him to embrace an acquisitive republic.

10. Aristotle, *Politics* 1253a7–17; Lord's translation, 37.

11. See also the discussion in Sullivan, *Three Romes*, 181–90.

12. Some Roman patricians placed a higher premium on their property than their honor (*D* 1.37), a fact that would suggest that such patricians actually belong to the class that Machiavelli designates as the people. Conversely, princes often must overcome the disadvantage of a low birth (*P* 6).

13. I have changed the translation of *le braccia* that Mansfield and Tarcov offer from "arms" to "limbs"; *Machiavelli: Tutte le opere,* ed. Mario Martelli (Florence: Sansoni, 1971), 129.

14. Aristotle, *Nichomachean Ethics* 1177b5–6; Irwin's translation, 285.

15. Aristotle, *Nichomachean Ethics* 1177b15–18; Irwin's translation, 286.

16. Aristotle, *Nichomachean Ethics* 1177a20–b1; Irwin's translation, 284–85.

17. Aristotle, *Politics* 1267a8–12; Lord's translation, 68.

18. There is a type of leisure associated with Christianity, which Machiavelli terms "ambitious idleness" in the preface to the first book of the *Discourses*.

19. See also Harvey C. Mansfield's discussion of Machiavelli's rejection of leisure in light of Aristotle's teaching (*Machiavelli's Virtue*, 14).

20. Aristotle, *Ethics* 1130b26–29.

21. Scipio failed at this type of judicious reading when he imitated Xenophon's depiction of Cyrus.

22. Livy, *Ab urbe condita* 1.14. I quote from the translation by Aubrey de Sélincourt (New York: Penguin Books, 1960), 49.

23. Thomas Hobbes, *Leviathan*, ed. Richard Tuck (Cambridge: Cambridge University Press, 1991), 70.

24. Hobbes, *Leviathan*, 461–62.

25. Thomas Hobbes, *De Cive* (Oxford: Clarendon Press, 1983), 74–75.

26. Hobbes, *Leviathan*, 90.

Part Two

Modernity and Problems of Ethical Reflection

Chapter Five

Rousseau on the Sources of Ethics

Clifford Orwin

In ethics as in other realms, Jean-Jacques Rousseau has exerted an extraordinary influence from his debut as a thinker down to the present day. As the founder of the counter-Enlightenment, he was the first to contend *on the basis of modern thought itself* that everything the Enlighteners had presented as auspicious for the future of mankind was deeply ominous for it. The first great modern critic of modernity, he brilliantly articulated the discontent with itself that has dogged it ever since.

Rousseau's contribution to ethical thought thus begins with his critique of his predecessors. They had promoted a new, more "realistic" morality of rational self-interest—more realistic, that is, than classical or Christian morality. Rousseau's first attack on the new morality, the *Discourse on the Sciences and Arts,* flashed like a thunderbolt across the painted skies of the salons of Paris.[1] There, responding to the question whether the spread of the arts and sciences had contributed to the purification of morals,[2] he insisted that in his time, as in all others, it had rather contributed to their decline.[3] In his own day the dissemination of Enlightenment rationalism had fostered behavior that was deeply pernicious. It had encouraged a narrow egoism which, together with the spread of commerce, learning, urbanity, and the inequality associated with them, had favored depravity and decadence. The dream of reason had brought forth monsters, not supporting but confounding the cause of virtue wherever rationalism had penetrated. Self-interested reasoning did not support morality: at most it sustained the appearance of it. Nor were human beings themselves as rational as such teachings presumed: civilized man offers "the disfiguring contrast of passion that believes that it reasons and the understanding that hallucinates."[4]

Yet if the outlook for civilized human beings was dismal, it was still the responsibility of a public-spirited philosopher to prescribe for them. This was true whether they groaned under the monarchies that went hand in hand with decadence or whether, as in Rousseau's native Geneva, a rearguard action might still be waged on behalf of republican virtue. And then there were more primitive peoples, some of whom dwelt on the margins of Europe (like the Corsicans and Poles, in whom Rousseau was to take an interest), who might yet benefit from his new wisdom. Everywhere, moreover, a few born to think resided among many who could not be troubled to do so and lived in the shade of opinion. This diversity of constituency partly explains the complexity of Rousseau's writings on morality.[5] There was, as he saw it, no one moral education appropriate to all learners; indeed, there was no one desired result.

Rousseau's canvass of the history of the West yielded two distinct models of moral education, which he called civic and domestic. Rousseau's exemplars of civic education were Sparta and republican Rome, small, tight, agrarian societies subject to the general will of their citizens. Such societies depended on virtue in the sense of the term that Rousseau had learned from Montesquieu: a passionate devotion to *la patrie* and to the freedom, equality, and simplicity that prevailed within its walls. Virtue so conceived implied unremitting public-spiritedness culminating in indifference to the fate of oneself and one's own. "Vile slave," declaims the Spartan mother informed by a helot that all five of her sons have perished in battle, "I asked you not about my sons but whether we won the victory."[6]

Rousseau was aware that such citizenship was not easily come by. Nor, however, was it simply utopian or fanciful.

The homeland cannot subsist without freedom, nor freedom without virtue, nor virtue without citizens. . . . Now training citizens is not accomplished in a day, and to have them as men they must be taught as children. Someone may tell me that anyone who has men to govern should not seek, outside of their nature, a perfection of which they are not capable; that he should not want to destroy their passions, and that the execution of such a project would not be any more desirable than it is possible. I will agree the more strongly with all this because a man who had no passions would certainly be a very bad citizen. But it must also be agreed that although men cannot be taught to love nothing, it is not impossible to teach them to love one thing rather than another, and what is truly beautiful rather than what is deformed. If, for example, they are trained early enough never to consider their own persons except as related to the body of the state, and not to perceive their own existence, so to speak, except as part of the state's, they will eventually come to identify themselves in some way with this larger whole; to feel themselves to be members of the homeland; to love it with that delicate sentiment that every isolated man feels only for himself; to elevate their soul perpetually toward this great object; and thereby to translate into a sublime virtue this dangerous disposition from which all our vices arise. Not only does Philosophy demonstrate the possibility of these new directions; but History provides a thousand stunning examples. If they are so rare among us, it is because no one cares whether there are any citizens, and still less does anyone think of doing something early enough to form them. It is too late to change our natural directions when they have become entrenched, and habit has been combined with *amour-propre*.[7]

Thus does Rousseau defend himself against the charge of utopianism: his "new directions" are not new but well attested in both theory and practice. If these "new directions" seem incredible to his contemporaries, it is because they no longer comprehend citizenship because they no longer grasp the indeterminacy of human selfishness. "Denaturing" thus proves ambiguous as a characterization of civic education. Rousseau's moral realism cuts both ways: man is naturally self-ish, but the self is naturally malleable.

While civic education, like other forms of moral education, depends on the dila-tion of the self (the *moi humain*), the self cannot be extended indefinitely, nor can its focus be successfully divided between the particular and the universal. Civic educa-tion as Rousseau conceives it is intensely political and particularistic, and it must pervade the entire society. He espouses the classical teaching that a city must remain small if it is to retain the intense allegiance of its citizens. "When the world became divided into nations too large to be well governed, [civic education] was no longer practicable; and other reasons that the reader can easily see have also prevented its being tried by any modern people" (*PE* [*OC* 3:261–62]). The chief of these other reasons is Christianity, which by dividing the human heart between heaven and earth and preaching a universalistic morality, has rendered impossible a moral education at the same time rigorously particularistic and rigorously this-worldly.[8] Rousseau himself proves to have mixed feelings about the particularism of civic morality, which drives men to shed the natural blood of their fellows in the name of what are ultimately conventional or accidental distinctions. Indeed he goes so far as to lament the division of mankind into distinct and warring societies; this is the "pacifistic" or proto-Tolstoyan side of Rousseau's ethics.[9] At the same time, Rousseau prefers civic morality with all its warts to the cosmopolitanism of the modern "humanitarian," which he never fails to denounce as fraudulent.

Every particular society, when it is narrow and unified, is estranged from the all-encompassing society (sc. of the human race). Every patriot is harsh to foreigners. They are only men. They are nothing in his eyes. This is a drawback, inevitable but not compelling. The essential thing is to be good to those with whom one lives. . . . Distrust those cosmopolitans who go to great length in their books to discover duties they do not deign to fulfill around them. A philosopher loves the Tartars so as to be spared having to love his neighbors.[10]

It seems that the feeling of humanity evaporates and weakens as it is extended over the whole world, and that we can't be moved by calamities in Tartary or Japan as we are by those of a European people. Interest and commiseration must in some way be confined or compressed to be activated. Now since this inclina-tion in us can be useful only to those with whom we have to live, it is good that the feeling of humanity, concentrated among fellow citizens, gains fresh force through the habit of seeing one another and through the common interest that unites them (*PE* [*OC* 3:254–55]). "Humanity is a political resource too valuable to squander on humankind."

As Rousseau was a moral realist, so was he a political one. He saw how demanding was the virtue required to sustain freedom and equality among human beings. He recognized how precariously human nature supported such virtue, how stringent an education was required to sustain it, and how susceptible, therefore, it must always be to corruption. While maintaining the possibility in theory (as well as the historical actuality) of the city of the social contract, he articulated it less as a blueprint for realization in his own day than as a rigorous demonstration of the illegitimacy of the kind of government we moderns had to put up with.[11]

The modern world, far removed from Sparta and Rome, was subject to a political destiny best described as post-Christian. This was the predominance of the large, enlightened, commercial society, with its progress, luxury, inequality, and corruption. The typical denizen of this society was the bourgeois, a term to which Rousseau imparted its distinctively modern and pejorative sense. Rousseau's critique of the bourgeois has proved his most durable legacy. Its core was that in comparison with natural man, who was solitary, and with the citizen, who was fully integrated into the larger whole of the city, the bourgeois "floated," neither wholly independent of others nor wholly integrated with them.[12] Ravaged by a thousand futile cares, divided between duties he does not love and passions he cannot satisfy, the bourgeois depends far too much on others to be entirely himself, yet is far too selfish for others to depend on him.

The predominance of the bourgeois furnishes the context common to Rousseau's projects of "domestic" education—education for an age in which citizenship was no longer possible. The challenge was not to reform a corrupt society—this Rousseau deemed impossible[13]—but to rescue some few from the general corruption. His scenarios for his contemporaries were, as the late Judith Shklar put it, so many "strategies" for coping with the strange combination of estrangement from his fellows and dependence on them that is the lot of post-Christian man.[14] Different human types required different forms of therapy. As a result, Rousseau stands at the source of not one but a range of moral alternatives. The alternative most suitable for most ordinary people was "domestic"; it substituted the family for the greater society as the locus of life, in morals as in other respects. For Rousseau's two couples, Emile and Sophie of *Emile* and Wolmar and Julie of *Julie,* the crucial moral arena is that of spouse, children, dependents, and neighbors. Rousseau was the philosophic patron of what we might call romantic domesticity and foreshadowed the nineteenth-century novel in both celebrating this alternative and disclosing some of its difficulties.[15]

Rousseau's domestic moral education acquiesces in the bourgeois revolution by recognizing that morality will be both a private matter and a this-worldly one. The question arises, "Which view of the world is most appropriate for fostering such a morality?" Rousseau regards his contemporaries as in need of two quite contrary moral rhetorics: that of the return to nature and that of the overcoming of nature. The rhetoric of the return to nature carries forward the critique of moral rationalism previously mentioned, promotes in its stead various pre- or subrational grounds of morality, and articulates a new post-Christian religion of nature. Here Rousseau preaches the retrieval of nature, already scarred by "a thousand forever recurring causes, by the acquisition of a mass of knowledge and errors, . . . by the continual impact of the passions" (*SD* [*OC* 3:122]).

The relevant moral distinction is between the natural, on the one hand, and the historical or factitious on the other, with the latter stigmatized as corruptions of the former. Rousseau's rhetoric of the overcoming of nature, on the other hand, exalts reason and will as the grounds of a morality of autonomy and dignity unavailable in nature. It preaches the subjection of desire as such to reason and will. By severing reason from natural inclinations no less than factitious ones, Rousseau bids farewell to practical reason as conceived by Hobbes, Locke, and Hume, and he anticipates the Kantian version.

The seeming contradiction between Rousseau's appeals to nature and senti-ment and to reason conceived as their antithesis has led to confusion among his critics and, not surprisingly, to the imputation of confusion to him. The two appeals are consistent, however, at least in regard to their practical intention. Each brings new arguments to bear in support of the moral life, and each seeks to restore the purity of that life over and against the argument from rational self-interest that Rousseau regards as so debasing to morality. Each, moreover, aims to further the possibility of human happiness by sketching a life distinguished by its goodness not only for others but for oneself. Each, finally, points beyond itself to a life combining the fullest development of reason and the other faculties per-fected only in society with a version of the return to nature. Here the opposites converge, in the life of which Rousseau himself—the Rousseau of the *Reveries of the Solitary Walker*—furnishes the first (and only?) exemplar.

Rousseau's rhetoric of the overcoming of nature is the less frequent of the two. It is, nonetheless, of the greatest historical importance, above all because of its impact on Immanuel Kant and through him on all subsequent moral philosophy. Rousseau's most famous statement in this vein occurs in *Social Contract* 1.8.

> The transition from the state of nature to the civil state produces a most remarkable change in man by substituting justice for instinct in his conduct, and endowing his actions with the morality they previously lacked. Only then, when the voice of duty succeeds physical impulsion and right succeeds appetite, does man, who until then had looked only to himself, see himself forced to act upon other principles, and to consult his reason before listening to his inclinations. . . . To the preceding one might add to the credit of the civil state moral freedom, which alone makes man truly the master of himself. For the impulse of mere appetite is slavery, and obedience to the law one has prescribed to oneself is freedom. (*OC* 3:364–65)[16]

Morality consists in emancipation from the tutelage of nature: the life accord-ing to nature is submoral. Morality is submission to self-legislation. Rousseau here differs from Kant in casting this self-legislation as collective rather than individual—hence its linkage with the social contract and the authority of the general will. And because it is thus political, its effectiveness among the citizens depends upon the civic education discussed above.

Also because Rousseau's morality of rational will is political, its substance is ultimately particular: the good of the political community in question. General (and hence moral) in relation to the citizens, it is particular in relation to outsiders (and so without authority for them). As we have already seen, Rousseau rejects moral cosmopolitanism as politically impracticable and largely hypocritical. The moral world of the Spartan does not extend beyond the walls of Sparta. This means, however, that on this level of Rousseau's moral teaching the opposition between morality and nature remains imperfect. The morality of the general will serves natural (albeit collective) selfishness even as the rhetoric of 1.8 suggests that morality is higher than natural selfishness. We overcome the (transient) impulsions of nature in obedience to our permanent ones, aware that we can secure what is good for us only by willing the general good. Rousseau's Kantian rhetoric embellishes a moralism that in its realism forgoes Kantian purity. He hymns an emancipation from nature that falls well short of true emancipation.

Finally, that the morality of the overcoming of nature as presented in the *Social Contract* is political in character means that although it can inspire the bourgeois, it cannot serve as an adequate guide for him. It instructs him as to what he lacks and what he, at least in principle, should hope for should a great revolution occur someday, but it cannot suffice to direct his daily life, deprived as he is of all opportunity of citizenship. Not surprisingly, then, while it is Rousseau's first formulation of morality in this vein, it is not his last.

Rousseau's second great statement of the opposition between morality and nature is found toward the end of *Emile*. With it we reach the climactic stage of Emile's education. Here the tutor, Rousseau's alter ego, must deal with a new problem, one arising from Emile's courtship of Sophie. Hitherto Emile has been a paragon of moderation and therefore of freedom, not because he is capable of overcoming his appetites but because his education has preserved his appetites in their natural moderation. Now, however, in thrall to his love of Sophie, Emile has lost both moderation and freedom. His passions are inflamed: he will brook no obstacle or setback to them. His very sanity is hostage both to fortune (which could snatch his beloved from him at any moment) and to the will of Sophie.

Emile's new situation discloses the limits of his education to date. As unbridled desire subjects him to misery and possibly wickedness, so he must subject it—to duty. The tutor calls his attention to the root of "virtue" in the Latin word for strength. To be virtuous is to be weak by nature and strong by will. This opposition of will and nature is to form the core of Emile's self-understanding. The will must be constructed: Emile is to believe that he has constructed it by his own efforts. The will is thus conceived as supernatural without being supernatural: we owe it not to God but to ourselves. Virtue is self-conquest; the virtuous man alone is truly his own master.

Here much foreshadows Kant. It is, however, revealing of Rousseau's distance from Kant that the means of Emile's moral education is a love affair.[17] The tutor plays Friar Laurence to the starstruck couple but, unlike his celibate predecessor, he succeeds in maneuvering them into a chaste marriage without indulging their unbridled passion—as he does in contriving a happy ending to it all. Emile gains morality; he also gets the girl. By demonstrating his willingness to relinquish Sophie, he proves his worthiness to possess her.

Virtue then is its own reward but by no means its only one. For the husband and father, as for the citizen, virtue makes a crucial contribution to his happiness. Even satisfaction that one has risen above one's nature figures in the argument as a contribution to happiness. Rousseau never presents happiness, however, as he sometimes does virtue, as supranatural. And Rousseau, unlike Kant, never denies that happiness is the authoritative goal for human beings. He thus casts doubt on the very opposition between nature and virtue, for if that contentment for which our nature longs is to be obtained through virtue, the latter's claim upon us would be not its superiority to our nature but its appropriateness to it. Behind or alongside the praise of virtue at nature's expense lurks the suggestion that all roads lead ultimately to nature, even that of virtue. Indeed, just this moral education of Emile that culminates in an injunction to transcend nature is repeatedly described throughout the work as the education most in accordance with nature. Rousseau's very rhetoric of morality as the overcoming of nature thus inevitably points to his rhetoric of morality as the return to nature.

Let us consider the return to nature. This strand of Rousseau's moral teaching commonly invokes conscience, sincerity, and compassion—all conceived as aspects of naturalness opposed to the artificiality of bourgeois society. Here virtue figures as something natural and universal, to be discovered within us all rather than to be imposed from outside as the capstone of a civic education or any other education.

> O virtue! Sublime science of simple souls, are so much trouble and equipment required to know you? Are not your principles engraved on all hearts, and is it not enough in order to learn your laws to return within oneself and to listen to the voice of one's conscience in the silence of the passions? That is the true philosophy, let us know how to be content with it. . . .[18]

Thus the conclusion of the *First Discourse*, the first of Rousseau's fusillades against enlightenment. Oddly, one seeks in vain in Rousseau for a straightforward exposition of these principles engraved on all hearts. Rousseau's version of conscience is post-Christian—natural rather than divine, or divine only insofar as we accept the natural as divine—and much about it remains obscure.

Rousseau's extreme empiricism, his nascent historicism, and his insistence on the perennial distinction in every society between the few true thinkers and the many captives of current opinion all tend against the quasi-Christian claim of an underlying substantive agreement common to human beings as such. The citizen, be it noted, lives not by the laws of conscience but by the general will, which is not universal but relative to the good of his particular society. Inasmuch as his heart is his guide, it is so not as the seat of nature within him but as the seat of the civic *moeurs* impressed upon it by the Legislator.[19] As for Emile, that "natural man within civil society," his morality, far from prompting him independently of his education, is, as we have already seen, the result of that long and arduous process.

Whether or not the sort of conscience that Rousseau preaches is compatible with Rousseau's principles, it alone can serve his rhetorical turn. Conscience can offer a clear alternative to the sway of opinion in defective societies only if it is universal, infallible, and audible to all who will but listen to it. Such moral populism also serves Rousseau well in his struggle to subvert the prestige both of the Church and of the Enlightenment. He claims to tell his readers only what they could have seen for themselves had they not been confused by the sophisms of his rivals. In repudiating these, they submit not to his tutelage but to that of their own hearts.

Rousseau's great set piece on the conscience is the Profession of Faith of the Savoyard Vicar in book 4 of *Emile*. The Vicar presents a view of the soul and conscience than which none could be more edifying or (in the sense already indicated) more populistic. It is all the more striking, then, that the rest of *Emile*, in which Rousseau presents his own account of nature and the soul, profoundly contradicts the view of the Vicar. (In particular, the Vicar's dualism of freedom and nature does not correspond with Rousseau's dualism of *amour de soi*—attachment to our particular existence—and *amour-propre*—sensitivity to our status relative to others.) Here, as elsewhere, our task in interpreting Rousseau on ethics is greatly complicated by his own ethical resolve to be alike truthful and edifying—while recognizing that the truth is not always edifying.[20]

In a brilliant recent article on the Profession of Faith, Arthur Melzer has argued that the Profession of Faith represents Rousseau's endeavor to replace Christianity with a religion of sincerity.[21] Insistence on faith in the proper doctrines, as preached by the one true Church outside which there is no salvation, yields to an emphasis on the sincerity of one's belief in whatever doctrines one holds. God requires not that we profess true beliefs but that we truly believe in what we profess. He likewise demands that we respect the sincerely held beliefs of others: the religion of sincerity is necessarily a tolerant religion. It also privileges natural over revealed religion, i.e., the teachings of reason as confirmed by conscience over those allegedly supernatural accounts about which both reason and conscience are silent.

Rousseau's elaboration of a religion of sincerity reflects his broader resort to this newly articulated virtue.[22] Earlier moralists had, of course, demanded sincerity in morality, but none had defined morality primarily in terms of sincerity. As already suggested, Rousseau's emphasis on sincerity is an aspect of his promotion of a return to naturalness within society—what Friedrich Nietzsche was scornfully to describe as the return to nature *in impuris naturalibus*. Nature in Rousseau's understanding is partly universal and partly particular: there is human nature as opposed to the vicissitudes of history and the distortions of society, and there is my nature as opposed to anyone else's. Because Rousseau champions nature in both senses, there is a certain ambiguity in his thought, too-hasty resolutions of which point us in contradictory ethical directions: toward what Nietzsche would despise as herd morality, on the one hand, and the ethics of authenticity, on the other. Neither is true to the complexities of Rousseau's position. Sincerity is indeed a matter of the real me, yet Rousseau's simultaneous resort to conscience—understood not as what distinguishes men but what unites them—greatly qualifies his emphasis on the idiosyncratic individual.[23] As for the herd, that figure in Rousseau who best succeeds at returning to nature within society—Rousseau himself in his persona of the solitary walker—is he who lives farthest from the herd.

If sincerity forms one prong of Rousseau's campaign for the renaturalization of morality, compassion forms the other.[24] In the *Second Discourse*, Rousseau presents compassion as the sole fully natural basis of morality within society, as it is the sole remnant of the putative gentleness of our vanished natural state. Much is unpersuasive about these claims (more than enough to persuade us that Rousseau himself remains unpersuaded by them), but their questionableness only underscores the enormous practical significance he attaches to them. Of his project to liberate morality from the stifling rationalism of his predecessors, his resort to compassion is the crown. Morality must rest on sentiment, according to Rousseau, and the preeminent moral sentiment is compassion. He advertises it not as the most perfect but as the most effective basis of morality: "While Socrates and minds of his stamp may be able to acquire virtue through reason, mankind would long ago have ceased to be if its preservation had depended solely on the reasonings of those who make it up."[25] Rousseau's understanding of compassion is nothing if not "realistic," and his promotion of it is, in fact, an aspect of his moral realism.

In advocating a morality of compassion, Rousseau breaks alike with the rationalism of the philosophic tradition and the otherworldliness of Christianity. The sensitive male was not Rousseau's exclusive creation: both the British novel of sensibility and the Scottish moral sense school of philosophy had anticipated him in this respect. Still, no thinker prior to Arthur Schopenhauer (who acknowledges his debt to Rousseau[26]) has gone so far in the direction of reconstructing ethics on the ground of compassion. And, to Rousseau's credit, none (certainly not Schopenhauer) has given so much thought to the problems and limits of this enterprise. Rousseau's articulation of the phenomenon of compassion is remarkably subtle, perhaps overly so.[27] Few ambiguities of compassion or of the relationship it forges between spectator and sufferer escape his notice. As his understanding of human nature is vitalistic, so he construes compassion as a manifestation of vitality, a temporary conferring on another of the benefits of our natural solicitude for ourselves. Indeed, Rousseau presents the most intense compassion as erotic in origin, depending on the sublimation of adolescent sexuality. Because our imagination transports us into the place of the other, we identify with him; because we remain aware of his otherness, we maintain our separateness from him. A complex welter of emotions results from this dialectic of coupling and decoupling. Discomfort, relief, satisfaction that our situation is superior to that of the sufferer, satisfaction that he needs our aid, satisfaction in providing it and in contemplating his consequent indebtedness to us—all enter into the experience of sympathizing with the ills of another. Compassion thus enlists both major currents of our vitality—*amour de soi* and *amour-propre*—in the service of our fellows. Compassion proves to have its limits as a moral guide—it requires to be bounded by a quasi-Kantian principle of generality[28]—but the emphasis of Rousseau's presentation is a highly positive one.

While there are other aspects of Rousseau's appeal to naturalism in ethics, conscience, sincerity, and compassion rank foremost among them. All partake of the ambiguities of Rousseau's treatment of the theme of nature generally. None of these qualities is clearly natural if we take that term in its narrowest sense: nature as the *terminus a quo*, or zero point, of the development of man's humanity—nature, therefore, as starkly opposed to reason and society. All of them figure in the problem of how to understand the Rousseauian alternative of a life of nature lived within the bounds of reason and society. This is not merely a rhetorical problem but a genuinely philosophical one with which few thinkers have wrestled as deeply.

For this the crucial work is again *Emile*. Part treatise, part novel; part account of a nondefective education, part a treasury of suggestions for mitigating defective ones; part Rousseau's account of his own experiences as an educator, part his account of his own experiences as a youth: the work is a genre unto itself. *Emile* describes the education of an imaginary youth by an imaginary tutor. It is a work of the greatest intellectual ambition. As the late Allan Bloom once put it, it is a *Phenomenology of Mind* posing as Dr. Spock.[29] It offers Rousseau's definitive account of the stages of human development within society. It aims to establish two principles, which appear to tend in opposite directions but are not, strictly speaking, incompatible.

The first of these principles is that the obstacles to a harmonious development of the human faculties are both more subtle and more pervasive, and the task of education thus more challenging, than previous thinkers realized. The very means employed by educators to teach their pupils to act well have actually taught them to act badly. Above all, in seeking to subject their pupils to their will, teachers have evoked in them a counterwill that ruins everything. Hobbes's "restless desire for power after power ending only in death" is not the natural human psychology that society must tame through education. Rather, it is the consequence of society's mistaken preoccupation with taming: it results from imposing on the pupil a will alien to his own. This problem pervades every stage of education from the cradle through adolescence and every aspect of it from the choice of the curriculum to the dress of the pupil. What usually passes for instruction is repression, and the lesson conveyed to the pupil is to dominate where he can and to submit where he must.

The education of a new man superior to the servility that reigns in society therefore requires a radical restructuring of the curriculum and an equally radical revolution in methods of pedagogy. Rousseau's proposals, which were to inspire "progressive" or "child-centered" education, command admiration, even if they sometimes strain credulity. Their general implication for moral education is clear. Rather than have his ethics imposed upon him, for reasons that he is incapable of conceiving and with a high-handedness he is bound to resent, the child is to discover it himself through his own experience. He is to learn necessity at the hand of nature rather than human willfulness at the foot of the teacher. The new duty of the teacher is to guide the child's experience. Stated more bluntly, it is to manipulate the child's environment so that he reaches the desired conclusions while ascribing them entirely to himself because he remains unaware of the manipulation.

The second of Rousseau's novel contentions is that despite the great complexity of the educator's task, nature poses no barrier to his success that is, in principle, insurmountable. The most intractable problems of education lie not in the matter (human nature) but in the method; their solutions are in principle within our reach. As Rousseau never tires of insisting, man is by nature good: not nature, but society's deformation of it, is to blame for the wickedness endemic to society.

Rousseau's thought lends itself to oversimplification, more so perhaps than with most other thinkers, because his polemical intention led him to incendiary oversimplifications of his own. His doctrine of the natural goodness of man has proved particularly susceptible to caricature. At its deepest level, this doctrine represents Rousseau's attempt to revise modern philosophical anthropology in the light of the implications of modern natural science. It underscores the folly of ascribing to nature (now understood biologically) problems more coherently attributed to society or culture.

I have stated the goodness of nature in negative terms: nature is not to be blamed for this, and it poses no insuperable obstacle to that. This seems to me true to what is most serious in the argument of *Emile*. Rousseau does not cast nature as a panacea or as a simply adequate standard for us in ethics or any aspect of life. True, so-called natural man—man whose native faculties have been least developed by accidents of history—offers a model of that wholeness and self-sufficiency that the bourgeois so conspicuously lacks. Yet any attempt to approximate that wholeness in society can be only a free rational project for which nature provides little direct guidance.

It follows that ethics in Rousseau can be natural neither as it is for Aristotle and Cicero (as an aspect of man's fulfillment of his natural end) nor as it is for our psychobiologists (as nature's genetically programmed prescription for us). Rousseau does contend that a harmonious or noncontradictory development of the faculties is possible, and that this outcome is "natural" precisely in its noncontradictoriness (for to be noncontradictory, it must not contradict nature). Just as nature was powerless to prevent man's deformation at the hands of society, so it does not impede the project to reconstitute him within society. Nature is good because it is blameless: it is neither responsible for our evils nor resistant to our efforts to cure them. But what then of society, on which devolves that onus of badness lifted from the shoulders of nature? Does it, too, pose no insuperable obstacle to the project of the reconstitution of our happiness and goodness? Is it, too, ultimately what we make it?

The answer to this question depends decisively on the status of *amour-propre*, the key alike to the problem of human unhappiness and to that of human immorality. This term defies English translation. We may render it literally as love of one's own, but its sense in Rousseau begins to emerge only from his distinction between it and another form of self-regard, *amour de soi-même* ("self-love").

> *Amour-propre* and *amour de soi-même*, two very different passions in their nature and their effects, must not be confused. Self-love is a natural sentiment which inclines every animal to attend to its self-preservation and which, guided in man by reason and modified by pity, produces humanity and virtue. Vanity [i.e., *amour-propre*] is only a relative sentiment, factitious, and born in society, which inclines every individual to set greater store by himself than by anyone else, inspires men with all the evils they do one another, and is the genuine source of honor. (*SD*, note xv [*OC* 3:219–20])

Through *amour-propre* we come to see ourselves as others see us and it matters to us how others see us. It sets us in competition with one another not only for the necessary goods of life but for esteem and all that signifies or attracts it. "Everyone began to look at everyone else and to wish to be looked at himself, and public esteem acquired a value. . . . From these first preferences arose vanity and contempt on the one hand, shame and envy on the other . . ." (*SD* [*OC* 3:169–70]). *Amour-propre* is the great complication of the human situation, which draws us out of the mute self-absorption of other beasts. As the source of that "vain pride and . . . self-admiration, [that] causes [man] eagerly to run after all the miseries of which he is susceptible, and which beneficent Nature had taken care to keep from him" (*SD*, note xv [*OC* 3:202]), *amour-propre* often figures in Rousseau's account as the bane of our existence and the villain of the human morality play. It is, among other things, the predominant passion of the bourgeois and the source of the falseness and baseness of his way of life.

> [T]he savage lives in himself; sociable man, always outside himself, is capable of living only in the opinion of others and, so to speak, derives the sentiment of his own existence only from their judgment. It is not part of my subject to show how such a disposition engenders so much indifference to good and evil together with such fine discourses on morality; how everything being reduced to appearances, everything becomes factitious and play-acting: honor, virtue, and often even vices in which one at length discovers the secret of glorying. (*SD* [*OC* 3:193])

Amour de soi-même or self-love, conversely, figures as the source of happiness and virtue, as in Rousseau's initial contrast of the two sentiments described earlier. On closer inspection, however, the implications of *amour-propre* for morality appear ambiguous. Already in the *Second Discourse*, Rousseau quietly concedes that morality is not, as he has first proclaimed, a phenomenon of *amour de soi-même* but one of *amour-propre*.

> If this were the place to go into details, . . . I would show that it is to this ardor to have ourselves talked about, to this frenzy to distinguish ourselves which keeps us almost always outside ourselves, that we owe what is best and worst among men, our virtues and our vices, our Sciences and our errors, our Conquerors and our Philosophers, that is to say a multitude of bad things for a small number of good ones. (*SD* [*OC* 3:188–89])

If the attractiveness of morality to human beings depends on *amour-propre*, then both Rousseau's moral rhetoric of return to nature and his moral rhetoric of ascent from it must be analyzed as appeals to *amour-propre*.

Rousseau's most thorough treatment of the role of *amour-propre* in the formation of human character occurs in *Emile*. There we come to see that *amour-propre* mediates all social relations, whether harmful or salutary. It defines that whole realm in which our happiness or misery, goodness or wickedness, depends not on our intrinsic situation but on our relations to others and our perception of these relations.

Amour-propre would be simply bad only if these relations were irremediably bad; that is, if education for a happy life in society were impossible. Such proves not to be Rousseau's position.

> Let us set down as an incontestable maxim that the first movements of nature are always right. There is no original perversity in the human heart. There is not a single vice to be found in it of which it cannot be said how and whence it entered. The sole passion natural to man is *amour de soi* or *amour-propre* taken in an extended sense. This *amour-propre* in itself or relative to us is good and useful; and since it has no necessary relation to others, it is in this respect naturally neutral. It becomes good or bad only by the application made of it and the relations given it. (*Emile*, book 2 [*OC* 4:322]; trans. Bloom, 92)

In *Emile*, Rousseau thus abandons the opposition between *amour-propre* and nature, and thereby the claim that while *amour de soi-même* is natural to us, *amour-propre* is factitious. (Indeed, he effectively abandons the opposition between *amour-propre* and *amour de soi-même*.) He admits that *amour-propre* is natural and in principle neutral as between human happiness and unhappiness. Where nature ceases being good, she at least remains malleable. If nature can be said to be good it is because *amour-propre* is not invincibly bad. The goodness of nature is the weakness of nature. *Amour-propre* is what we make of it: the most important thing Rousseau would make of it is morality.

Since my Emile has until now looked only at himself, the first glance he casts on his fellows leads him to compare himself with them. And the first sentiment aroused by this comparison is the desire to be in the first position. This is where *amour de soi* turns into *amour-propre* and where begin to arise all the passions dependent on this one. But to decide whether among these passions the dominant ones . . . will be humane and gentle or cruel and malignant, whether they will be passions of benefi-cence and commiseration or of envy and covetousness, we must know what position he will feel he has among men, and what kinds of obstacles he may believe he has to overcome to reach the position he has to occupy. (*Emile*, book 4 [*OC* 4:523–24]; trans. Bloom, 235)

The principle of the crucial stages of Emile's education, then, is not that the tutor should prevent him from living comparatively—this is by nature both unnecessary and impossible—but that he should manipulate the comparisons Emile makes so as to obtain the desired results. Everything depends on Emile's perception of his standing vis-à-vis others and of the impediments to his arriving at the position he understands to be suitable for him. Frustration in these regards will harden Emile's heart to others by fanning resentment toward them, while success will preserve his natural benevolence toward them. These statements require elaboration: what the tutor will teach Emile to regard as success is quite different from what passes as such in society. Not the satisfaction of ambition, but freedom from it; not prominence in society but an obscure life of domesticity and autarky on its margins: such will be the brass ring for which Emile will reach and which his education will place within his grasp.

Emile's moral education proceeds in stages: Rousseau's approach to education is that of a founder of developmental psychology. These stages are beyond the scope of this chapter. Very generally, we may say that Emile proceeds from learn-ing the sanctity of property relations through an appeal to his self-interest to a morality of interpersonal relations based on a complex development of compas-sion to a morality centered in the home and family and anchored by his love for Sophie.[30] The reference in the passage just cited to the dependence of the moral passions of beneficence and commiseration on *amour-propre* confirms just how far-reaching is the empire of the latter, and how misleading the rhetorical oppo-sition of *amour-propre* and nature and thus of nature and morality. At the same time, the appeal to nature as the basis of morality must be reinterpreted: if moral-ity is natural, it is so because *amour-propre* is natural.

It was on and through Kant that Rousseau exercised his greatest influence as a pedagogue of ethics. It would be a mistake, however, to think of Rousseau as himself a Kantian in ethics. As already suggested, Rousseau intends his ethical teaching as an alternative to the miseries and corruptions of the bourgeois. His thought is what philosophy professors call eudaemonistic: his primary concern is happiness. He never wavers in his conviction that for human beings, the good is prior to the right. He never presumes that there can be a sufficient argument against injustice short of a proof that it inevitably entails unhappiness. He never values the dignity attendant upon justice except as an ingredient of happiness. True, the greatest happiness—whether of natural man or of the solitary walker— requires complete indifference to one's dignity. Yet for that vast majority of human beings in society for whom freedom from the incubus of status is no longer possible, Rousseau proffers the incomparable status of the moral life.

Rousseau is aware of the power of the summons to eschew happiness as our primary goal in life and to pride ourselves on our willingness to sacrifice happiness to the demands of morality. Ultimately, however, this appeal is intelligible to him only as attesting to the primacy of *amour-propre*. Human social life, in its unimproved version, is a restless quest for status after status ending only in death. Rousseau agrees with Hobbes that "all the mind's pleasure is but glory (or to have a good opinion of oneself), or refers to glory in the end . . . [but] glory is like honor, if all men have it, no man hath it, for they consist in comparison and precellence."[31] He seems to have concluded, however, that there is no status like moral status, no precellence like moral precellence. By casting morality as self-conquest, the triumph of the true self (which is the moral self) over nature (which is but dross), Rousseau devises a lure irresistible to *amour-propre*. The contest pits us not against one another but against subhuman nature, the common enemy of the dignity of us all. By reserving a status above all others for those who opt for morality over status, Rousseau enlists *amour-propre* against itself. To rise above nature to autonomy confers infinite dignity on each of us, and Rousseau, like Hobbes, understands dignity as status.

The place of morality in *Emile* thus recalls a quip of the early Woody Allen, who, in devising a spoof of a college catalogue, included a course entitled "The Categorical Imperative—and Six Ways to Make it Work for You."[32] In the later stages of Emile's ethical education, the tutor preaches the doctrine of generality: something very like the categorical imperative is to serve as his ward's ethical standard. Yet all of this is indeed with an eye to Emile's happiness: its ultimate justification is the more than six ways it works for him.

It may seem inappropriate to discuss so coldly that moral integrity which Rousseau extols so fervently. The moral person views morality and its motives as *sui generis*, as unconditional and unconditioned, and Rousseau the moralist willingly indulges him in this. Rousseau the philosopher, however, insists on the exhaustiveness, in matters of morals as in all others, of the dichotomy of *amour de soi-même* and *amour-propre*. He thereby suggests that the virtuous person's aspiration to transcend *amour-propre* is, like all human ambitions for transcendence, a symptom of *amour-propre*. Rousseau grasps the tension between the praise of morality, on the one hand, and psychological analysis of morality, on the other. Where he offers the former, he generally abstains from the latter. Yet both figure prominently in his writing. And just as he makes clear in his account of civic education how public spirit arises from the manipulation of *amour-propre*, so he shows how the same passion grounds the more private virtues of Emile and Sophie. An adequate consideration of the sufficiency of *amour-propre* to account for the phenomena of morality, particularly the deeply entrenched human sense of justice, would exceed the bounds of this chapter.[33]

Having considered both the citizen and Emile, there is one last ethical alternative we must not overlook, one of which Rousseau himself was the first (and perhaps only) exemplar: that of the solitary walker (*promeneur solitaire*). This possibility defies easy characterization by any term familiar to us. In an earlier draft of this chapter I ventured "bohemian." The bohemian, however, despises society and his duties to it: Rousseau, while free of the illusions of society, never repudiated his duties to it. He would never have given over his efforts to benefit society had it not proscribed him so thoroughly as to render all such efforts impossible.[34] Unlike the bohemian, then, the aged Rousseau neither chose his marginality nor prided himself on it.

On the other hand, the typical bohemian has not relinquished his hopes for the improvement of his society: he not only esthetically but politically regards himself as a member of the avant-garde. The bohemian generally conceives of the eventual improvement of society in terms of those very principles of equality and liberty proclaimed by the society itself (if it is a modern society): the modern bohemian is usually (although not invariably) on the left. The aged Rousseau, however, has entirely overcome his hopes for the improvement of his society as a result of his efforts; indeed, he has come to reject hope of any kind as a torment.[35] Unlike the bohemian, he has not chosen his marginality, but he conceives of that marginality as more complete.

Another point of contrast between the Rousseauian solitary and the bohemian relates to the previous one. The bohemian frequents not dense shady groves but coffeehouses. He is a member in good standing, if not of the "culture," then of a "counterculture." "Bohemia" identifies a social milieu, a society within a society. The aged Rousseau, however, is never in such good company as when he is entirely alone. He looks for companionship without commitment, congenial societies that dissolve as easily as they form.[36] The primacy for the solitary of his reveries signals his deepest rupture with society.

To be sure, the solitary cannot entirely avoid intercourse with his fellow members of society. Nor is it wholly devoid of pleasure for him or of benefit for them. One pleasure of a life of marginality is beneficence. Paradoxically, only the man who has burned his bridges to society will find that nothing stands in the way of his benefiting it. His is a spontaneous and therefore easy beneficence, however. He "practice[s] random kindness and senseless acts of beauty"—as the bumper sticker has it— which costs next to nothing in money, time, practical obligation, or emotional commitment. His beneficence is as limited as his means and threatens no permanent encroachment on his solitude. Rousseau's example of it is the purchase of wafers from a vendor for some schoolgirls whom he chances to encounter.[37]

Let us not forget, however, that by staying clear of injustice, the solitary avoids many evils to himself. He recognizes society as a comprehensive system of unhappiness in which those who think themselves masters are no less slaves.[38]

Excused of responsibility for society by its utter rejection of him, he cultivates the maximum freedom from it compatible with enjoying its minimal benefits. Shunned by it, he is free to enjoy the pleasures of shunning it. As for opposition to the injustices of society, this is no longer within the solitary's power. He limits himself to observing what Rousseau declares the first maxim of justice in an unjust society: to do as little harm as possible (which almost always implies, he says, refraining from attempts to do good).[39] In this avoidance of complicity lies the solitary's peculiar integrity. Neither citizen nor bourgeois, he lives on the fringes of society as both parasite on it and reproach to it.[40]

As the founder of the ethics of the outsider, Rousseau also purveyed a permanent and general suspicion of insiders. He was the first to conceive of society as a "system" in the modern pejorative sense. Oppression and vice, inequality and misery, were "systemic." Men are as society makes them; they play the roles society imposes on them. Rousseau would scratch his head at the earnestness of our ethicists; don't they know that integrity would be the last resort of a public official even if circumstance permitted it to him? Where corrupt elites oppress corrupted peoples, it is vain to debate principles of governance. Should the good by some chance find themselves in positions of authority, they will not succeed in improving society; rather they will be lucky to escape with their own virtue intact.[41] As for so-called professional ethics, discussion of which is so popular today, Rousseau would reject it as a contradiction in terms. You can guess what he thought of the public officials of the *ancien régime*, those pillars of inequality and servants of the rich. He was particularly hard on doctors and priests, the "caring professions" of his day. Indeed he argued that the very practice of a caring profession invariably inured one to caring. "It is by dint of viewing suffering that priests and doctors become pitiless." Compassion is easily exhausted, and a requirement of any education in it is that the pupil not be subjected to the sight of *too much* suffering. Rousseau preferred paternalism to reliance on the caring professions; his characters Wolmar and Julie take far better care of their servants and dependents than any outsider could be paid to do.[42]

Having completed our survey of Rousseau as a source of ethics, we may venture some tentative conclusions. Rousseau's vices in matters of ethics are arguably the same as his virtues: he was both impracticably strict and bewilderingly eclectic. He held up a tarnished mirror to society and called it to view itself from every unflattering angle. He was a genius at discovering such angles. So was he at fashioning images of societies of an impossible rectitude as a rebuke to the corruption of those he knew. Whether these images have proved salutary is at best an open question.

As a recent defender of Rousseau's moral teachings has insisted, we must avoid the opposite but complementary misinterpretations of them as counseling either fanatical engagement with society to impose moral purity on others (the alternative of Robespierre) or complete withdrawal from society in order to preserve one's own.[43] Still, as Grant concedes, Rousseau's teachings lend themselves to misinterpretation. While his ethics may be both more moderate and more flexible in practice than is generally recognized, the tone of his denunciation of every actual modern society is shrill and uncompromising, and his own example seems to confirm that under such conditions, we can preserve our integrity only by opting for marginality.

Here we must take note of Rousseau's greatest shortcoming as a prophet: his failure to foresee the advent of liberal democracy. As the disciple of Montesquieu, Rousseau could never grant the possibility of combining democracy with liberalism. Democracy depended above all on virtue of the Spartan or Roman sort, while liberalism, with its commerce, inequality, and enlightenment, was deadly to virtue. That this position is not wholly implausible even today is confirmed by the proliferation and durability of leftist critiques of liberal democracy. Even the most ardent defender of modern Western societies would have to admit that they fall far short of the standard for democracy set by Rousseau, and that misgivings on this score are bound to haunt our societies as long as they aspire to combine liberalism and democracy, inequality with equality.

Rousseau's failure to provide us with a clear ethical standard, as Kant was to do, follows necessarily from his repeated indications of the priority of the good to the right. Different readers will cleave to different visions of the good. Some will even yearn to be told that the right is prior to good—as the basis of a dignity transcending nature—and because it is good for them to be told this, it is right for Rousseau to tell it.

Rousseau thus refrains from offering the sort of public ethics with which we are familiar from the theorists of today: an ethics of "impartiality" or "fairness," a liberal morality off the rack, one size fits all. Such moralities necessarily presuppose the priority of the right to the good and its compatibility with radically different visions of the good. Rousseau teaches, however, that there can be no morality impartial as to ways of life, no notion of the right that does not imply one of the good, both for those who practice it and for those upon whom it is practiced. "Neutrality" is not an option. In particular, liberal neutrality is not an option, for liberalism too defines a way of life, which, like every other, promotes a particular human type for whom alone its morality is suitable. That type is, mutatis mutandis, the bourgeois. A bourgeois who has undergone psychotherapy, who has read Richard Rorty, who "celebrates diversity," or who worries about the ozone layer is still a bourgeois. Like all great writers, Rousseau compels us to face our shortcomings, ethical and otherwise. As he exposed the smugness of the liberalism he knew, so he can help us challenge our own—including the claim to ethical impartiality. So often derided by liberals as utopian, he thus provides us with a much needed reality check.

NOTES

I am grateful to David Bromwich and Victor Gourevitch for their critiques of an earlier version of this chapter.

1. *Discours sur les sciences et les arts*, in Rousseau, *Oeuvres complètes*, under the general editorship of Bernard Gaganebin and Marcel Raymond (Paris: Bibliothèque de la Pléiade, 5 vols., 1959–95) (cited hereafter as *OC*), 3:330. Hereafter the *First Discourse* or *FD*. Two excellent translations are available, one by Judith R. Bush, Christopher Kelly, and Roger D. Masters in *"Discourse on the Sciences and Arts" ("First Discourse") and "Polemics,"* ed. R. D. Masters and Christopher Kelly (Hanover, N.H.: University Press of New England, 1992), and the other by Victor Gourevitch, *"The Discourses" and Other Early Political Writings* (Cambridge: Cambridge University Press, 1997). As the pagination of both of these editions is keyed to that of *OC*, citations of the latter apply equally to them. In what follows we cite the *First Discourse* in the Bush, Kelly, and Masters translation.

2. "Morals" here translates French *moeurs*, which embraces both manners and morals; no single English word offers an adequate translation.

3. For recent defenses of the plausibility of this famous argument of the *Discourse*, see Victor Gourevitch, "Rousseau on the Arts and Sciences," *Journal of Philosophy* 69 (1972): 737–54; Victor Goldschmidt, *Anthropologie et politique*, 2nd ed. (Paris: Vrin, 1983), 45–104; Claude Lévi-Strauss, "Rousseau fondateur des sciences de l'homme," in S. Baud-Bovy et al., *Jean-Jacques Rousseau* (Neuchatel: La Baconnière, 1962), 239–48.

4. This last citation is from the *Discours sur les origines et fondements de l'inégalité parmi les hommes* (*OC* 3:122; cf. 125–26, 141–44 and notes [the denial of reason as the human species characteristic], 154–57). Again the best translations are those of Gourevitch and of Bush, Kelly, and Masters in their *"Discourse on the Origins of Inequality" ("Second Discourse"), "Polemics," and "Political Economy"* (Hanover, N.H.: University Press of New England, 1992), keyed like that of Gourevitch to the pagination of the *OC*. Here and throughout cited as *Second Discourse* or *SD* in the Gourevitch translation. See also *Emile, ou de l'éducation* (*OC* 4:502–10, 522–23, and note; tr. Allan Bloom [New York: Basic Books, 1979], 220–27, 234–35, and note).

5. On this see Arthur M. Melzer, *The Natural Goodness of Man: On the System of Rousseau's Thought* (Chicago: University of Chicago Press, 1990), 253–82 ("Rousseau's 'mission' and the practical intention of his writings").

6. For this and other examples in the same vein, *Emile*, book 1 (*OC* 4:248–49; tr. Allan Bloom, *Emile, or on Education* [New York: Basic Books, 1979], 39–40).

7. *Discours sur l'économie politique* (*OC* 3:259–60); cited hereafter *Political Economy* or *PE*. I have used the rendition of Bush, Kelly, and Masters published in their version of *SD*. There is also a version by Gourevitch available in his edition of Rousseau, *"The Social Contract" and Other Later Political Writings* (Cambridge: Cambridge University Press, 1997). Cf. *SD* (*OC* 3:9–15, 24); *Du Contrat social* (hereafter *SC*), II, 78, 12; IV, 7 (*OC* 3:381–86, 393–94, 458–59).

8. See *SC* 4.8 (*"De la religion civile"*) [*OC* 3:460–69]).

9. *SD* (*OC* 3:178–79); *L'Etat de guerre* (ibid., 601–16, tr. Gourevitch in *SC* etc., 162–76). Rousseau was ultimately unable to solve the ethical dilemma posed by his acknowledgment of the arbitrariness of the division of the human race into separate societies, on the one hand, and his belief that all decent political life necessarily presupposed this division, on the other. For a brilliant elucidation of this difficulty, see Pierre Hassner, "Rousseau and the Theory and Practice of International Relations," in *Legacy of Rousseau*, ed. Clifford Orwin and Nathan Tarcov (Chicago: University of Chicago Press, 1997), 200–19.

10. *Emile*, book 1 (*OC* 4:248–49); tr. Bloom, 39. For further comment on this passage and the problem it identifies, see my "Distant Compassion: CNN Borrioboda-Gha," *National Interest* 43 (Spring 1996): 42–49.

11. For arguments for the realism of Rousseau's political thought, see Ramon Lemos, *Rousseau's Political Philosophy: An Exposition and Interpretation* (Athens: University of Georgia Press, 1977), and Melzer, *Natural Goodness of Man.* For the intended (nonrevolutionary) effects on Emile of the study of the principles of the social contract, see *Emile*, book 5 (*OC* 4:855–60; tr. Bloom, 471–75).

12. *Emile*, book 1 (*OC* 4:249–51; tr. Bloom, 39–41); this critique recurs repeatedly throughout Rousseau's writings. For its centrality for Rousseau and his subsequent influence, see Karl Löwith, *From Hegel to Nietzsche: The Revolution in Nineteenth Century Thought*, tr. David Green (Garden City, N.Y.: Doubleday, 1967), 230–32; Werner J. Dannhauser, "The Problem of the Bourgeois," in *Legacy of Rousseau*, ed. Orwin and Tarcov, 20–44.

13. *FD* (*OC* 3:10); *Lettre à l'Abbé Raynal* (ibid., 33); *Observations* (ibid., 55–57); *Préface du Narcisse* (*OC* 2:971–74). This material is translated in the Masters and Kelly edition of *FD* and in Gourevitch, *Discourses* etc.

14. Judith N. Shklar, *Men and Citizens: Rousseau's Social Theory,* 2nd ed. (Cambridge: Cambridge University Press, 1985). On the variety of Rousseau's proposals as expressing not the disunity but the unity of his thought, see also Stephen Ellenburg, *Rousseau's Political Philosophy: An Interpretation from Within* (Madison: University of Wisconsin Press, 1976), 16–17.

15. On this aspect of Rousseau's thought, see the magisterial treatment by Allan Bloom, *Love and Friendship* (New York: Simon and Schuster, 1993), 38–156, and the discussion of romanticism following. For a sympathetic but critical treatment of Rousseau's presentation of female domesticity, see Claude Habib, *Pensées sur la prostitution* (Paris: Belin, 1994).

16. Note, however, the disclaimer with which the passage concludes: "But I have already said too much on this topic, and the philosophical meaning of the word *freedom* is not my subject here." All translations of *SC* are from Gourevitch, ed., *SC* etc. For a careful treatment of the problem of freedom in Rousseau, see Daniel E. Cullen, *Freedom in Rousseau's Political Philosophy* (De Kalb: Northern Illinois University Press, 1993).

17. Bloom, *Love and Friendship*, 138–39.

18. *FD* (*OC* 3:30).

19. See Christopher Kelly, "'To Persuade without Convincing': The Language of Rousseau's Legislator," *American Journal of Political Science* 31 (1987): 32–135.

20. On Rousseau's doctrine of truth telling, according to which one owes only useful truths (the reasoning for which conclusion implies that one equally owes useful falsehoods), see Victor Gourevitch, "Rousseau on Lying: A Provisional Reading of the Fourth *Reverie*," *Berkshire Review* 15 (1980): 93–107.

21. Arthur M. Melzer, "The Origin of the Counter-Enlightenment: Rousseau and the New Religion of Sincerity," *American Political Science Review* 90, no. 2 (1996): 344–60. On the prehistory of this doctrine in Locke, see Robert P. Kraynak, "John Locke: From Absolutism to Toleration," *American Political Science Review* 74, no. 1 (1980): 53–69.

22. See Arthur M. Melzer, "Rousseau and the Modern Cult of Sincerity," in *Legacy of Rousseau*, ed. Orwin and Tarcov, 274–95.

23. For a persuasive argument against interpreting Rousseau's own position in terms of "authenticity," see Ruth W. Grant, *Hypocrisy and Integrity: Machiavelli, Rousseau, and the Ethics of Politics* (Chicago: University of Chicago Press, 1997), 58–59.

24. Having written extensively on compassion elsewhere, I will treat it only briefly here. See my "Rousseau and the Discovery of Political Compassion," in *Legacy of*

Rousseau, ed. Orwin and Tarcov, 296–320, and "Moist Eyes from Rousseau to Clinton," *Public Interest* 128 (Summer 1997): 3–20.

25. *SD* (*OC* 3:156–57).

26. Arthur Schopenhauer, *On the Basis of Morality*, tr. E. J. F. Payne (Indianapolis: Bobbs-Merrill/Library of the Liberal Arts, 1965), 183–87.

27. The principal thematic treatment occupies the first quarter of book 4 of *Emile*.

28. *Emile,* book 4 (*OC* 4:547–48), tr. Bloom, 252–53.

29. Bloom, "Introduction" to his translation of *Emile*, 3.

30. For a magisterial exposition of the stages of Emile's moral education, see Bloom, *Love and Friendship*; for a brief sketch, see Bloom's introduction to his translation of *Emile*, also published as "The Education of Democratic Man: *Emile,*" *Daedalus* (Summer 1978): 135–54.

31. Thomas Hobbes, *De Cive, or Philosophical Rudiments of Man and Society* ed. Howard Warrender (Oxford: Clarendon Press, 1983), chap. 1, sec. 2.

32. Woody Allen, *Getting Even* (New York: Random House, 1977).

33. For a brilliant treatment of this question, see Eve Noirot [Grace], "Nature and the Problem of Morality in *The Reveries of the Solitary Walker,*" doctoral thesis, University of Toronto, Department of Political Science, 1996.

34. *Reveries du promeneur solitaire*, First Walk (*OC* 1:995–1001); *The Reveries of the Solitary Walker,* tr. Charles E. Butterworth (Indianapolis: Hackett, 1992), 111.

35. *Reveries*, First and Eighth Walks (*OC* 1:995–1001, 1074–84; tr. Butterworth, 1–11, 110–21).

36. *Reveries,* Fifth Walk (*OC* 1:1041–42, 1048; tr. Butterworth, 64, 70); *Emile*, book 4 (*OC* 4:678–91; tr. Bloom, 344–55).

37. *Reveries,* Ninth Walk (*OC* 1:1090–92; tr. Butterworth, 127–29).

38. *SD* (*OC* 3:174–75); *Emile*, book 2 (*OC,* 4:310–11; tr. Bloom, 85); *SC* 1.1 (*OC* 3:351); Geneva Manuscript (*OC* 3:28–182; tr. Gourevitch in *SC* etc.

39. *Emile*, book 2 (*OC* 4:340, tr. Bloom, 104–5); cf. book 5 (*OC* 4:849, tr. Bloom, 467).

40. My thanks to Victor Gourevitch for persuading me that "bohemian" is misleading as applied to the Rousseauian solitary.

41. *Emile*, book 5 (*OC* 4:849, 860; tr. Bloom, 467, 474–75).

42. *Emile*, book 4 (*OC* 4:517; tr. Bloom, 231); *Julie, ou La Nouvelle Héloïse,* part 5, letter 2 (*OC* 2:527–57). On Rousseau's critique of the notion of a therapeutic profession, see Orwin in *Legacy of Rousseau*, ed. Orwin and Tarcov, 312–15.

43. Grant, *Hypocrisy and Integrity,* 102–41, 167–70.

Chapter Six

Without Foundation:
A New View of Kant

Susan Neiman

It wasn't until the night before I sat down to write this chapter that I realized I'd lost my grasp, if I ever had one, on what foundationalism is. And since I'd been asked to write about Immanuel Kant and the foundations of ethics, it seemed that I ought to recover it, at least in a conventional sense. I reached for the *Encyclopedia of Philosophy,* preparing to give silent thanks to the Book of the Month Club, but to my surprise found neither the word "foundation" nor any of its cognates. (And this, as readers nostalgic for graduate school humor will recall, in a publication that devotes a good page to the entry "nothing.") Puzzled, I began to look further, reaching for the indexes of half a dozen classic texts of contemporary philosophy, only to draw the same blank. Not even Richard Rorty has an entry devoted to foundationalism.

There is an easy explanation for this perplexity, namely, that the question of foundationalism, in ethics as elsewhere, has become so pervasive as to defy straightforward treatment, let alone indexing. I incline to a different view. Despite the general sense that something called a problem of foundationalism stands in the forefront of contemporary ethics, there is a conspicuous absence of serious and sustained discussion of it. For at least in the classical texts for which I assume responsibility (and I suspect in the ones I do not know), there is very little resembling the foundationalist position, which comes under frequent attack. Foundationalism, that is, may exist only in the minds of those postmodernists who need to create spectres in order to be daring. The question of courage plays a role in classical ethics, as we will see, but I believe we have enough to fear from real dangers without inventing conceptual ones.

These general remarks are meant to raise questions, not to answer them; in Kant's case they are not hard to defend. Let's begin by reconstructing what might be meant when it's said that Kant tried to put ethics on a firm foundation. At least two different projects that could be called foundationalist have been blamed on Kant. The first is straightforwardly practical. In the Categorical Imperative, Kant was often thought to have provided the moral principle from which all other moral principles followed, a sort of metarule for deriving other rules. Thus, the originality of Kant's ethics lay not in any matters of content.[1] Rather, Kant's service was thought to consist in providing a formula that would test and ground the moral intuitions embodied in tradition as in ordinary moral consciousness. Much like a compass, the Categorical Imperative could be dropped into the thickest of woods and still point due north, telling us effortlessly how to go on.

The second foundationalist project that might be ascribed to Kant is a more theoretical one, though it may have practical consequences. Having given us rules for determining moral decisions, Kant is also thought to have tried to give a proof of their validity. Demonstrating that we cannot live coherently—whatever this comes to—without some version of the moral law, just as we cannot without the causal law, would be a sort of transcendental deduction of morality. This project would be of primary interest to professional philosophers, who can see themselves as offering defenses against relativism. If the first project is meant to provide a practical tool, the second is a weapon to use against those who might want to take it away. Should a skeptic decide to doubt the results provided by the infallible compass, the Kantian can guarantee that those results are truly grounded. Thus, Kantian ethics would aim at a fail-safe system, providing a sort of double grounding. Moral principles would all be derivable by a sort of logic, so that any decisions we need to make could be determined according to rule. Furthermore, that moral logic itself could be seen to be grounded, if not in the nature of a Platonic Good-in-Itself, then surely in the nature of humanity. If this is foundationalist, it's not hard to see why one might seek it. Life would surely be easier if you could tell your children, Saddam Hussein, and the tireless sophomore in the back row of your intro course that certain elementary forms of moral behavior are not open to discussion.

Tempting as this picture may be, it has very little to do with Kant. Indeed, on both counts it is diametrically opposed to crucial features of Critical Ethics. The view that the Categorical Imperative means to provide a formula for deciding hard cases comes close to Leibniz's vision of a universal calculus enabling warring parties to settle disputes with a sovereign "Come, let us calculate"; but it loses every resonance of the injunction to think for yourself. And the metaphysical grounding Kant is thought to have sought, if not offered, runs counter to his fundamental and absolute distinction between "is" and "ought." Far from deducing their indisputable truth, Kant argues that moral principles are *not* true.

Let us examine each of these claims in more detail. The idea that Kant's ethics are not intended to provide mechanical rules is a gift of the excellent recent work on Kantian ethics. Generations of readers attacked the Categorical Imperative as an exceptionless machine that did not even work properly, spending much time showing how it failed to exclude or include the right sorts of cases. Only quite recently has it been widely suggested that the Categorical Imperative was never intended to function automatically in the first place. Onora O'Neill argues that the Categorical Imperative cannot in principle work as an algorithm. Barbara Herman charts the ways in which our knowledge of moral relevance enters into judgment even before the Categorical Imperative can be applied and shows the centrality of open-ended moral casuistry in Kantian ethics.

It has often been noted how much recent Kantian ethics is indebted to John Rawls, whose own work explicitly attempts to eschew questions of metaethical grounding in favor of substantive moral and political debate. But it is interesting to note the similarity of positions argued by philosophers whose work was influenced by Jürgen Habermas as well. So Seyla Benhabib explicates Hannah Arendt's use of Kant's notion of reflective judgment as a crucial political principle, and emphasizes the role of contextualization in moral judgment, as does Thomas McCarthy in discussing the inherent indeterminacy of Kant's notion of practical reason.[2] The presence of so much agreement between German- and American-educated neo-Kantians may suggest that the views they are expounding are just good sense. The Categorical Imperative should be viewed neither as a device meant to crank out general moral truths ("Lying is always wrong") nor as a set of directions for determining individual moral action ("x may not lie at time t in order to achieve y").[3] Rather, it should serve as a reminder of perspective that helps us to shape and refine our own moral judgment, but never to substitute for it.

This ground has been well covered by others. I wish to add only, first, the very general reminder that the indeterminateness of the Categorical Imperative is a feature not only of Kant's moral principles but also of all his principles of reason. The need for choice and judgment to give meaning and use to moral principles is not thus an ad hoc requirement, but part of Kant's systematic and wide-ranging theory of reason, according to which such indeterminacy is necessary to maintain that freedom that is reason's fundamental characteristic.[4] I have argued for this view elsewhere; here I wish only to suggest, additionally, that instead of focusing on Kant's weakest examples, we attend to one of his better ones. The view of the Categorical Imperative as a malfunctioning machine has often seemed confirmed, at the latest, by Kant's last essay "On the Supposed Right to Lie from Altruistic Motives." Were there a prize to be given for the worst piece of philosophy ever written by an author of significance, this essay must deserve it. It not only proposes a conclusion that does violence to all our moral intuitions, namely, that it is unacceptable to lie to the murderer who comes to your home demanding the whereabouts of your innocent friend, but, even worse, it does so by appealing to an argument that verges on the ridiculous and is at odds with the very structure of Kant's moral theory: Kant suggests that the friend whom you believe to be hiding in your basement might have slipped out the back door, where your lie could unwittingly deliver him straight into the hands of the murderer. This discussion is more appropriate to slapstick cartoon than to philosophy, and only false piety has devoted so much space to it: either by showing why this example completely undermines the Critical Ethics, or why it is, on the contrary, permissible to disagree with Kant's conclusion.

Much more helpful light is shed on Kant's ethics by an example that is not mentioned in the standard literature, though it comes from his mature and important *Metaphysics of Morals*. Those who believe that the Categorical Imperative provides us with proof that lying is unacceptable even to save a life will be surprised to find the discussion of falsehood leaves open, under casuistical questions, such examples as the following: "An author asks one of his readers, 'How do you like my work?' One could merely seem to give an answer, by joking about the impropriety of the question. But who has his wit always ready? The author will take the slightest hesitation in answering as an insult. May one, then, say what is expected of one?" (*Metaphysics of Morals*, Ak. 431).

I find this example explosive. If we take it seriously we must acknowledge that Kant's ethics not only refrain from providing rigid solutions to complex moral problems, but also insist that the problems remain open. The ordinariness of the example reminds us that any occasion can serve as an occasion for moral thinking, for the issues it can raise are far from trivial. Provoked by it, students in my graduate seminar recently discussed whether one could tell a friend that poetry written in grief over the death of a beloved is still bad poetry and whether literary categories can be applied to eyewitness accounts of mass murder. A musician for the Israeli Philharmonic used the example to raise issues concerning demoralization, standards of excellence, and the maintenance of group cohesion, and mentioned Leonard Bernstein's solution: shout "bravo" to every performance; then go on to subject each phrase to the sharpest critique. We can continue the reflections indefinitely: as authors, considering the opportunities for abuse of authority, or confidence, we probably have a duty to refrain from questions that could tempt another to prevaricate. (This includes not merely the vulgar challenge Kant mentions but the more tasteful "Have you had a chance to read it yet?") This example shows how much thought may be demanded by the simplest of interactions between reasonable beings. If this case is uncertain, so is everything else. In this sense, Kant's ethics leave us without foundation.

In beginning to answer the question of what, if anything, it does leave us, I want to turn to the more theoretical foundational question. The search for foundations of ethics proceeds from the problem most elegantly formulated in David Hume's observation that the "ought" has such an entirely different character than the "is" that it seems inconceivable that the former can be deduced from the latter.[5] In one way or another, attempts to answer moral skepticism propose to conceive the inconceivable, to prove that moral laws are really true. Otherwise, it is feared, we are left with some version of emotivism, according to which your taste for torturing children is, metaphysically speaking, no different than my taste for lemon tarts.

Here as elsewhere it is useful to view Kant as turning Hume on his head. Kant not only accepts Hume's claim that "ought" cannot be derived from any claims about nature; "ought," he tells us, *has no meaning in nature.* Here Kant can be said to acknowledge the critical thrust of emotivism: as claims about the nature of reality, moral claims are quite literally senseless. Every attempt to prove that the moral law is true must end in failure. For morality is not a matter of truth, the way the world is; it is, like every principle of reason, a matter of the way the world ought to be. This distinction, between the "is" and the "ought," is for Kant the most fundamental, structuring any experience that is recognizably human.

It is crucial to see that for Kant, this distinction is essential to all aspects of human experience, in particular that it is as important to the practice of science (in the broadest sense) as it is to morality. For the presupposition of creative activity, the idea that the world can and should be made intelligible, is itself not a fact about the world but a demand on it. That is, we cannot make sense of reality without going beyond it. It is this capacity to go beyond given experience, to prescribe laws for reality rather than passively accept it, that constitutes human dignity itself. If this general capacity for autonomy is, for Kant, the thing that makes us human, we can understand why Kant was viewed for generations as the metaphysician of the French Revolution. Where reason's natural task is to propose standards and structures that are not read off the world of experience, it is easy to argue that the reigning order of custom and tradition should be overthrown in accordance with "natural" laws of reason. Conservative theorists like Edmund Burke, who dismiss such arguments as dangerously utopian, take for granted just the Humean metaphysics that Kant will call into question. In ridiculing radical demands for social change as inconsistent with the sorry facts of past experience, the empiricist assumes, without argument, that experience is the measure by which ideals are to be judged. Kant's entire Critical Theory, by contrast, argues that this order is exactly backward: it is human reason's function to derive meaning through its opposition to experience.

If this is the metaphysics that allows us to understand Heinrich Heine's description of Robespierre as tame and humdrum (*spiessbürgerlich*) when compared to Kant, it is one that disallows any attempt at ethical grounding. For all Kant's talk of architectonics, and his evident fondness for building metaphors, his insistence on the depth of the gap between "ought" and "is" is an insistence on the impossibility of giving ethics foundations, by natural means or any other. In particular, Kant makes no appeal to necessary *facts* about human nature. To say that the capacity to make demands on experience is constitutive of human dignity is not to say that experience would be incoherent without it. As history all too perilously reminds us, this feature of human nature is one we may choose to discard. Dignity and self-respect are not themselves neutral notions: morality is normative all the way down. Conversely, one who tries to reject moral skepticism by showing that ethics is objective has misunderstood something crucial about discourse: "objective" is a term that makes sense to use about objects, and nothing else.

A proof that morality is by its very nature groundless is an unpromising offer for those interested in instilling ethics. The fact that it is a deep proof may make matters seem all the worse. It is all very well to insist that most demands for ethical foundations would undercut what Kant called the cardinal maxim of Enlightenment: to think for yourself. At a time when most principles of Enlightenment are violated with abandon, such thinking may be a luxury we cannot afford. Do Kantian ethics offer anything distinctive that might be of interest to those whose primary problems are not metaphysical ones? If not, one must wonder: it may be more fun to read Nietzsche.

First, we must note that while Kant denies that moral statements can be true, he allows that they can be necessary. Indeed, he makes the puzzling and difficult claim that only statements of reason carry genuine necessity. Moral principles, as principles of reason, are those that even God could not conceive to be otherwise. We can begin to understand Kant's meaning if we try to negate what he called the Unconditioned in the practical realm, the highest principle of practical reason: the claim that there should be a systematic connection between happiness and virtue. Try denying an implication of this—for example, say that people who help other people ought to be tortured—and you will find yourself speaking nonsense.[6] You can say such words, but they will be as unintelligible as the denial of "A = A." Like "A = A," however, the claim that happiness and virtue should be systematically connected forms a limit rather than a signpost. If there *are* morally necessary principles, they will give about as much guidance in the practice of ethics as "A = A" tells us how to proceed in the progress of science.

And yet we know that the question of moral education occupied Kant deeply and often.[7] There were only two events in Kant's uneventful life, two departures from routine: first was his reading of Rousseau's *Emile*; second was hearing the news of the French Revolution. If Rousseau's general conception of moral education lurks in the background of much of the Critical Philosophy,[8] Kant returns to the question in detail at the end of his major ethical writings.[9] The *Critique of Practical Reason* proposes a method of moral education that Kant himself states to be unusual, used so seldom that we can make no appeal to experience to prove or cast doubt on its efficacy. Its distinctive features are two. The first may seem surprising: Kant insists that moral education proceed not by lecture, nor by a study of general principle, but through a dialogue that examines particular cases of possible moral behavior. The second feature will seem more familiar: Kant insists that virtue be always presented in its purest form, without any appeal to the practical advantages it may offer. Standard moral education proceeds by showing that ethics is good business: in Kant's own example, a grocer may decide to be honest so as to attract more customers, acquiring a reputation that will bring even children to shop at his store. Kant, by contrast, insists that ethics be taught by reference to heroes: those who do justice for the sake of justice though it threaten their lives. Reverting for a moment to merchant metaphors, Kant argues: "Virtue is here worth so much because it costs so much."[10]

Knowing he proposes methods opposed to accepted practice, Kant can give no evidence for their success. He believes, however, he finds evidence of our openness to such methods in the pleasure we get from the lively discussion that arises around questions of ethical character. One need only consider the speculation recently dominating living rooms across the globe about what the possible lie of a political leader might reveal about his moral character to confirm Kant's claim that "in mixed companies consisting not merely of scholars and subtle reasoners but also of business people and women," we entertain ourselves by "exact, meticulous and subtle [argument] about the moral worth of this or that action from which the character of some person is to be made out."[11]

Let us note, for those inclined to view Kant as dour and ascetic, that he *wants* us to enjoy moral reasoning, and hence, morality. The *Metaphysics of Morals* explicitly condemns "cheerless, gloomy and sullen" reflection that leads us to hate virtue and says of Kant's own method: "Its advantage lies especially in the fact that it is natural for a man to *love* a subject which he has, by his own handling, brought to a science (in which he is now proficient); and so, by this sort of practice, the pupil is drawn without noticing it to an *interest* in morality" (*Metaphysics of Morals*, Ak. 484).

We are, therefore, not to tell our children stories about greengrocers, but about the supporters of Anne Boleyn. Kant mentions this case as one of persecution that will make a natural impression on a ten-year-old child. By presenting the story of someone who defends innocent but powerless people, and suffers for it deeply, we lead the child to a sense of awe and wonder at the capacity for moral personality that can overcome even the strongest of natural desires, love of life itself. Examples like these, Kant tells us, lift us out of the world of sense. Let us ask, in closing: "Why is it important to be thus exalted?"

Secondary literature offers little discussion of such examples, and it is easy to dismiss Kant's emphasis on them as relics of an earlier age, when children were raised on Plutarch's *Lives,* and the sort of sentimental exhortation to virtue that makes us nostalgic and uneasy. Against such dismissal we should read Kant's warning, in the Anne Boleyn discussion, against the "fleeting and ephemeral elevation of soul, the longing for unattainable perfection which produces mere heroes of romance."[12] Even more important is Kant's own insistence that the method he proposes is not the usual one: even in the Stoic circles of eighteenth-century Prussia, moral education proceeded more by reference to the advantage of duty than to its sublimity. The repeated presence of such examples is therefore not an anachronistic curiosity. I suggest that we understand the force and meaning of such examples by looking at the place accorded to the first of them, Kant's discussion of the gallows in the second *Critique.*

Kant himself initially looked for just the sort of proof of the objectivity of ethics that his later work showed to be impossible.[13] Instead, he offers what he called the Fact of Reason—the claim that reason *just is* morally authoritative for us.[14] To offer as brute fact what seemed on the verge of proof was so disappointing that it became the object of straightforward ridicule for authors as otherwise inclined to disagreement as G. W. F. Hegel and Arthur Schopenhauer. Yet just at the point where we hoped for proof, Kant gives us an example. We are asked to consider a person who claims to be unable to resist temptation. Were a gallows erected in front of the bordello where he would be immediately executed after satisfying his lust, he would, Kant assures us, quickly find his love of life sufficient to withstand every sensual desire. Now we are asked to imagine the same man, the same gallows. This time his life is threatened by an unjust ruler, who wishes to force him to give false testimony to destroy an innocent person. None of us can say with certainty what he would do, but Kant holds it to be equally certain that all of us know that we *should* defy the unjust ruler, though it cost us our lives—and that we are perfectly capable of doing so. The moment after describing the example, Kant concludes: "(7) *Fundamental Law of Pure Practical Reason* So act that the maxim of your will could always hold at the same time as a principle establishing universal law" (*Critique of Practical Reason*, Ak. 31). One thought experiment we all can perform; ergo, the moral law. Q.E.D.

The experiment thus carries a great deal of weight. To begin with, it is meant to answer those conservative or cynical critics who argued that even if some enlightened few are able to act according to principles of reason, the mass of humankind is motivated by simpler and cruder passions.[15] Ethical instruction, and political organization, must therefore proceed by manipulating those passions through some form of benevolent despotism. One cannot found a social order grounded in appeals to the dignity of those whose motives are consistently base. If here or there exists a greengrocer who cherishes honesty for its own sake, most value it, at best, as good policy. Here only life and death examples will help us. For on Kant's account of morality it is crucial that we have no insight into the motives of action, our own or anyone else's. Thus, the greengrocer who refrains from cheating customers to keep them away from his competitor's market looks just the same as the one who does so out of simple decency. You will never know what motivates your greengrocer; neither, in the end, will he.

When we consider a hero, however, we have to stop short. The willingness to give up one's life, the basis of all other desire, bears witness to our awesome capacity to transcend nature itself. Anyone can turn up instances of false heroism: places and times when one performed the wrong act for the right reasons, or the right act for the wrong reasons, and died with an air of unearned glory. It is easy enough to deflate other people's heroes, pointing out that what seemed to be noble was a complex sort of vanity, what looked like disinterest was merely bad faith. Such discussion belongs precisely to that analysis of moral character in which Kant holds us to take such an interest. This is why, with the curious exception of an anonymous defender of Anne Boleyn, Kant refrains from listing concrete examples of heroism. We cannot be certain that any particular person, in history or fiction, acted purely from respect for morality; each of us must find our own heroes. When we engage in this sort of dialogue we will find that each of us can imagine, at the least, one person whom we believe to have defied death rather than accept injustice. And where we view the attempt to reduce that person's motives to banal ones as resentful and petty, we see that it is possible to act for the sake of the moral law. Note that this procedure—for Kant the central one of moral education—is not in conflict with his claim that morality cannot be derived from examples. Examples are not the source of morality, but the confirmation of its real possibility. There is a point to leaving each one to fill in the blank for herself, for any six-year-old is capable of thinking: if Hannah Senesch did it, so could I.

In his often mistaken and always wonderful *Geschichte der Religion und Philosophie in Deutschland*, Heine contrasts Kant with Robespierre.

> But although Kant, the great destroyer in the realm of thought, far surpassed Robespierre in terrorism, he had many similarities which invite a comparison between the two men. First, we find in both the same unrelenting, cutting, unpoetic, sober honesty. We also find in each the same talent for mistrust; only the one exercises it against thought and calls it critique, the other uses it against men and calls it republican virtue. In the highest degree, however, we find in both the model of the bourgeois: nature determined them to weigh coffee and sugar, but fate would have them weigh other things, and put on the scales a king for one, and for the other a God. . . . And they both got it right!

It is impossible to guess whether Heine was thinking of the greengrocer passage, but perhaps we must grant him that Kant was something of a *Kleinbürger*.[16] He was, after all, the metaphysical herald of the bourgeoisie revolution. Suddenly the life of a far more miserable sinner than Augustine can have widest significance; any son of a saddle maker can turn out a genius. In seeking to instill ethics through awesome examples Kant reminds us that we do not wish to remain, finally, a society of greengrocers; and he asks us to consider the conditions in which shopkeepers turn heroes. Resolution, courage to reason, are given to all.[17]

One remaining worry needs to be raised, though space makes it impossible to do much more than that. I have argued that Kant's ethics do not give us hard rules or firm foundations; that Kantian moral instruction proceeds as much by example and inspiration as by principle. If one cuts out so much that seemed part of the Critical Theory, does anything distinctly Kantian remain? I recently heard a talk whose title placed the author between Kant and Aristotle; he was also moving between analytic and continental philosophy. The lecture was good, but I couldn't help feeling a sort of dismay: while this sort of catholicism is far preferable to the rigid caricatures through which most of us studied, one wonders if late-twentieth-century philosophy will dissolve into mush. A little character, a little principle, a little virtue ethics, a little rule. If the features I've emphasized are part of Kant's ethics, what remains to give it force?

Kant's ethics get unique power from two distinct features: his reminder of the claims of universalism and his insistence that virtue is hard. The meaning of Kant's appeal to the universal is still far from clear.[18] His insistence on the difficulty of virtue is easier to sketch. Kant's ethics are often received as ascetic, the world they inhabit relentlessly harsh. I believe he is simply honest. Not Kant's ethics but the world itself has moments of ineluctable bleakness. Righteous people often suffer; wicked people often thrive. Reason and nature are not in tune.[19] This is an ordinary truth we'd prefer to disregard. Denial can take many forms: from the Stoic self-deception that the only happiness that really counts is the consolations of philosophy to Epicurean appeals to prudence designed to make us think that goodness and self-interest can be merged like a family business. Like no one before or after him, Kant underscores the disjunction between happiness and virtue and rejects all attempts to collapse one to the other. Moving from greengrocers to gallows compels us to remember the depth of the gap between "is" and "ought," the actual and the ideal. Yet it also compels us to wonder and awe. And if cynicism is the greatest threat to an ethical standpoint, that is reason enough to consider a method that has not been tried.

NOTES

This chapter was written while I was a fellow of the Institute for Advanced Studies of the Shalom Hartmann Foundation, whose resources have enabled me to write it. I am also indebted to discussions of the Institute's political philosophy research group, in particular with Ruth Gavison, Menachem Lorbeerbaum, and Yael Tamir.

1. As Kant himself replied, just a trifle defensively, to an early critic who accused him of offering nothing more than a souped-up version of the Golden Rule: "A critic who wished to say something against that work really did better than he intended when he said there was no new principle of morality in it but only a new formula. Who would want to introduce a new principle of morality and, as it were, be its inventor, as if the world had hitherto been ignorant of what duty is or had been thoroughly wrong about it?" Immanuel Kant, *Critique of Practical Reason,* trans. Lewis White Beck (Indianapolis: Bobbs-Merril, 1956).

2. See, among other sources, Onora O'Neill, *Acting on Principle* (New York: Columbia University Press, 1975); Barbara Herman, *The Practice of Moral Judgement* (Cambridge: Harvard University Press, 1993); Seyla Benhabib, *Situating the Self* (Cambridge: Polity Press, 1992); Thomas McCarthy, "Kant's Enlightenment Project Reconsidered," in *Proceedings of the Eighth International Kant Congress,* ed. Hoke Robinson (Milwaukee: Marquette University Press, 1995), 1049–65.

3. For discussion of the latter point see Herman, *Practice of Moral Judgement,* chap. 7, who points out not only that this kind of view presents philosophical problems, but also that it is unsupported by Kant's texts.

4. See Susan Neiman, *The Unity of Reason: Rereading Kant* (New York: Oxford University Press, 1994).

5. David Hume, *A Treatise of Human Nature,* 2nd ed., ed. L. A. Selby-Bigge and rev. P. H. Nidditch (Oxford: Clarendon Press, 1992), book III, part 1, sec. 1.

6. The philosophically interesting aspect of de Sade is that he does try to deny this in, for example, *Juliette and Justine,* complete with the hand of Providence holding a bolt of lightning to back him up in conclusion. But thousands of pages cannot, of course, provide a substitute for consistency, though they do provide a backhanded comment on how hard it is to get, even with the best of wills.

7. See also Herman, *Practice of Moral Judgement*, on this score.

8. See Susan Neiman, "Metaphysics, Philosophy: Rousseau on the Problem of Evil," in *Reclaiming the History of Ethics: Essays for John Rawls,* ed. Barbara Herman, Christine Korsgaard, and A. Reath (Cambridge: Cambridge University Press, 1997).

9. Indeed, the *Metaphysics of Morals* tells us that the very concept of virtue implies that virtue is not innate and must therefore be taught, so that questions of how to teach it become of particular importance on a Kantian view. This has to do with Kant's conception of virtue as being only acquirable through struggle. See *Metaphysics of Morals,* Ak. 477.

10. Kant, *Critique of Practical Reason,* Ak. 157.

11. Ibid., Ak. 154.

12. Ibid., Ak. 156.

13. On the history of Kant's attempt to deduce the moral law see Dieter Henrich, "The Concept of Moral Insight and Kant's Doctrine of the Fact of Reason," in Henrich, *The Unity of Reason,* ed. Richard Velkley and tr. Jeffrey Edwards (Cambridge: Harvard University Press, 1994), 55–87.

14. On interpreting the Fact of Reason see John Rawls, "Themes in Kant's Moral Philosophy," in *Kant's Transcendental Deductions*, ed. Eckhart Förster (Stanford: Stanford University Press, 1989), 81–113.

15. On conservative critics of Kant see Frederick Beiser, *Enlightenment, Revolution and Romanticism* (Cambridge: Harvard University Press, 1992), (part 3 [281–362] deals with conservatism); and Neiman, *Unity of Reason,* 105–44.

16. Heine actually uses the word *Spiessbürger,* but that is too much for this Kantian to swallow.

17. The first *Critique*'s crucial chapter, "The Canon of Pure Reason," concludes thus:

But, it will be said, is that all that pure reason achieves in opening up prospects beyond the limits of experience? Nothing more than two articles of belief? Surely the common understanding could have achieved as much, without appealing to philosophers for counsel in the matter. . . . I may at once reply: Do you really require that a mode of knowledge which concerns all men should transcend the common understanding, and should only be revealed to you by philosophers? Precisely what you find fault with is the best confirmation of the correctness of the above assertions. For we have thereby revealed to us, what could not at the start have been foreseen, namely, that in matters which concern all men without distinction nature is not guilty of any partial distribution of her gifts, and that in regard to the essential ends of human nature the highest philosophy cannot advance further than is possible under the guidance which nature has bestowed even upon the most common understanding. (A831/B859)

18. Here I wish only to suggest that the emphasis on universality is less interesting than often thought to be on the level of individual ethics. One might say that teaching ethics in early childhood starts with the smallest scale universal; generalizing from one's own case to that of another is the first moral act. We internalize the Golden Rule when we repeat, more often than it seems anything ought to be necessary, that anyone who thinks it is wrong for Johnny to hit them should not begin by hitting Johnny. But it cannot have been Kant's intention to do something that is already done quite well in kindergarten. Ruling out individual self-interested exceptions is too clearly just the opposite of moral thinking. I

believe that Kant is more interested in questions concerning universalist questions of social and political organization, where we are still inclined to stay where we started, viewing justice as helping our friends and hurting our enemies.

19. This is a general claim that lends Kant's vision of the human an air of deepest and general *Zerrissenheit*. The few great passages of prose that he could not refrain from writing all express the ways in which we are torn: between the starry heavens above me and the moral law within me, between reason's fate to be driven and its awareness of limit. So being human, in general, is hard, for Kant, and nobody stresses this more. But then, as his *Anthropology* states categorically: "There is *no merit* in doing what is easy."

Chapter Seven

History as Psychology/Morality as Pathology: Nietzsche and the Ethical Tradition

Dwight David Allman

In *Beyond Good and Evil*, Friedrich Nietzsche prefaces his discussion of the new breed of philosophers whom his writings aim to cultivate with the proclamation, "For psychology is now again the path to the fundamental problems."[1] In his playfully bombastic but profoundly earnest self-portrait, *Ecce Homo*, he likewise announces "[t]hat a psychologist without equal speaks from my writings."[2] One could multiply these examples with selections from almost any of Nietzsche's mature works to illustrate his predilection for describing himself and his life's labor by reference to the word *psychology*. To be sure, what might be termed the psychological cast of Nietzsche's thought has long been appreciated; moreover, its influence on the development of modern psychology has become increasingly evident.[3] However, the import of Nietzsche's self-representation as a "psychologist," indeed, as one without precedent or rival—"Who among the philosophers before me was in any way a *psychologist*?"[4] —stands in need of clarification.

Nietzsche's identification of his conception of philosophy with psychology bears directly on the fate of our moral and ethical traditions. That it has for us today become difficult, perhaps impossible, to take up the issues of morality without finding ourselves inevitably swept into the territory of psychology is at least partly Nietzsche's doing. To grapple seriously with the problem of ethics at the end of the twentieth century demands at some point a reflection on the contemporary propensity to translate this question into a problem for psychology, and that reflection in turn points back to Nietzsche's persistent conflation of philosophy and psychology.

Between the foregoing passage from *Beyond Good and Evil* (published in 1886), which identifies Nietzsche's central concern as having to do fundamentally with psychology, and his self-presentation in *Ecce Homo* (the last work finished before his breakdown in early 1889) as the world's foremost psychologist, an obvious tension exists. On the one hand, Nietzsche represents his philosophical undertaking as some kind of *return* to psychology; on the other hand, he portrays himself as the *first and only* student of the human psyche: "Before me there simply was no psychology."[5] How are we to understand these conflicting claims? Is it possible to conceive of Nietzsche's thought, at one and the same time, both as a return to a psychological engagement with "the fundamental problems" and as an entirely new, uniquely psychological approach to these very problems? By seeking an answer to this question, we ready ourselves to assess the relevance of Nietzsche's philosophical project for the ethical tradition from which he both descends and departs. What finally resolves this apparent dilemma is Nietzsche's treatment of the problem of history. It is, moreover, Nietzsche's attempt to contemplate life in the light of his understanding of history that constitutes the basis of his remarkable appeal in late modernity.

THE FATE OF THE SOUL IN MODERNITY

To bring fully to light the passages in which Nietzsche defines and describes himself in terms of psychology, I begin with a somewhat novel account of a familiar story about the modern course of political philosophy. At the beginning of the seventeenth century, Europeans still assailed or defended political power in terms, typically, of religious and theological *auctoritas*.[6] Making the case for a given policy or regime involved demonstrating, first and foremost, its agreement with scripture and with received authorities like Aristotle, whom scholasticism had baptized into the canon.[7] By century's end, however, Europeans looked more and more to nature as the basis of political legitimacy. Leading political thinkers of the seventeenth century had orchestrated a return to nature for normative guidance in politics, even while they spurned the naturalism of the ancient philosophers.[8] A primary target of Thomas Hobbes's *Leviathan* (published in 1651), with its distinctively modern and incipiently liberal formulation of politics, is Aristotle's *politike episteme* (political science). In *Leviathan*, Hobbes sought to do for the science of politics what he saw Francis Bacon, René Descartes, and others doing in the investigation of the physical universe. He hoped to rest politics on the same mechanistic-materialist and universalizable foundations on which the modern students of nature sought to erect a new order of physical sciences. Hobbes would establish political science not on the authority of venerable texts of ancient wisdom or prophetic revelation, but on technical observation of bodies and their motions.[9] In Part One of *Leviathan*, Hobbes therefore sets out to supply a strictly materialist account of man himself, the one indisputably natural element within the realm of politics.

Hobbes's departure from the well-trod path of Aristotle's *politike episteme* is nowhere more evident than in this bold proclamation from *Leviathan*: "For there is no such *Finis ultimus* [utmost aim]nor *Summum Bonum* [greatest good] as is spoken of in the books of the old moral philosophers."[10] For Aristotle, the greatest good or "happiness," as *eudaimonia* is usually rendered, has a determinate structure, making it possible, first, to give an explicit account of the *Summum Bonum*, and, then, to label it the "final end," or *Finis ultimus*, around which human action properly orients and orders itself. By contrast, Hobbes here defines "felicity" as "a continual progress of the desire," making clear that he sees no eudaemonistic resolution of human endeavor in and through what "the books of the old moral philosophers" deemed the ethical life. Consistent with his rejection of Aristotle's determinate conception of the human good, Hobbes likewise explains the terms *good* and *evil* as mere conventions that denominate "the object of any man's appetite or desire" and "the object of his hate and aversion," respectively.[11] By implication, Hobbes commits himself to a hedonistic conception of human action and to a reductive view of ethics as resting ultimately on whatever brings pleasure.

Aristotle brought order to the perennial and fundamental concern of how one might best lead one's life with an ethics built upon the concept of the *Summum Bonum*. Behind Hobbes's dissolution of this order stands a pivotal challenge to the moral and political thought bequeathed by antiquity. To an important extent, the early modern revolution in moral and political philosophy instigated by Hobbes revolves around a rejection of the doctrine of the soul—the linchpin holding together being and becoming for the tradition of moral philosophy inaugurated by Socrates and perpetuated by medieval Christian thinkers. Deploying a favorite trope of medieval political thought, Hobbes cues attentive readers to this radical element of his teaching by representing the "great Leviathan" or "Commonwealth" as an "artificial man," in which "the *sovereignty* is an artificial soul [that] giv[es] life and motion to the whole body."[12] With this orienting image of "the body politic," Hobbes links sovereignty, the central issue within the theory of state he intends to develop, to a traditional (idealist) notion of the soul as the source of life and motion in the body.[13] As a result, when the account "Of Man" that follows lacks any parallel treatment of the soul, the discrepancy appears especially conspicuous. Hobbes thus quietly raises the question of the soul, inviting readers to seek out his answer. In the one passage within Part One where the word *soul* appears, Hobbes wholly rejects (though in a somewhat roundabout way) the established sense of the word as denominating something noncorporeal. In short, Hobbes insists that all substance has dimension and, as such, body. The universe harbors no "spirit incorporeal" and the idea of the soul as an immaterial substance is dismissed as a self-contradiction.[14]

The early modern attempt to conceive of human beings in strictly material terms would prompt Jean-Jacques Rousseau to instigate the initial philosophical revolt against the modern political project, in particular against the abandonment by modern social and political thinkers of the issues of the soul. As an epigraph to his monumental *Discourse on the Origin and Foundations of the Inequality among Men* (1754), that frequently sardonic "Citizen of Geneva" thus selected a passage from his Latin translation of Aristotle's *Politics* that runs as follows: "Not in depraved things but in those well-oriented according to nature are we to consider what is natural."[15] Rousseau maliciously chooses Aristotle to introduce an essay that would begin a pivotal reorientation of modernity to signal his challenge to early modern political thought.[16] Aristotle represented the perfect symbol by which Rousseau might presage his quarrel with the fathers of the modern project, since it was against Aristotle (not to mention his scholastic enthusiasts) that the founders of modern science and modern philosophy had originally defined themselves. Rousseau thus points back to Aristotle as a way of pointing beyond the encompassing materialism and empiricism that defined the emergent political thought of the early modern world.

The passage from the *Politics* with which Rousseau chooses to identify his *Second Discourse* expresses a view of nature and, in particular, of human nature that is based on Aristotle's attempt to bring the world into focus through the lens of a purposive conceptualization of the natural whole—that is, through final causation. Things that are "well-oriented according to nature" (as Rousseau's Latin text puts it)[17] are those that stand in consistent relation to the guiding purposes and aims of nature—in short, those in which there exists a harmony of the actual with the potential, of what is with what ought to be. Aristotle goes on to complete this thought as follows: "Therefore, the human being whose state is best both in body and in soul is the one who ought to be studied, and in him this maxim [namely, that one should not look to what is depraved but to what is 'well-oriented according to nature'] is clear; for in the case of the depraved, or those in a depraved condition, it might often seem that the body rules over the soul on account of being in a condition that is bad and contrary to nature."[18]

Aristotle's approach to the study of nature is thus inextricably linked to the idea that the natural realm has nonmaterial dimensions that must be taken fully into account before one can hope to determine what is "according to nature." For this reason, the idea of the soul is fundamental to Aristotle's understanding of what the realm of nature encompasses because it governs his very attempt to conceptualize the natural as such. By extension, Aristotle's contention that the *polis*, though plainly a human construct, is nevertheless a natural phenomenon depends on the idea that human nature has what might be termed a spiritual essence. Only in and through the mode of existence uniquely available within the *polis* does it become possible for man to make actual the natural but intangible purposes that manifest themselves in his generic features and faculties and that thereby define the state of his flourishing. When Hobbes banishes the nonmaterial from the realm of serious inquiry into the nature of human beings, he necessarily constricts the political to the level of human artifice.

By recalling Aristotle, however, Rousseau clearly does not mean to invoke a conception of nature rooted in final causation. Rousseau looks back to Aristotle, as to the ancients in general, to gain critical purchase on modernity, but the extent of his commitment to a discernibly modern framework manifests itself even in this appeal to Aristotle. In the final analysis, Rousseau calls not for a fresh engagement with ancient philosophy and science, but for a newly critical investment in the modern social and political project. To be sure, Rousseau indicates that early modern materialism is insufficient to the task of a genuine science of man, and therefore to a politics predicated on scientific knowledge. But Rousseau would not so much abandon the materialism of modern science as reconfigure it within the original, modern historicism. He stands, in effect, as the first in modernity to delineate a concept of the human sciences that necessarily removes them from the realm of the physical sciences.[19] In Rousseau's hands, Aristotle becomes the herald of a uniquely modern quest to come to terms with essential, nonempirical dimensions of human being. In this way, the problem of the soul returns but in an entirely new form. History is now identified as the medium through which insight into the immaterial and vital core of human nature becomes finally possible.

THE IDEA OF PROGRESS AND THE PROBLEM OF THE SOUL

Rousseau is rightly credited with having first placed the matter of human nature, and therein the issues of social and political life, within a historicist frame. In the final analysis, however, this achievement amounts to a novel extension of a rationale introduced, curiously enough, by early modern materialists like Hobbes. The Hobbesian reconceptualization of happiness as "the continual progress of desire" entails the rejection of the ancient idea that the soul constitutes the spiritual ground of the structure of human vitality. Indeed, one might further conclude that it entails the rejection of the idea that there is any spiritual order to happiness. For Aristotle, on the other hand, the concept of the soul elaborates the proper and hierarchical configuration of the psychic dimensions of human being. As such, the doctrine of the soul prescribes a certain spiritual condition—based on an ordering of appetites, aspiration, and the like under the sovereignty of reason—as given by nature for man. In his *Nicomachean Ethics*, Aristotle thus broadly defines the life of virtue as "the soul's activity that expresses reason."[20] The modern materialist doctrine of happiness, by comparison, identifies a radical indeterminacy at the core of human being. Human existence is propelled, as it seems, by a perpetual flux and consequent redefinition of its primary objects. At the same time, however, Hobbes suggests that happiness follows essentially a linear (as opposed to circular) trajectory, that there is a "progress" to the sequence of desires directing the course of an individual's life. In short, Hobbes's articulation of a notion of human happiness to complement the materialist politics with which he gives impetus to modern liberalism establishes at the same time the basis for the modern ideology of progress.

Hobbes discovers in the interest each has in bodily well-being the surest foundation for political life. He thus identifies within the flux of psychic experience the "fear of death" (security) and the desire for "commodious living" (prosperity) as the most constant and reliable passions upon which to base the calculations of his universal science of politics.[21] Hobbes seeks, in other words, to predicate on his hedonistic materialism a program for political governance that partakes implicitly of the spirit of idealism.[22] In this way, he sets the stage for a modern politics of the body[23] that makes the ongoing and even unlimited prospect of bodily satisfactions the basis of social/political contentment and tranquillity. Hobbes thus inaugurates a strategy for political order around which the modern liberal state and the modern capitalist economy gradually emerged. As Jean Bethke Elshtain explains, "The founders of modern liberalism embraced an argument that posited human wants and needs as expandable, indeed, nearly insatiable," making both possible and necessary the "indefinite growth of the productive forces of economic life [in order] to satisfy and continually fuel the restless cycle of the creation and satiation of needs."[24] From this vantage point, Hobbes's displacement of the traditional idea of the soul in favor of a continuum of ceaselessly mutating desire looks to establish what we might call the spiritual preconditions of modern social, political, and economic life. And one key precondition appears to be a metaphysics of progress that necessarily leads to a distinctive formulation of the idea of history. The ground for such a metaphysics is the idealist underpinnings of Hobbes's political hedonism; moreover, the advent of the concept of progress within modern social and political thought prefigures the conflation of the question of the soul and the question of history that, in turn, marks the advent of historicism.

Rousseau is prompted to conceive of the question of human nature as a version of the problem of history by the fact that eighteenth-century thinkers had constructed an elaborate doctrine of progress around Hobbes's political hedonism, and by the fact that Rousseau's philosophical awakening is sparked by the question of progress as posed in 1749 by the Academy of Dijon—"whether the restoration of the sciences and the arts contributed to the purification of mores?"[25] What primarily concerns Rousseau in the *First Discourse* is the spiritual condition of modern man and, in particular, the distinctively modern conviction that this moment in time represents the pinnacle of a history of progress. His argument thus builds itself not simply around a comparison of corrupt societies with healthy ones, but around a persistent comparison of the modern with the ancient world: "Ancient politicians spoke incessantly about mores and virtue; ours speak only of commerce and money."[26] A guiding concern of Rousseau's social and political thought is the nobility of man, which he believes has been degraded by what modern men hail as "progress." He insists that "our souls have become corrupted in proportion as our sciences and our arts have advanced toward perfection."[27] The challenge posed by the *First Discourse* to the idea of progress thus begins a search for the original modern politics of the soul. And historicism is born with Rousseau's attempt in the *Second Discourse* to recover an image of the soul in its original state.[28] To a significant extent, however, Rousseau simply follows the lead of Hobbes, whose reconsideration of the idea of the soul pioneered a new way of thinking about the relation of the present state of man to past and future states. In this light, Rousseau's polemic with modernity clearly appears to be not so much a rejection as a radicalization: the natural man of Hobbes's *Leviathan* is swallowed up by the indeterminacy that Hobbes himself posits at the core of that nature and that Rousseau, wrestling with the modern thesis of progress, subsequently elaborates as history.

HISTORY AS PSYCHOLOGY

If Rousseau is the first great critic of the civilizational order that the most original thinkers of the sixteenth and seventeenth centuries had attempted to conceptualize, Nietzsche is the first great antagonist of that modern world. Yet Nietzsche's antagonism, like Rousseau's criticism, takes vital nourishment from an intellectual food chain winding directly back to the first moderns. Both figures define themselves vis-à-vis modernity by extending in original and radical ways premises that are distinctly modern in origin. With respect to the question of the soul, in particular, Nietzsche represents the full flowering of seeds planted by Hobbes.

Nietzsche sends his prophet-sage, Zarathustra, to proclaim that the modern scientific quest to ameliorate the temporal condition of man has eventuated in a profound spiritual crisis. Zarathustra's well-known observation that "God is dead" is Nietzsche's provocative shorthand for describing the unhappy predicament of late modernity. But it is necessary to emphasize several points to bring this curt assessment fully into focus. Broadly speaking, Nietzsche means to suggest that Western civilization has lost its way; the modern world no longer knows whence to take its bearings. A histrionic passage from *The Gay Science*, in which Nietzsche first allegorizes the spiritual crisis of modern civilization in terms of the death of God, dramatizes this point:

> The madman jumped into their midst and pierced them with his eyes. "Whither is God?" he cried; "I will tell you. *We have killed him*—you and I. All of us are his murderers. But how did we do this? How could we drink up the sea? Who gave us the sponge to wipe away the entire horizon? What were we doing when we unchained this earth from its sun? Whither is it moving now? Whither are we moving? Away from all suns? Are we not plunging continually? Backward, sideward, forward, in all directions? Is there still any up or down? Are we not straying as through an infinite nothing? Do we not feel the breath of empty space? Has it not become colder? Is not night continually closing in on us? Do we not need to light lanterns in the morning? Do we hear nothing as yet of the noise of the gravediggers who are burying God? Do we smell nothing as yet of the divine decomposition? Gods, too, decompose. God is dead. God remains dead. And we have killed him."[29]

God, whom Nietzsche here represents as the sun that anchors the orbit of human existence, has not simply expired but has been quietly killed off by the very community dependent on this star for light, warmth, and direction. The unfolding of modern civilization has somehow subverted the ideals, beliefs, and pieties that made this civilization possible. The madman comes therefore bearing grim news. The proclamation that "God is dead" describes a pervasive and existing condition in which the community as a whole is implicated: "All of us are his murderers." At the same time, the bearer of this news is looked upon as a "madman"; the community to which he reports what he sees obviously does not yet view itself through his eyes. Nietzsche thus prompts us to consider whether this brief tale representing the condition that confronts the modern world is not likewise meant to provoke and thereby to hasten, if possible, that confrontation. To be sure, Nietzsche takes the crisis of modernity to be ultimately an unprecedented opportunity.

The account of the madman contained in *The Gay Science* turns out to be the initial rendition of the story Nietzsche tells as prologue to *Thus Spake Zarathustra*, in which Zarathustra takes the place of the madman and comes heralding the *Übermensch* as a resolution to the modern condition.[30] In both cases, Nietzsche chooses to detail the cultural and metaphysical crisis of modernity in an allegory woven around the announcement that "God is dead." In its most immediate sense, the phrase suggests that belief in the personal deity of the Bible has disappeared. Nietzsche elsewhere indicates that modern consciousness is the product of a scientific *Bildung* (a word variously translated as "education," "breeding," or "culture" that denotes a comprehensive molding of human faculties and sensibilities) that has supplanted the authority of the traditional sources of meaning, even while eschewing the question of meaning. As a result, the once architectonic "Why?" goes unanswered,[31] and a civilization predicated on the scientific quest for truth must face the fact that the value of truth has become uncertain. A debilitating nihilism seems at hand. Both allegories make clear, however, that the dissipation of traditional belief is hardly news to the inhabitants of this modern world. In the allegory from *The Gay Science*, the crowd to whom the madman reports his findings mocks his consternation over the death of God. Similarly, Zarathustra comes expecting to find an audience desperate to resolve its spiritual predicament but discovers a community comfortably reconciled to the loss of belief and hostile to anything that might unsettle its self-contentment. In this way, Nietzsche gestures toward a second, somewhat more intricate, signification for the idea that "God is dead."

In all of his mature works, Nietzsche represents the present moment as one characterized not only by an almost pervasive atheism but also by a renewed faith in moral order. This seeming paradox finds its explanation in Nietzsche's account of modern philosophy, in particular of modern German philosophy. Part One of *Beyond Good and Evil*, entitled "On the Prejudices of Philosophers," includes a discussion of German philosophy's vital role in supplying the modern world with a moral philosophy to supplement its scientific orientation. The account begins with Immanuel Kant and his decisive influence on the subsequent development of German idealism, which Nietzsche traces, with malicious wit, to Kant's discovery of "a moral faculty in man." In this way, Kant seemed to have rescued the ethical tradition from the critical, empiricist eye that modern science increasingly cast in its direction.[32] As a result,

> The honeymoon of German philosophy arrived. All the young theologians of the Tübingen seminary went into the bushes—all looking for "faculties." And what did they not find—in that innocent, rich, and still youthful period of the German spirit, to which romanticism, the malignant fairy, piped and sang, when one could not yet distinguish between "finding" and "inventing"! Above all, a faculty for the "suprasensible": Schelling christened it intellectual intuition, and thus gratified the most heartfelt cravings of the Germans, whose cravings were at bottom pious.[33]

Nietzsche here indicates that modern German philosophy initially sought to address itself to what the ancients held to be the issues of the soul through an approach ("looking for 'faculties'") that reflects the preeminence of modern science and scientific materialism. But he also suggests that Kant's discovery of a faculty upon which moral existence might properly and materially ground itself involved a certain sleight of hand, enabling Kant to rehabilitate in the guise of an empirical discovery the idealist faith in a natural moral order. The civilizational influence of German philosophy thus issues from Kant, but, in particular, from Kant's formative influence on "the young theologians of the Tübingen seminary." The mention of Tübingen is an oblique reference to the German idealists. Friedrich Schelling and G. W. F. Hegel spent their student years together in Tübingen. Kant, then, gave decisive impetus to a modern tradition of idealism nourished, at the same time, by what Nietzsche here describes as the "[pious] cravings of the Germans" and elsewhere as a "theologian's instinct" characteristic of the German intellectual classes.[34] While Nietzsche declares that this "exuberant" moment in the history of German culture was part of a "youthfulness" that has since passed away—"Enough, one grew older and the dream vanished"—he also contends that Kant, and the tradition of German philosophy deriving from Kant, have exercised an "enormous influence . . . throughout the whole of Europe."[35] He implies, moreover, that this influence remains an active one. The self-contentment exhibited by those in the marketplace to whom the madman (and, in turn, Zarathustra) reports his discovery that "God is dead" finds its explanation in modern philosophy's renewal of this idealist faith.

With his own philosophical labors, Nietzsche thus seeks to confront and to contest this prevailing (German) metaphysical orientation. He notes that German culture has aged since Kant inspired a generation of seminarians to take up philosophy; he clearly hopes it has also seasoned. The generation that came of age with Nietzsche in the 1860s was as likely to espouse pessimism as idealism. Nietzsche therefore concludes this passage from *Beyond Good and Evil* by unceremoniously dismissing the search for "faculties" or physiological foundations upon which to ground moral existence, calling instead for an inquiry into the spiritual dynamics motivating such a search in the first place. He intimates that what follows is directed to an audience prepared and conditioned by, but now become

somehow uncertain of, the idealist quest to mark the spiritual boundaries of existence. Nietzsche thus proposes his own return to the question of the soul, a return
that marks a radical departure for moral philosophy and, at the same time, for the
course of Western social and political thought. He would account for the intangible dimensions of material existence through "new versions and refinements of
the soul-hypothesis,"[36] through "versions and refinements" that take what might
be termed an extramaterialist approach to the matter of the nonmaterial. This
opening segment of *Beyond Good and Evil* thus concludes with the statement that
instigated our inquiry, the proclamation of a new spiritual orientation for philosophy: "For psychology is now again the path to the fundamental problems."[37]

What we might call the original premise of Nietzsche's philosophical enterprise, namely, the claim that "God is dead," thus finds its elaboration at least
partly in his account of the impact of German philosophy on the modern European world. The philosophy of Hegel marks the high tide of German idealism,
and it is against the pervading influence of Hegel that Nietzsche, like others of his
generation, labored through his early years to define himself.[38] His youthful identification with Arthur Schopenhauer and with Schopenhauer's philosophical pessimism represents, among other things, an initial stance against a Hegelian configuration of historicism that buttressed what the mature Nietzsche repeatedly
disparages as modernity's decadent optimism and faith in progress. Throughout
his works of the 1870s, moreover, Nietzsche can be found struggling to free himself not only from the reins of discipleship, first to Richard Wagner and finally to
Schopenhauer, but also from the vast influence of the tradition of German philosophy that he associates, in particular, with Kant and Hegel.

In an "Attempt at a Self-Critique," composed in 1886 to introduce a second
printing of his first book, *The Birth of Tragedy*, a mature Nietzsche describes this
initial work as handicapped by the fact that he sought to articulate with "Schopen-
hauerian and Kantian formulas" something that is "at odds with Kant's and
Schopenhauer's spirit and taste."[39] Later, however, in the review of his works
contained in *Ecce Homo* (1889), Nietzsche determined that "the cadaverous per-
fume of Schopenhauer sticks only to a few formulas," but that the work "smells
offensively Hegelian" with its central teaching seemingly modeled on the historical dialectic introduced by Hegel: "An idea—the antithesis [*Gegensatz*] of the
Dionysian and the Apollinian—translated into the realm of metaphysics; history
itself as the development of this 'idea'; in tragedy this antithesis is sublimated
[*Aufgehoben*] into a unity; and in this perspective things that had never before
faced each other are suddenly juxtaposed, used to illuminate each other, and comprehended [*begriffen*]—opera, for example, and the revolution."[40]

Two years after writing *The Birth of Tragedy*, Nietzsche took up the question
of history directly in an assessment of modern culture that implicates contemporary historicism in the crisis of the modern soul. Nietzsche's ruminations "On the
Use and Disadvantages of History for Life," the second of his *Untimely Meditations*, lead him to conclude that modernity's scientific engagement with the past,

encouraged and sustained by an idealist reading of history as the conduit of reason itself, has eventuated in a paralyzing state of consciousness beset by nihilistic despair. He implies that the modern (Hegelian) faith in history's process has been seriously misplaced and calls for a reconceptualization of the relation between history and life—in short, for a new kind of historical consciousness.

In sum, Nietzsche comes increasingly to identify German philosophy, and particularly Hegel, with the historical consciousness that Zarathustra attributes to the "last man" in his well-known description of that peculiarly modern creature at the beginning of *Thus Spake Zarathustra* (1883).[41] Last men have lost faith in the God of the Bible but continue to believe in human progress and in a moral order that presides over existence. Such men therefore poke fun at the madman's questions concerning the fate of a world that can no longer take its traditional faith seriously; likewise, they mock and foment hostility toward Zarathustra's proposal of the *Übermensch*—an attempt to define anew man's relation to existence in an age without God. Another, lesser-known passage from *The Genealogy of Morals* (1887) returns to the image of the last man to answer the question "[w]hat today constitutes *our* antipathy to 'man'?" Here Nietzsche describes the being marking the culmination of the modern project as a maggotlike creature whose historical self-understanding nevertheless leaves him supremely content with his station and circumstance, for this "hopelessly mediocre and insipid man has already learned to feel himself as the goal and zenith, as the meaning of history."[42] Nietzsche thus emphasizes that a certain conception of history underlies the spiritual state he identifies with the last man.

Hegel found in historicism the means of rehabilitating the idea of progress, which Rousseau had so deflated through his original appeal to history. And it is upon a teleology of progress that the self-satisfaction and contentment of the last man ultimately rests itself.[43] With this passage from *The Genealogy of Morals* (not to mention others),[44] Nietzsche brings to the foreground what Zarathustra's original portrait of the last man left in the background, namely, that the last man is at bottom a type of Hegelian. The proclamation "God is dead" thus appears to have the additional function of expressly delineating those, like the madman and Zarathustra, who take the disappearance of traditional faith to signal a spiritual crisis of civilizational dimensions, from those who consider it merely another marker along the road to the end of history. In this way, Nietzsche would both affirm his break with the preponderant tradition of German philosophy and attack the progressive historicism that he associates with the condition of the last man.[45] Opposition to the (essentially Hegelian) historicism of a self-satisfied modernity, moreover, appears to be a defining feature of Nietzsche's own existential outlook. "God is dead" means that both the personal God of biblical revelation and Hegelian Reason must be rejected as a basis for moral and spiritual life. By extension, Zarathustra's teaching on the *Übermensch*, which Nietzsche locates in antithetical relation to the idea of the last man, takes on the aspect of an anti-Hegelian stance. In short, a reworking of the problem of history necessarily stands at the center of Nietzsche's philosophical project. And the stage is thus set for a complete subsumption of the issues of the soul into the problem of history—a development that describes, at the same time, the radicalization of historicism generally identified with Nietzsche.

Against the backdrop now in place, Nietzsche's description of psychology as "now again" [*nunmehr wieder*] the venue for serious philosophical inquiry is at last readily intelligible. The historical turn in modern social thought, initiated by Rousseau, but carried forward by the German idealists to the point where a sensibility to history—a "sixth sense," as Nietzsche sometimes calls it—became the precondition of understanding in human affairs, opened the way for a new kind of account of the soul, a new psychology. With Nietzsche, historicism takes a psychological turn. The challenge posed by Rousseau to the early moderns gave new life to the study of history, especially in Germany. But, thanks in great part to Kant, nineteenth-century German historiography, like philosophical idealism, preserved the priority accorded by modern science to rational inquiry and the quest for truth. Nietzsche, however, takes Rousseau's assessment of the moral corruption fostered by modern science to a new level, arguing that the commitment to truth (which he traces back as far as Socrates) now threatens the possibility of civilization. Nietzsche's attempt to explain and to remedy this condition rests on his identification of philosophy with psychology. In his role as the *first* psychologist of Western civilization, Nietzsche must likewise reconceive the practice of philosophy: not the matter of truth as such but our interest in and need for truth become its concern.

On the one hand, Nietzsche translates philosophical historicism into an exploration of the interiority of existence and experience, an exploration, as he puts it, of "[t]he world viewed from inside."[46] On the other hand, he dissolves the constitutional divide between the inner and the outer realms of being and experience, between subject and object, into an enveloping complex of becoming. As Nietzsche explains it in a provocative passage from *On the Genealogy of Morals*, "There is no 'being' behind doing, effecting, becoming; 'the doer' is merely a fiction added to the deed—the deed is everything."[47] There is no essential agent that can be isolated from (and thereby made accountable for) action; the discrete configuration of forces that we recognize as a human being is a flux of drives, impulses, motions. Nietzsche's psychological rehabilitation of the question of the soul thus appears to be also an extension of the materialist orientation of early modernity. No core or essence denominates human beings; rather, all is a continuum of becoming. Like Hobbes, moreover, Nietzsche will brook no thought of transcendence. Fully historicized, the soul defines what might be described as the relational aspects of the material forces constitutive of the experience of bodies. As such, the idea of the soul is usefully construed "as [the] social structure of the drives and affects."[48]

Nietzsche linked modern science to an emerging atheism that he deemed modernity's proudest legacy. By returning to the idea of the soul, he by no means sought to recover a premodern concern with the exclusively corporeal dimensions of the modern universe. On the contrary, his vehement denial of a realm of Being transcending corporeality represents something of a continuation of the modern campaign against the nonmaterial. In this light, it is possible to view Nietzsche as a radical extension of Hobbes, but as one that leaves well behind any attempt to rest political life on a regulative-normative connection between the nature of man and the cosmic order. However, Nietzsche likewise contends that with him philosophy marks a *return* to psychology; he thereby points back beyond Hobbes and the early modern dismissal of the issues of the soul to an ancient tradition that identified the soul as the distinctive ground of the ethical life.[49] Here Nietzsche emphasizes an antithetical side to his engagement with modernity, bringing to the foreground his antipathy for the modern project, including modern politics. He variously identifies himself, in fact, with the Greek god Dionysus, the pre-Socratic philosopher Heraclitus, and even with the "noble" Plato in articulating opposition to the modern world.[50] One might therefore conclude that Nietzsche brings together vital elements of both ancient and modern philosophy for a reconfiguration of the spiritual dimensions of moral, social, and political life.

MORALITY AS PATHOLOGY

But Nietzsche's antagonism toward modernity deserves further consideration. Reflecting "On the Prejudices of the Philosophers" in the opening part of *Beyond Good and Evil*, Nietzsche declares "materialistic atomism" to be "one of the best-refuted theories there [is]." He goes on to celebrate the achievement of an eighteenth-century Jesuit thinker named Ruggiero Boscovich for teaching us "to abjure the belief in the last part of the earth that 'stood fast'—the belief in 'substance,' in 'matter,' in the earth-residuum and particle-atom."[51] In a subsequent passage, Nietzsche ranks himself among the "five or six minds" who have come to understand modern physics as nothing more than "an interpretation and exegesis of the world." Still later, he condemns the "mechanistic doltishness" of "natural scientists," for it leads them to "reify 'cause' and 'effect.'" He explains: "In the 'in-itself' there is nothing of 'causal connections,' of 'necessity,' or of 'psychological non-freedom'; there the effect does *not* follow the cause, there is no rule of law."[52] In this light, Nietzsche appears to stand in fundamental if not extreme opposition to modern materialism. His call at the end of this section for a return to psychology thus appears to point to an endeavor altogether antithetical to modern science.

An important thread of Nietzsche's apparent rejection of mechanistic materialism, however, leads directly back to the early modern formulation of the scientific project. Hobbes's attempt to conceptualize a science of politics based itself on the uniquely modern (in a word, Cartesian) solution to the uncertainty hovering perpetually around the canon of ancient and medieval science. In his 1637

Discourse on Method, Descartes advocated building all claims to knowledge on a generalized doubt. In effect, Descartes invites and indulges all skepticism concerning the teachings of received authority in the interest of establishing a science based on a new standard of certainty. In the *Discourse*, he speaks of thereby arriving at conclusions that "presented [themselves] so clearly and distinctly to my mind that there was no reason or occasion to doubt [them]."[53] Four years later, in the *Meditations Concerning First Philosophy*, Descartes based his inquiries into the question of the existence of God and nature on what became the paradigmatic example of such a conclusion—*cogito ergo sum*. In short, only conclusions predicated entirely on one's own powers of thought meet Descartes' standard of certainty; knowledge derives strictly from the unaided operations of the mind. And, as both Descartes and Hobbes well understood, such knowledge "consists in comparing figures and motions only."[54]

The early moderns thus conceived of a new model of science based on a demand for certainty hitherto available exclusively in mathematics. While Aristotle prefaces his study of *politike episteme* and the ethical life with the observation that different subject matters are amenable to different degrees of clarity,[55] Hobbes invokes geometry as the model for a modern science of politics.[56] But building a science of politics on the model of mathematics amounts to the construction of a mechanistic and materialistic account of human existence out of the most stringent idealism. It is only here that Hobbes's project comes fully into view as resting on the incongruous but absolutely necessary (and quintessentially modern) combination of idealism and materialism.[57] Hobbes necessarily formulates his political science in terms of bodies and motions because the Cartesian demand for a mathematical kind of certainty leaves only extension and motion as possible subjects for scientific investigation. As a result, all concern with ends, as also with the nonmaterial or incorporeal (which necessarily exhibits no extension), must be dismissed by serious science and genuine philosophy. Hobbes, then, conceives of a materialist politics, whose matter is nevertheless strictly conceptual, that requires at the same time the unqualified rejection of the incorporeal soul.

Within the paradigm of science established by Descartes, therefore, only a strictly cognitive—purely conceptual and, as such, ideal—world is true and knowable. But the idea of the incorporeal soul can have no part in the modern materialist version of this world. And yet, it is the idealist rigor of Hobbes's materialism that leaves his account of man particularly vulnerable to the challenge posed by Rousseau, who aims to make comprehensible vital (spiritual) dimensions of our humanity that defy reduction to body or motion. It might nevertheless be argued Rousseau's turn to history has the aspect both of a protest against the materialist politics of the early moderns and of an attempt to account for the soul in a way that remains compatible with the materialist frame of modern science. The historicist turn initiated by Rousseau had the consequence of highlighting the fact that the "true world" of Cartesian science is not a human world.

Nietzsche, in turn, radicalizes this conclusion by extending the historicist case against the idealist dimensions of modern science and politics.

Several passages from Nietzsche's examination of "The Prejudices of the Philosophers" serve to illustrate this point. In his discussion of modern physics, mentioned earlier, Nietzsche contends that the abstract world of Cartesian science must be viewed not simply as an isolated realm into which the genuinely human cannot venture, but more importantly as "only an interpretation" conditioned by and contained within finite historical boundaries.[58] He implies that all thinking is subject to the same limitations. In a subsequent passage, Nietzsche takes up the Cartesian *cogito* to demonstrate that it is not an incontrovertible fact but an interpretive construct of readily contestable dimensions:

> When I analyze the whole process that is expressed in the sentence "I think," I find a whole series of daring assertions that would be difficult, perhaps impossible, to prove; for example, that it is *I* who think, that there must necessarily be something that thinks, that thinking is an activity and operation on the part of a being who is thought of as a cause, that there is an "ego," and, finally, that it is already determined what is to be designated by thinking—that I *know* what thinking is.

At the same time, he unpacks the irreducible unity of the "I" to reveal a "synthetic concept" shaped by "grammatical habit."[59] In sum, Nietzsche seeks to deconstruct the cognitive foundation on which Descartes would build his "clear and distinct" conclusions to persuade us that we can have no access to a world or realm beyond the thoroughly subjective confines of human consciousness.

But, if every idea, chain of thought, or insight amounts to no more than a species of interpretation, that is, to an inescapably subjective event, it follows that the only world with which we have (and can have) any experience is a thoroughly human world of our own making. This world is a kind of fiction, for it is necessarily an expression and reflection of ourselves—in a word, it is anthropomorphic;[60] but it is also a projection of what we might somewhat problematically label the *inner* dynamic and the only reality accessible to us. It thus becomes possible to comprehend why Nietzsche characteristically reads every claim about the world as such as "the personal confession of its author and a kind of involuntary and unconscious memoir,"[61] and why he consistently translates questions concerning the order of nature into claims about a given psychological constitution.[62] The anthropomorphic structure of consciousness amounts to the vantage point best described by Nietzsche as "[t]he world viewed from inside." And he conceptualizes this world in terms of the will to power "and nothing else."[63] Here, finally, Nietzsche's identification of philosophy with psychology comes fully into focus. Limited to the view from "inside," philosophy has come with Nietzsche to recognize itself as nothing more than an account of the invisible constellation (*psyche*) that delineates and defines each individual, as nothing more than psychology. Nietzsche returns to the idea of the soul to suggest that bodies and motions are only the palpable manifestation of a distinctive configuration of what might be termed *submaterial forces*,[64] which alone explain the physical experience of existence. And, as earlier noted, Nietzsche views body, motion, and "underlying" forces as part of a continuum of becoming; consequently, "the deed is everything."

The return to the soul via Nietzschean historicism leads not only to the complete subjectivism of thought and the consequent transmutation of philosophy into a kind of psychology, but also translates the matter of the ethical life into a question of pathology. With Nietzsche, the logic of historicism threatens to devour utterly the tradition out of which it arises, leaving modern men to confront the unprecedented task of self-consciously re-creating the world from scratch. Zarathustra thus insists, "Man is something that shall be overcome. What have you done to overcome him?"[65] The historical-psychological enterprise that now defines philosophy culminates in a genealogical conception of the "soul" that reduces our tradition of moral thought and practice to a record of civilizational pathology. Nietzsche's relevance to the ethical tradition thus resides most fundamentally in the challenge that his radical extension of historicism poses to the perpetuation of that tradition.

The course that Nietzsche charts "beyond good and evil" takes its bearings from a genealogy of morals that tracks the morality of agency back to pathologies emanating from the experience of weakness and oppression. Under the impetus of "submerged, darkly glowering emotions of vengefulness and hatred [the weak] exploit this belief [in the agent-subject] for their own ends and in fact maintain no belief more ardently than the belief that *the strong man is free* to be weak and the bird of prey to be a lamb—for thus they gain the right to make the bird of prey *accountable* for being a bird of prey."[66] It should be evident, however, that the conflation here of doer and deed necessarily follows from Nietzsche's construction of human consciousness, according to which thinking and willing are indivisible. In short, the identity of actor and action is a direct result of the attempt to account for the intricacies of spiritual life without reference to anything beyond the physio-psychological interaction of what I have called submaterial forces over time. It is hardly surprising, then, that the concept of the self-responsible agent appears deviant and pathological from such a vantage point.

Nietzsche approaches our tradition of moral thought and practice as a kind of genealogical Rosetta stone by which historical insight into the relations of the different human "quanta" of force becomes possible. And the account that Nietzsche thereby decodes reveals the moral tradition of Western civilization to be largely a product of "darkly glowering emotions of vengefulness and hatred," in a word, of *ressentiment*.[67] If we follow Nietzsche in his radical historicism to the conclusion that "God is dead," a pronouncement by which Nietzsche means to signal his turn toward a philosophy of history that leaves no possibility for an irreducibly spiritual dimension to existence, then we can only conclude with Nietzsche that our moral/cultural tradition, which has been largely defined by this idea, must be "overcome." If, however, we see in Nietzschean historicism a final, fateful expression of a self-consuming dynamic within the modern reflection on the question of the soul, perhaps the vigorous resuscitation of that question in its traditional guise could finally lead us beyond this all-too-Nietzschean moment.

NOTES

1. See Friedrich Nietzsche, *Beyond Good and Evil*, #23, tr. Walter Kaufmann (New York: Random House, Vintage Books, 1989), 31–32.

2. See Friedrich Nietzsche, *Ecce Homo*, "Why I Write Such Good Books," #5, tr. Walter Kaufmann (New York: Random House, Vintage Books, 1969), 266–68.

3. Walter Kaufmann, one of the first scholars in the postwar period to engage Nietzsche's writings and legacy in a serious way, entitled his groundbreaking work from 1950 *Nietzsche: Philosopher, Psychologist, Antichrist* (Princeton: Princeton University Press). For Nietzsche's influence on psychology in the twentieth century, consider Carl Jung's extensive study of and seminar on *Thus Spake Zarathustra* as documented by *Nietzsche's Zarathustra: Notes of the Seminar Given in 1934–39*, ed. James L. Jarrett (Princeton: Princeton University Press, 1988). See also Graham Parkes, "A Cast of Many: Nietzsche and Depth-Psychological Pluralism," *Man and World* 22, no. 4 (1989): 453–70.

4. *Ecce Homo,* "Why I Am Destiny," #6, 331.

5. Ibid.

6. On the medieval concept of *auctoritas*, see Ernst Robert Curtius, *European Literature and the Latin Middle Ages*, tr. Willard R. Trask (Princeton: Princeton University Press, 1973), 49–53, 203–7; and A. J. Minnis, *Medieval Theory of Authorship: Scholastic Literary Attitudes in the Later Middle Ages* (London: Scholar Press, 1984), 10–12 and *passim*.

7. Consider, as an example, Robert Filmer's scholastic defense of monarchy in his *Patriarcha*. See Robert Filmer, *"Patriarcha" and Other Writings*, ed. Johann P. Sommerville (Cambridge: Cambridge University Press, 1991), 12–18.

8. The tradition of modern political thought that begins with Hobbes can be represented as a combination of what in antiquity stood in fundamental opposition—political idealism and materialism, Plato and Epicurus. As Leo Strauss explains, "[b]y being both mathematical and materialistic-mechanistic, Hobbes' natural philosophy is a combination of Platonic physics and Epicurean physics." It is doubtful, however, that Hobbes understood his project in these terms, for "[h]e was fully aware that his thought presupposed a radical break with all traditional thought, or the abandonment of the plane on which 'Platonism' and 'Epicureanism' had carried on their secular struggle." See Leo Strauss, *Natural Right and History* (Chicago: University of Chicago Press, 1953), 170.

9. See Thomas Hobbes, *Leviathan*, introduction and part 1, chap. 2, ed. Edwin Curley (Indianapolis: Hackett, 1994), 3–5, 8.

10. *Leviathan*, part 1, chap. 11, 57–58.

11. See Hobbes's earlier chapter on "The Passions, and the Speeches by Which They Are Expressed," *Leviathan*, part 1, chap. 6, 28–29.

12. *Leviathan*, introduction, 3–4.

13. Compare Aristotle's account of the soul at *De Anima*, 406b.26–407a.2; 413a.21–413b.1; 415b.9–28.

14. See *Leviathan,* part 1, chap. 12; compare the same passage from the Latin version that Hobbes published in 1668: "but that the same thing might be both a *spirit* and *incorporeal* cannot be understood. For a spirit is determined by place and figure, i.e., by limits and some size of its own. Therefore, it is a body, however rarefied and imperceptible." Compare also *De Anima*, 412a.1–412b.13.

15. The Latin version that appears on Rousseau's original text reads: "*Non in depravatis, sed in his quae bene secundum naturam se habent, considerandum est quid sit naturale.*" The passage is found in book 1 of the *Politics* at 1254a.36–38. It occurs in the context of Aristotle's defense of natural slavery, that is, within an argument that functions as a kind of paradigm for Aristotle's teaching on natural right. Rousseau's repeated and unconditional rejection of the notion that slavery could have a natural basis underscores the fact that on the central question of natural right he stands very much with the moderns and against Aristotle. See also Roger D. Masters, *The Political Philosophy of Rousseau* (Princeton: Princeton University Press, 1968), 112–13.

16. It is safe to say that Rousseau chose his epigraphs with great care. He makes clear, in fact, that he intends with these liminary quotations to encapsulate the work as a whole. See *Rousseau Juge de Jean-Jacques*, Dialogue 3 (Pleiade, 1, 941); also Masters, *Political Philosophy*, 15, n. 56.

17. The Latin text that Rousseau cites renders the original Greek somewhat loosely. The most reliable Greek manuscripts do not contain a word corresponding to the adjective "well-oriented," but simply read "in things which are in accord with nature" (*dei de skopein en tois kata physin exousi mallon to physei . . .*). One might, however, argue that the addition only helps to bring out the full sense of what Aristotle means by *kata physin*.

18. Aristotle, *Politics* 1254a.38–54b.3 (my translation).

19. In his great work on the human sciences, *Truth and Method*, Hans Georg Gadamer explains that "[t]he experience of the socio-historical world cannot be raised to a science by the inductive procedure of the natural sciences. . . . Its ideal is rather to understand the phenomenon itself in its unique and historical concreteness." Gadamer's elaborate account of the evolution of this ideal, however, fails even to mention Rousseau's seminal contribution to this development. See Hans Georg Gadamer, *Truth and Method* (New York: Continuum, 1975), 5–6, 153–92.

20. See *Nichomachean Ethics*, 1098a.8–17.

21. See *Leviathan,* part 1, chap. 13, 78.

22. In this same vein, Leo Strauss observes that "[Hobbes] tries to instill the spirit of political idealism into the hedonistic tradition. He thus became the creator of political hedonism, a doctrine which has revolutionized human life everywhere on a scale never yet approached by any other teaching." See *Natural Right,* 169

23. Compare John Locke's subsequent attempt to limit politics to *care of the body* in his *Letter Concerning Toleration* from 1689. See, in particular, John Locke, *A Letter Concerning Toleration*, ed. James Tully (Indianapolis: Hackett, 1983), 23–30.

24. Jean Bethke Elshtain, *Democracy on Trial* (New York: Basic Books, 1995), 12–13. Elshtain is herself paraphrasing a description of the idea of progress with which Christopher Lasch prefaces his book *The True and Only Heaven: Progress and Its Critics* (New York: Norton, 1991), 13. Lasch concludes this description as follows: "Insatiable desire, formerly condemned as a source of frustration, unhappiness, and spiritual instability, came to be seen as a powerful stimulus to economic development. Instead of disparaging the tendency to want more than we need, liberals like Adam Smith argued that needs varied from

one society to another, that civilized men and women needed more than savages to make them comfortable, and that a continual redefinition of their standards of comfort and convenience led to improvements in production and a general increase in wealth," 13–14. See also Lasch's discussion of eighteenth-century thinkers David Hume and Bernard Mandeville, as well as Adam Smith, in chapter 2.

25. It was this question that Rousseau addressed in his prizewinning *First Discourse*. For Rousseau's famous account of the sudden inspiration that led to the composition of the essay, see his *Confessions*, chap. 8.

26. Jean-Jacques Rousseau, *The Basic Political Writings*, tr. Donald A. Cress (Indianapolis: Hackett, 1987), 12.

27. Rousseau, *Basic Political Writings*, 5.

28. ". . . the human soul, altered in the midst of society by a thousand constantly recurring causes, changes that took place in the constitution of bodies, by the constant impact of the passions, has, as it were, changed its appearance to the point of being nearly unrecognizable." Rousseau, *Basic Political Writings*, 33.

29. Friedrich Nietzsche, *The Gay Science*, #125, tr. Walter Kaufmann (New York: Random House, Vintage Books, 1974), 181–82.

30. See Friedrich Nietzsche, *Thus Spake Zarathustra*, prologue: 3–4, tr. Walter Kaufmann (New York: Penguin Books, 1978), 12–16. Hereafter cited as *Zarathustra*.

31. See Friedrich Nietzsche, *The Will to Power*, book 1, #2, tr. Walter Kaufmann and R. J. Hollingdale (New York: Random House, Vintage Books, 1968), 9. As is well known, *The Will to Power* was not written by Nietzsche but is a posthumous compilation by Nietzsche's sister of unpublished materials from his notebooks for the years 1883 to 1888 according to a plan he once sketched out but later abandoned. See Kaufmann's account of the work's origins and significance in the "Editor's Introduction," xiii–xxix.

32. For other passages in which Nietzsche suggests that Kant and, subsequently, "German philosophy" amount to an attempt at rescuing the moral order identified with biblical religion from the loss of faith, see *The Antichrist*, especially sections 9–11, in *The Portable Nietzsche*, tr. Walter Kaufmann (New York: Penguin Books, 1976).

33. *Beyond Good and Evil*, #11, 18.

34. In *The Antichrist*, Nietzsche exclaims, "The Protestant parson is the grandfather of German philosophy. . . . Why was Kant's appearance greeted with jubilation among German scholars—of whom three-fourths are the sons of parsons and teachers—and whence came the German conviction, echoed even today, that a change for the *better* began with Kant? The theologian's instinct in the German scholars divined *what* had once again been made possible . . . the conception of morality as the *essence* of the world." See *Portable Nietzsche*, tr. Kaufmann, 576.

35. *Beyond Good and Evil*, #11, 18.

36. See *Beyond Good and Evil*, #12, 19–20.

37. *Beyond Good and Evil*, #23, 31–32.

38. On the intellectual climate of the Germany in which Nietzsche came of age, see Peter Bergmann's excellent chapter on "The Generation of 1866" in his *Nietzsche: "The Last Antipolitical German"* (Bloomington: Indiana University Press, 1987), 32–58.

39. See "Attempt at a Self-Critique," #6, in Friedrich Nietzsche, *The "Birth of Tragedy" and the "Case of Wagner"*, tr. Walter Kaufmann (New York: Vintage Books, Random House, 1967), 24–25.

40. *Ecce Homo, The Birth of Tragedy,* #1, 271. I include in brackets several of the German words Nietzsche uses here that are readily associated with Hegel.

41. See *Zarathustra*, prologue, #5, 16–19.

42. Friedrich Nietzsche, *On the Genealogy of Morals*, 1:11, tr. Walter Kaufmann (New York: Random House, Vintage Books, 1969), 43. Nietzsche's depiction of this contemporary man as a kind of insect is clearly meant to link this passage imagistically to Zarathustra's lengthier account of the last man, who is likewise represented as an insectlike being that is "as ineradicable as a flea-beetle" at *Zarathustra,* prologue, #5, 17.

43. "'Formerly, all the world was mad' say the most refined, and they blink. . . . 'We have invented happiness,' say the last men, and they blink." *Zarathustra,* prologue, #5.

44. Consider, for example, this statement from book 5 (added only in a second edition published in 1887) of *The Gay Science,* in which Nietzsche speaks of those who "delayed this triumph of atheism most dangerously and for the longest time. Hegel in particular was its delayer par excellence, with his grandiose attempt to persuade us of the divinity of existence, appealing as a last resort to our sixth sense, 'the historical sense.'" See *Gay Science,* #357, 304–10.

45. It should be noted that Nietzsche describes the philosophies of Leibniz, Kant, and Hegel as necessarily German in that each philosophy represents "a thoughtful piece of self-knowledge, self-experience, self-understanding," but the "unconditional and honest atheism" of Schopenhauer is declared "a European event." See *Gay Science,* #357, 304–10.

46. See *Beyond Good and Evil,* #36, 47–48.

47. *Genealogy of Morals,* I, #13, 45.

48. See *Beyond Good and Evil,* #12, 20.

49. See *Nichomachean Ethics,* 1098a.8–16.

50. See, for example, *Ecce Homo,* preface, #2, 217–18; *Beyond Good and Evil,* #10, #14, and #204, 16–17, 21–22, 121–23.

51. *Beyond Good and Evil,* #12, 19–21.

52. *Beyond Good and Evil,* #14 and #21, 21–22, 28–30.

53. See René Descartes, *"Discourse on Method" and "Meditations",* tr. Laurence J. Lafleur (Indianapolis: Bobbs-Merrill Educational Publishing, The Library of Liberal Arts, 1960), 15.

54. See Thomas Hobbes, *Elements of Law, Natural and Politic,* ed. J. C. A. Gaskin (Oxford: Oxford University Press, 1994), 19; also Descartes, *Discourse on Method,* 118–20.

55. See *Nichomachean Ethics,* 1094b.13ff.

56. See *Leviathan,* part 1, chaps. 4 and 5, 19–27.

57. Leo Strauss thus describes Hobbesian political science as "the classic example of the typically modern combination of political idealism with a materialistic and atheistic view of the whole." See *Natural Right,* 170.

58. See *Beyond Good and Evil,* #14, 21–22.

59. See *Beyond Good and Evil,* #16, #17, and #19, 23–24 and 25–27.

60. See the following passage from Leo Strauss's "Note on the Plan of Nietzsche's *Beyond Good and Evil*": "What Nietzsche claims to have realized is that the text in its pure, unfalsified form is inaccessible (like the Kantian Thing-in-itself); everything thought by anyone—philosopher or man of the people—is in the last analysis interpretation. But for this very reason the text, the world in itself, the true world cannot be of any concern to us; the world of any concern to us is necessarily a fiction, for it is necessarily anthropomorphic; man is necessarily in a manner the measure of all things" in Laurence Lampert, *Leo Strauss and Nietzsche* (Chicago: University of Chicago Press, 1996), 191.

61. See *Beyond Good and Evil,* #6, 13–14.

62. "It is almost always a symptom of what is lacking in himself when a thinker senses in every 'causal connection' and 'psychological necessity' something of constraint, need,

compulsion to obey, pressure, and unfreedom; it is suspicious to have such feelings—the person betrays himself." *Beyond Good and Evil,* #21, 29.

63. See *Beyond Good and Evil,* #36, 47–48. Nietzsche understood that his reading of things could claim no more for itself than that it too was an interpretation, encumbered by the same contingencies that he had identified with the very condition of human consciousness. He believed, however, that his teaching on the will to power placed him in the unique position of being able to receive any manifestation of its status as "only an interpretation" and at the same time confirming its validity. See Lampart, *Strauss and Nietszche,* 192.

64. I use the term *submaterial* here to emphasize the fact that Nietzsche views these forces as essentially physical. He thus links philosophy not only to psychology but also to physiology. See, for example, *Beyond Good and Evil,* #3 and #15, 11, 22–23.

65. *Zarathustra,* prologue, #3, 12.

66. *Genealogy of Morals,* I, #13, 45.

67. For a discussion of Nietzsche's use of this term, see Walter Kaufmann's introduction in *Genealogy of Morals,* 5–10.

Chapter Eight

Deconstructing Darwin

Stephen R. L. Clark

It is not irrational to criticize Darwinian theory as, in its developed form, an incitement to crime. The message of Darwinism in the abstract is that species are not natural kinds and that there is no reason to expect "evolutionary progress." In its concrete manifestations, in Charles Darwin's writings, as well as in those of his followers, it is more usually assumed that the poor, sick, savage—and Irish—are "unfit" and will be eliminated soon (unless a misguided compassion delays the process). Even a more sociable Darwinism than Herbert Spencer's (emphasizing the value of social feeling, and even of self-sacrificing heroism) insists that we can "really" mind only about our kin, and should for that reason act to prevent the poor or sick or "savage" from breeding. Darwinists, though inconsistently, allege that we are always bound to be enduring the Malthusian tragedy and cannot expect people to be more rational, generous, or compassionate than they would be in such dire conditions. Because there "must" be such a struggle for survival we "civilized" folk initiate it. These ethical effects do not flow from the bare bones of Darwinian theory (that we are all related, with four thousand million years of history, and that populations change their character because of differences in the number of viable offspring resulting from the particular traits of the parent population), but they are so entangled with Darwinism as this is popularly presented that we have good reason to complain when our children are taught such "Darwinism" as the only rational theory. On the contrary, if Darwinism were true, we could have no interest in the Truth, nor in any reliable way of uncovering it.

Darwin was not the first to speculate that there were forms of life before us, nor yet that all forms of life, both past and present, were genealogically related. He was not the first to try to exclude all final causes from his account of nature. He was not the only one to notice that in a Malthusian struggle for life, it is generally those with some obvious superiority (of strength, or wit, or versatility) that survive to breed. Conversely, he was not himself responsible for every element of the neo-Darwinian synthesis that has come to dominate mainstream biological circles and the mind of the chattering classes. Notoriously, he was himself "Lamarckian," in allowing for the inheritance of acquired characteristics, and pre-Mendelian in that he did not know how inheritance could pass particular characteristics down, rather than blending, and thus homogenizing, variations. He was neither the first to find it difficult to reconcile natural evil and orthodox theism, nor as militantly atheistical as some of his disciples. There are traces in his writings of an intolerable racism but also clear evidence that he was personally and politically humane.[1]

Scientists regularly, and properly, insist that any new theory must be examined critically, and tested to destruction, before it is at last accepted as a working model for the profession. They will often also agree that the motives that particular scientists bring to that inquiry may be mixed. People with a personal and imaginative attachment to the Steady State theory of cosmology, or even a personal antipathy toward their academic rivals, are likely to devise all manner of ingenious objections to the Big Bang theory, and yet more ingenious ad hoc solutions to the objections others raise to them. In this way, each side assists the other to appreciate what else must (or may) be the case if their preferred doctrine is to be approved.

Science does not demand that every scientist be honest, open-minded, and self-critical, but that the institutions of peer review and team rivalry, fueled by whatever personal emotion, prevent too ready an acceptance of a plausible but faulty view. Oddly, when the same thing happened to Darwinian theory, it is assumed that the squabble must have been, and must be, between "true scientists who see that the theory is obviously, unanswerably and uniquely true" and "shabby obscurantists who are either mad, or ignorant, or evil."[2] To state the obvious: Darwin's contemporaries, including the unfortunate Samuel Wilberforce, had every right to identify difficulties in Darwin's theory. Indeed, it was their duty to do so, even if they relished the task for "non-scientific reasons." Those who do not want a theory to be true are always likeliest to think of the best objections and thus to compel those who do want it to be true (namely, the original theorists) to refine or to abandon what they had said. There may be a moment when the argument is closed: no one feels like arguing the point again, and no one wants to pay for more research. Until that moment is reached, the argument is not closed, whichever side is right.

It is, unfortunately, necessary to emphasize this point. In the present climate of academic discourse, anyone who is prepared to consider objections to Darwinian theory, or even to contemplate revised versions or alternatives to that theory, is automatically supposed to be either a "creationist" or a "deconstructionist," and "therefore" culpably anti-intellectual. I myself belong to neither camp: as a rational realist I merely claim the right to question Darwinists and seek to understand the arguments of anti-Darwinists. There are several points at issue. I think it very likely that the history of life-on-earth extends back four thousand million years, and that all contemporary living creatures here on Earth are genealogically related. It is also clear that, on certain plausible assumptions, Darwinian change is bound to occur. It is less clear that Darwinian processes are all that are involved in the production of life's present diversity. The metaphysical and ethical implications frequently drawn from Darwinian theory are ones that I reckon we have good reason to reject: if that required me to reject Darwinian theory, I would do so as readily as Wilberforce did.

Exactly what Wilberforce said in his debate with T. H. Huxley is obscure. He made, it seems, a joke about Darwin's ancestry, and Huxley retorted rudely. But the main thrust of Wilberforce's case was probably to do with an issue that still troubles theorists. It is all very well to say, quite plausibly, that (other things being equal) the faster antelope will live to breed.[3] It does not follow that successive generations of antelope can therefore be expected to get ever faster, even if there is still the same pressure to get away from ever-faster, ever-craftier, ever more cooperative predators. Even if only very fast antelopes breed (and in all real situations this will not be true), the result will be, at best, to ensure that the range of antelope speediness is narrower.

No antelope will ever break the sound barrier, however long and forceful is the evolutionary pressure. We cannot make giants, or geniuses, or immortals by allowing only the tall, the clever, or the long-lived to breed. That may eliminate the congenitally short, stupid, or short-lived, but it does not make anyone taller, cleverer, or longer-lived than anyone was before. To get something new out of the breed, something that was not already part of the range of that breed's variation, demands a change that cannot be predicted and should not—by Darwin's own account—be expected. It may be that evolutionary pressure for, say, size, will create the circumstances in which a radical variation can find breeding partners. As long as most of the breed are less than six feet tall, an extraordinary ten-footer will probably not breed, even if his or her size does constitute a personal advantage. Once most of the breed are already more than six feet tall, the ten-footer may more easily find partners and propagate that trait. It does not follow that any successor generation will produce a *twenty*-footer. Only if there is some external tug toward increasing size, speed, complexity, or intelligence can we reasonably expect successive generations of any particular lineage to experience any such steady increase. Oddly, even those evolutionary theorists who denounce any appeal to final causes, or to evolutionary progress, will often themselves expect that creatures get quicker, smarter, and "more complex" over generations, just because "it pays." But the fact that it *would* pay explains why it occurs only if we concede a strength to "final causation" that it was the Enlightenment effort to deny.[4]

Darwin lacked any account of how such sudden variations beyond the previous range of a given character might occur or how they were not blended back into that range within a generation. He was entitled to insist that, somehow, it could happen, since exactly such mutations did visibly occur within domesticated breeds and could be preserved. That most such mutations were, on their own, injurious (for example, being born without a tail or an important layer of fur)[5] was not an objection to the developed theory, but some confirmation of it. If the mutations were designed, or guided, we could expect that they were ones a designer wanted: as it was, they appear to occur "at random," and only a few turn out to bring eventual advantages. This does not establish that they were *not* designed: our own thoughts, so some have argued, occur at first "at random," and those few that survive conscious and unconscious culling are the remnant of uncounted "really bad ideas." Maybe that is how every designer works: pushing at the boundaries of the immediately given in the hope that something, somewhere, works a little better.

Wilberforce and others may also, with some justice, have objected that the one thing Darwin did not explain was the origin of species. Maybe, as others (including Herbert Spencer) had suggested, a given variety of living creature would, over the long run, be descended from those creatures of that kind that had some obvious advantage. But what reason was there to suppose that this variation *within* a species would at some point generate a genuinely different species? Greyhounds may get faster with the generations (at least to the limit of their kind's capacity), but a very fast greyhound is still of the same species as a bulldog. Left to themselves, our dogs would probably revert to the standard "mongrel" dog shape, occasionally producing an unusual example and maybe having regional varieties. Black moths may outperform white moths upon soot-darkened trees (and be outperformed in turn when the trees get cleaner), but the species survives precisely because it still contains both varieties. As long as we hold an essentialist or typological account of species, this objection seems conclusive. An individual dog cannot become a cat, however catlike it may be; neither can a dog, in the natural course of events, ever give birth to a cat. If there were an especially catlike puppy either it would fail to breed at all (and that would be the end), or it would contribute its own catlike character to the breeding pool of dogs (and not be a new species). Science fiction writers like to play with the notion that a genuinely new species might start to be born of older stock—but it seems that this could be the result only of divine, or alien, intervention.

The mainstream response is to deny essentialist or typological accounts of species. If a species is only a set of interbreeding populations, then a new one comes about when there are barriers to interbreeding. At first, perhaps, these barriers might be merely external (perhaps a newly impassable river), or merely temperamental (some variations just don't fancy each other much). Once any such barriers exist, the populations can begin to drift apart to the point where there are mechanical or chemical obstacles to any successful interbreeding. This need not be because "it pays": it is enough that there is no strong advantage in retaining a capacity to interbreed with creatures we shall never meet. Irish wolfhounds and Chihuahuas are a single species, but that is only because there are so many intervening sorts of dog. What we now know as genetic information can flow, albeit slowly, between even such disparate lineages.

But suppose all other dogs died off: the remaining sorts of dog would then be different species, since they would not, could not, breed. (Most probably they would be more different, more isolated than are lions and tigers—which can, on occasion, produce live, though probably rather confused, hybrids). If two creatures were once of the same species and now are not, merely because some other creatures have been killed, it is clear that a species difference is not an *essential* one. In general, creatures are not of different species because they look different, or even because they have "sufficiently different" genomes: they look different and may also differ substantially in their genomes because they are of different species (they belong to different breeding pools). Different lineages of Darwin's Galápagos finches have developed distinct adaptations: once they were isolated from each other and had adopted somewhat different habits, different variations were selected. Nothing rules out the possibility that one pair of creatures, of the same species, is more different phenotypically and genotypically than another pair of different species.

Speciation, in fact, has much the same effect as geographical or temporal isolation, allowing somewhat different sets of genetic variations to come into being. There is perhaps an evolutionary advantage in the habit of speciation: lineages that divide themselves may, under certain circumstances, be more fruitful than lineages that remain a single breeding pool (and thus cannot easily occupy so many specialized niches). Some later commentators have remarked that the creation of such small, isolated populations, whose initial characters have not been "selected," may be an important engine of evolutionary change. "Natural selection," in short, may not be the only explanation for endemic characters: they may merely be the ones a chance-met bunch of ancestors actually had (though they could as easily have had a different set).

The pregnant windborne finch that, perhaps, engendered all the Galápagos finches was not necessarily "fitter" than any of her sisters: on the contrary, she was the one stupid enough to get swept out to sea and lucky enough to land. "Being lucky" is not a heritable condition. Of course, it may be that such "luck" is always merited and that *every* general character of a given lineage is one that has played an important role in propagating that particular lineage. We have no sound empirical reason to believe that claim, of course; in any case it does not truly establish that all such characters are best explained by their success. The chance that no superior mutation has occurred is just, from that character's point of view, as lucky as its own survival.

Typological or essentialist thinking is not wholly dead. Even if biological species are not natural kinds, it does not follow that there are none. Some of the variations that occur within those kinds erect barriers against interbreeding and so create biological species, but it remains an open possibility that there are, after all, more serious divisions. Among mainstream biologists in the West such essentialism is associated with the supposed errors of "creation science," whose advocates believe that there is good reason to identify discrete kinds as God's initial creation. But the idea has been supported elsewhere and for other reasons. In German palaeontology, "typostrophism" seems to have been the most successful form during much of this century.[6] For typostrophists, evolution "unfolds" the potentials of a type achieved in a single jump, and such types have life cycles analogous to those of individuals.

One particular difference between typostrophists and mainstream neo-Darwinians is that the sudden beginning of a new type (by drastic changes in an organism's early development) is the organism's response to a changing environment (perhaps cosmic radiation from a supernova?): "It is not a direct adaptation to environmental stimuli, but is determined only by the norm of reaction of the organism."[7] On this account new forms do arise all of a sudden without alien or divine intervention: "the first bird hatched from a reptile's egg."[8] Selection operates only at a low level of taxonomic diversification ("microevolution"), and it is irrelevant to the origin of higher taxa ("macroevolution"). It is easy to suspect that this typostrophism has mystical, vitalist, or Platonic overtones (which are not the same), but it is worth recording that O. H. Schindewolf himself, and other theorists of this type, actually repudiated all such associations. What they had in mind could be accommodated within an ordinarily rationalist perspective and might even contribute to the mainstream synthesis.

One of the main engines of change that Darwin posited was the "reversion" or "throw-back" to an earlier, "primitive" or "savage" state. In typostrophist terms this would be a reversion to the basic type, from which some novel variation could unfold. More plausibly, perhaps, what serves as an adaptive variation will depend, for example, on what the organism is already choosing to do: a longer, thinner beak will be of no use to a Galápagos finch unless it has already elected to probe for insects rather than crack nuts. It follows that evolution is not simply driven by environmental change but also by the organism's preference (as non-Darwinians have often hoped).

Darwin's theory was originally advanced in opposition to catastrophism: the view that earlier forms of life were swept away by natural disaster or (equivalently) divine fiat, and the earth restocked. Instead, vast differences were engendered by infinitesimal variations over aeons. Macroevolution was no different from microevolution. On this account our own relationship to (say) *Homo habilis*, or yet earlier ancestors, is just like that of a wolfhound to a Pekingese: if all ancestral types had actually survived, genetic information could flow back and forth without any abrupt halt. Although the eventual products of genetic change may look strangely dissimilar, they are linked through generations that were hardly unlike at all. The difference between ourselves and, for example, chimpanzees is simply that the intervening types are now defunct: human beings, chimpanzees, and bonobos, it turns out, are even more closely related, genealogically, than any of us are to gorillas.

Because our ancestors are defunct, we do not see that we are, in a way, of a single species, just as wolfhounds, greyhounds, Pekes, and Chihuahuas are a single species. "In a series of forms graduating insensibly from some ape-like creature to man as he now exists, it would be impossible to fix on any definite point when the term 'man' ought to be used. *But this is a matter of very little importance.*"[9] Just such an impossibility, when comparing populations synchronically rather than diachronically, is employed a few pages earlier to show that distinct varieties are not different species.[10] Our ancestors and ourselves are, obviously, members of a single population (though we cannot pass genes backward to our ancestors), and for that reason every living organism on Earth is one of our relations. We are not "essentially" of another kind than they are. "If man had not been his own classifier, he would never have thought of founding a separate order for his own reception."[11]

This is a conclusion with which I have some sympathy (and have indeed written to similar effect to Richard Dawkins in *The Great Ape Project*).[12] What is strange to me is how few devoted evolutionists are really comfortable with that conclusion. If humankind is not a "natural kind," and species membership does not constitute an essential difference, what justifies insistence that all human beings "have rights" that no nonhuman being does? What justifies even the weaker conviction that all human beings share important characters only with one another? Nothing in the notion of a biological species requires that any two members of one species resemble each other more (whether phenotypically or genotypically) than either resembles any member of a different species. It is an axiom of civilized society that there are no subvarieties of human being whose characters are sufficiently different as to justify distinctive treatment or excuse differing behavior. Darwin was himself impressed by the surprising similarity of Tierra del Fuegians and Europeans, but nothing in his theory demanded that result. Rather the contrary: he believed that man had ascended from a savage state given visible form in those same Fuegians.[13] If there are enormous physical differences between different "subspecies," there may also be enormous mental and moral differences.

The point can be given additional force by contemplating Olaf Stapledon's imagined future. Long after Earth and the inner planets have been destroyed, he feigns, our immensely remote descendants will inhabit a terra-formed Neptune — but not only as creatures vaguely humanoid. All the vertebrate inhabitants of Neptune will be our descendants.

Two hundred million years after the solar collision innumerable species of subhuman grazers with long sheep-like muzzles, ample molars, and almost ruminant digestive systems, were competing with one another on the polar continent. Upon these preyed the subhuman carnivora, of whom some were built for speed in the chase, others for stalking and a sudden spring. But since jumping was no easy matter on Neptune, the cat-like types were all minute. They preyed upon man's more rabbit-like and rat-like descendants, or on the carrion of the larger mammals, or on the lusty worms and beetles. . . . On [the] marine flora fed certain highly developed marine worms; and of these last some in time became vertebrate, predatory, swift, and fish-like. On these in turn man's own marine descendants preyed, whether as sub-human seals, or still more specialised sub-human porpoises. Perhaps most remarkable of these developments of the ancient human stock was that which led, through a small insectivorous bat-like glider to the great diversity of true flying mammals, scarcely larger than humming birds, but in some cases as agile as swallows.[14]

A humanoid form eventually develops out of pseudorabbits. Stapledon's fantasy is flawed—or at least it is motivated by a conviction that the world is bound to reinvent the human intellect, and even the human form, if given half a chance. Later fantasists (such as Dougal Dixon) have been less confident that "human" characteristics would reappear. If they would, we might inquire, why didn't they appear long since? An older view supposed that dinosaurs were lumbering monsters well surpassed by agile and quick-witted foes, our ancestors. More recent revivals of a sort of catastrophism have suggested that the dinosaurs were killed by an accident that might as easily have killed off others. Either some small population of small mammals accidentally survived (not because of any heritable character), or else there was a heritable reason (they were hiding, or they were better adapted to a sudden frost) that had not previously given them any great advantage. Either way the dinosaurs were at least as successful in their way as mammals are in theirs. But in that case, if it is obvious the humanlike intelligence appears when given half a chance, why wasn't there a humanoid saurian?

The thesis (which Stephen Jay Gould has defended with no anti-Darwinian intent)[15] that sheer accident played a larger part in evolutionary history than Darwin thought is offered as a further blow to anthropocentric arrogance. Catastrophe—which isolated small, chance-met populations with their accidental, non-adaptive characters—engendered novel species. There are creatures with human characters (namely, us), but not because there need to be, nor even because our special ancestors were bound to win. It just so chanced that some small population of hominids survived where others did not. The thesis is less strange to orthodox religion than Gould supposes: "a wandering Aramaean was my father." It has never been sensible to think that God was required to select Israel, or Adam, or that they survived because they were, of themselves, "more fit." Saying that they just happened to survive is only a different way of saying that God willed that they survive but for no earthly reason.

What is it, in any case, to be "more fit"? "Social Darwinists" followed Spencer in conceiving that individual organisms that managed to secure a larger share of relevant resources would leave more descendants and thus propagate the heritable characteristics that had enabled them to prosper. We should expect that stronger, swifter, smarter organisms had more children or more grandchildren. Strangely, this led some of Darwin's followers, including his own children, to conclude that the state should take "eugenic" measures to ensure that the fitter were not outproduced. Very unfortunately, it was said, human societies helped the "unfit" to survive and reproduce: if the human species was not to regress, or vanish, we should take all appropriate steps to sterilize, or kill, the weak and stupid.

Or as Mr. Greg puts the case (so Darwin tells us):

The careless, squalid, unaspiring Irishman multiplies like rabbits: the frugal, fore-seeing, self-respecting, ambitious Scot, stern in his morality, spiritual in his faith, sagacious and disciplined in his intelligence, passes his best years in struggle and in celibacy, marries late, and leaves few behind him. Given a land originally populated by a thousand Saxons and a thousand Celts—and in a dozen generations five-sixths of the population would be Celts, but five-sixths of the property, of the power, of the intellect, would belong to the one-sixth of Saxons that remained. In the eternal "struggle for existence," it would be the inferior and *less* favoured race that had pre-vailed—and prevailed by virtue not of its good qualities but of its faults.[16]

It is understandable that those who were described as weak or stupid (namely, the poor, the savage, the Irish, or the Catholic) regarded Darwinism as an excuse for tyranny. It is also understandable that others reckoned that "the upper classes," defended from Darwinian competition by ancestral privilege, were destined in the end to be replaced. Fortunately, or unfortunately, the aristocracy, by marrying heiresses, were selecting for sterility, "and noble families are continually cut off in the direct line."[17] A similar accident has befallen Spain: by demanding priestly celibacy and burning heretics, the Catholic Church has damaged Spanish stock.[18] "Looking to the distant future, I do not think that the Rev. Mr. Zincke takes an exag-gerated view when he says: 'All other series of events—as that which resulted in the culture of mind in Greece, and that which resulted in the empire of Rome—only appear to have purpose and value when viewed in connection with, or rather as sub-sidiary to . . . the great stream of Anglo-Saxon emigration to the west.'"[19]

The war of each against all, which Hobbes had identified as the "state of nature," might result in occasional lucky victories. But the natural assumption must be that those who secured a larger share of the relevant resources for them-selves and for their descendants were not simply lucky: rather they shared some winning character. Spencer thought that individually successful entrepreneurs would win—and if they did not, it must be because they had been cheated of their due reward. An alternative view, associated with Peter Kropotkin but also, so it seems, truer to Darwin's own convictions, was that the winning character was social. Tribes whose members worked together were more successful than tribes whose members fought one another to the death. Tribes that allowed every mem-ber an equal stake in the common resource were more successful—or so Kropotkin and all right-thinking liberals supposed—than tribes that rationed resource by rank or ancestry, excluding the lowliest from any good beyond what they could grab for themselves. Darwinian competition, commonly so called, occurs only at the fringes of society or in society's collapse. In more usual times and places, whether human or nonhuman, the successful types are those that man-age to cooperate.

Huxley supposed—as some modern evolutionists also suppose—that "human morality" is at odds with "natural order." The law of the jungle tells us to compete without a qualm for relevant resources, but the social law requires us to restrain our greed. Kropotkin—and some modern evolutionists—retort that solitary, selfish predators are very rare; the social law and the law of the jungle are agreed: better cooperate than compete. In any such social species the occasional free rider is detected and restrained: the road to survival and to successful reproduction is by agreement. Even if we choose to identify the "gene," rather than the individual organism, as what, in the abstract, competes for space in later generations, the moral is not that "selfish genes" survive by making selfish creatures. The most successful genes have made themselves indispensable to larger groups; they are neither "selfish" in themselves nor do they encourage "selfishness" in their agents. This remains a Darwinian theory: those creatures that are themselves successful can be expected to have more descendants, but the grounds of success, in life and in the reproductive stakes, is not entrepreneurial egotism but the capacity to work with others to a common goal. It is simple-minded to insist, against available evidence, that greedy and coldhearted millionaires have more descendants, over the long run, than do the poor but honest. It is also simple-minded to suppose that honesty and kindness are reliably heritable characters. According to Darwin, "some elimination of the worst dispositions is always in progress even in the most civilized nations."[20] In saying so, he assumes far too rapidly that there is a simple correspondence between phenotype and genotype: the truth is that the same genotype under different circumstances engenders different phenotypes, which will be more or less successful in reproducing their genotype. The enterprise that in one context earns a prison sentence may, in another, earn a peerage—and which has more descendants is another matter entirely.

Kropotkin is far more plausible than Spencer and more in tune with Darwin's own likings. "A nation which produced during a lengthened period the greatest number of highly intellectual, energetic, brave, patriotic, and benevolent men, would generally prevail over less favoured nations."[21] The virtues that Darwin expected to succeed are not simply those of individual energy: only if that energy is deployed for "patriotic" and "benevolent" ends can the nation benefit. "Selfish and contentious people will not cohere, and without coherence nothing can be effected."[22] But patriotism and benevolence are not quite the same, nor is "social coherence" just the same as justice.

The sort of heritable virtues that—shall we call them—*Sociable* Darwinians have in mind are nepotistic. The truly selfish and coldhearted leave no heirs: to succeed in the Darwinian struggle, we must ally ourselves with others and provide for those likeliest to be our kin. Equivalently, we must not establish a social order in which our rivals breed "like rabbits," nor allow "a few wandering savages" to occupy good fertile land. "Both sexes ought to refrain from marriage if in any marked degree inferior in body or mind. . . . All ought to refrain from marriage who cannot avoid abject poverty for their children; for poverty is not only a great evil, but tends to its own increase by leading to recklessness in marriage. . . . There should be open competition for all men; and the most able should not be prevented by laws or customs from succeeding best and rearing the largest number of offspring."[23]

Darwin was, personally and politically, humane—and yet:

> We civilized men do our utmost to check the process of elimination; we build asylums for the imbecile, the maimed, and the sick; we institute poor-laws; and our medical men exert their utmost skill to save the life of every one to the last moment. There is reason to believe that vaccination has preserved thousands, who from a weak constitution would formerly have succumbed to small-pox. *Thus the weak members of civilized societies propagate their kind.* No one who has attended to the breeding of domestic animals will doubt that this must be highly injurious to the race of man. It is surprising how soon a want of care, or care wrongly directed, leads to the degeneration of a domestic race; but excepting in the case of man himself, hardly anyone is so ignorant as to allow his worst animals to breed.[24]

Darwin goes on to say that we cannot "check our sympathy" without "deterioration in the noblest part of our nature" and must therefore be less ruthless than that passage might suggest. Just what justifies this unnatural enthusiasm for a damaging "nobility" he does not explain. It also does not seem to have occurred to him (or to his disciples) that until there is a hospitable environment for all, we simply cannot tell what "faults" may be inherited.[25] Darwin's own health was not of the strongest: if he had been born into a lower layer of society, he might have died untimely. How many other "Darwins" did? Once again, this is to confuse genotype and phenotype.

Darwin's peroration extols "man's noble qualities, with sympathy which feels for the most debased, with benevolence which extends not only to other men but to the humblest living creature, with his godlike intellect which has penetrated into the movements and constitution of the solar system,"[26] but nothing in his theory makes it likely that there would be such a creature. The energetic Anglo-Saxon of his dreams will cherish his own kin and look with equanimity on the elimination of savage races or the sterilization of the "unfit." "At some future period, not very distant as measured by centuries, the civilised races of man will almost certainly exterminate and replace throughout the world the savage races. At the same time the anthropomorphous apes, as Professor Schauffhausen has remarked, will no doubt be exterminated. The break [between man and his nearest allies] will then be rendered wider, for it will intervene between man in a more civilised state, as we may hope, than the Caucasian, and some ape as low as a baboon, instead of as at present between the negro or Australian and the gorilla."[27] That is why, as G. Stanley Hall suggested, there is a gap between the fossil apes and us: our ancestors eliminated all the "missing links."[28] H. G. Wells looked forward with relish to sweeping away "those swarms of black and brown and dirty-white and yellow people."[29]

So a "higher morality" is, after all, at odds with a "natural ethic"? Darwin's fierce hostility toward the notion of priestly celibacy—a hostility he passed down to his children[30] — is evidence of his preference for a "natural" ethic, one that permitted or encouraged the "fittest" to hand on their heritable qualities. How can it be that there are celibates at all? Any tendency toward celibacy must surely be one of the strongest candidates for deselection. More recent Darwinists have suggested that such cultural forms are parasites, "mental microbes," "memes," that ensure their own proliferation even at the expense of sterilizing or otherwise damaging their hosts.[31] Alternatively, if celibacy (or a liking for celibacy) were an ordinarily heritable trait, perhaps it survives by giving some "advantage" to the bearer's relatives. As Darwin himself noted, even if especially sagacious members of an early tribe "left no children, the tribe would still include their blood relations."[32] Again: "There can be no doubt that a tribe including many members who, from possessing in a high degree the spirit of patriotism, fidelity, obedience, courage, and sympathy, were always ready to give aid to each other and to sacrifice themselves for the common good, would be victorious over most other tribes; and this would be natural selection."[33]

It does not seem to have occurred to Darwin that celibate priests might give that sort of advantage to their tribes. If it is sensible to propose that "the gay gene" survives because gay men have more time and energy to spare to look after their sisters' children (really?),[34] the same might be said of a "celibacy gene." It can also be argued that even genes that, occurring homozygously, inflict disaster may survive and prosper just because, in their heterozygous form, they contribute some special excellence: if the gene for sickle-cell anemia survives because it is lethal only when it is inherited from both parents and actually advantageous (as securing resistance to malaria) when inherited only from one, the same can be said for any gene at all (and rarely refuted). The distinction between genotype and phenotype is too often forgotten: a genotype that is selected, at one remove, because its usual phenotype is—for whatever reason—more successful than its rivals, may have quite different effects in other circumstances. Most of those who are now gay or even celibate might easily, in other circumstances, have been more fertile than those with other genes. Only very recently have gay men had the option of refusing heterosexual intercourse (and thus fatherhood). Breeding couples have not had to like each other or the act of intercourse. Would-be celibates may well have fathered (or mothered) just as many children as more amorous folk: maybe they fathered or mothered more ("profligate women bear few children, and profligate men rarely marry").[35]

Hardly anyone, till very recently, would have seriously said that copulation was his or her only goal, and those who did (like Don Juan) were not necessarily most fertile. Is it remotely plausible to think that every heterosexual male desires to impregnate as many women as he can, and everything he does is guided to that end? Is every fertile woman really surrounded by a horde of competing suitors? Even the Ik don't act like that.[36] To ask the obvious question: did Richard Dawkins really write his books only so there might be many little Dawkinses, and does he believe his theories only to promote that end? Has he succeeded? And if that is the explanation, and also the explanation for the theories' popularity, must we not begin to disbelieve them? If I believe that I believed a theory only because it was in my interest to do so, I have already begun to disbelieve.

David Stove has pointed out that the Malthusian axiom is clearly false for humankind (and probably false for most other animals). It is just not true that all human populations are *always* at the very limits of sustainable growth, constantly battling to achieve a bare share of the available resources. If that were our situation, then we could indeed predict that those who did not seize whatever they could for themselves and for their relatives, as well as those who did not bother to have children, would quickly find their distinctive heritable traits eliminated from the population. But there are—even nowadays—far fewer actual people than there are possible people, and famine conditions have always been the exceptions (nor are such famines produced by a simple increase in the population). It has not been true for humankind in all recorded history that "of the many individuals which are periodically born, but a small number can survive."[37] Nor has it been true—indeed, Darwin complains that it is not true—that the poorest and weakest members of society have the fewest children. It is not even clearly true that "the struggle for existence" is going on, remorselessly, among the poorest, and each new generation of the poor, accordingly, is fitter, stronger, quicker, healthier than the last.

Some regions of late-Victorian Britain perhaps offered a model for the Malthusian tragedy: my own great-grandfather was the last survivor of twenty-two siblings. But the others were not starved to death; neither did he survive just because he was the stronger. He simply survived some childhood illnesses for who knows what contingent reason and was not down the mine when the roof fell in. Those ideologues who chose to regard class stratification, overcrowding, and careless mine owners as necessary tools for the betterment of the species were choosing to believe that there was no alternative arrangement, that any attempt to improve the lives of the urban (and the rural) poor would leave us all worse off. They were mistaken.

By believing that we were all really, and permanently, enduring the Malthusian tragedy, Darwinians could excuse such treatment of the poor as they would not, being sympathetic souls, have wished to engineer: they could, in fact, pretend to themselves that it was something that they had not engineered. Harder-headed and harder-hearted Darwinians could go that one step further: claiming that they were "doing good" (or at least doing good for them and theirs) by seizing whatever advantage beckoned. Behavior that we might all forgive in desperate men, condemned to a bleak subsistence, was suddenly unavoidable and "right," because we must be always in that desperate state. "The Darwinian theory of evolution *is* an incitement to crime: that is simply a fact" (says Stove).[38] It incites to crime because it suggests that people are bound, "really," to be no better than nepotistic and bound to disguise what is really going on with talk of self-restraint, propriety, nobility, or righteousness.

Darwin himself preached sympathy (even for such savages as he supposed he had seen in Tierra del Fuego and for such careless, squalid, unaspiring, and superstitious Irishmen as English ideology demanded must exist).[39] But he offers no clear reason *why* such sympathy should be appropriate: a harder-headed Darwinian might have responded to an advocate of laissez-faire that it was indeed in our interests that "no poor Briton should be forced to beg or steal, or take any other vicious course for bread, . . . and that none of our commonalty who are willing to work should on working days be obliged to be idle, but that all such persons of both sexes and all capacities may know where they may be received and employed."[40] But that national interest need not extend beyond the nation's borders: if nations are weakened by the presence of the idle or the helpless poor, we have some national interest in helping them to work—and an equal interest in weakening other nations. There is a reason for the Opium Wars and every other underhand device to seize an available advantage. Those who say they will not must have some deeper plot in mind or else themselves be misled by their masters, the mad molecules. All any of us "really" want to do is what will maximize the chances of our genes taking up more space in the next generation's gene pool. The brutal route to this event is war: kill our competitors and rape their women. More subtle routes are preferable, perhaps, but only because they evoke less resistance.

What is inevitable cannot be avoided. If human beings, like every other creature, are always bound to have produced as many children as they can possibly support and bound to procure whatever further advantage for their children, nieces and nephews, and second cousins twice removed can be obtained by an appropriate outlay,[41] then they will do so. The fact that Darwinians so often seem obliged to reveal the error of our ways (in having fewer children than we might or giving help to unrelated strangers) is reason to suspect the theory. Not all the difficulties for Darwinian theory are real. Stove is a little unfair to E. O. Wilson and to Dawkins, for example, in suggesting that they do not appreciate why animals accept submission signals (rather than killing their rivals when they have the chance) or why they do not allow others to abduct and rear their children.[42] The point is not that Wilson and Dawkins cannot themselves feel the appropriate emotions (and so are puzzled by behavior that makes no sense to them), but that it may seem, at first, that the behavior they describe is less "fit" than it might be. The answer may be simple enough: fighting to the death is always damaging (even for the victor), and willingly abandoning one's child to an abductor is incompatible with the attentive care that must be given to children if they are to survive at all. Cuckoos, of course, do abandon their children, but not to other cuckoos.

"Natural selection follows from the struggle for existence; and this from a rapid rate of increase."[43] Since Darwin immediately goes on to deplore the sad result when "the struggle for existence [is not] sufficiently severe to force man upwards to his highest standard," and "a few wandering savages" occupy "enormous areas of the most fertile land . . . capable of supporting numerous happy homes," it seems strange that he continued to believe in any such constant natural increase or in natural selection. Elsewhere he contends only that "man tends to increase at a greater rate than his means of subsistence; consequently he is *occasionally* subjected to a severe struggle for existence, and natural selection will have effected whatever lies within its scope."[44] The argument seems to be that since we *have* evolved, and evolution demands that some traits have been favored at the expense of others, we *must* have been subject to the Malthusian nightmare (even though we manifestly were not). On these terms evolutionary pressure must be only intermittent: much of the time human (and probably other) populations are well within the carrying capacity of their habitat, and there will be no "struggle for existence" to eliminate the less fit. This does not mean that evolution stops dead: it may still be true that heritable characters that offer even the slightest increase in the number of viable descendants will spread through the population.[45] We simply have no way of saying what those characters might be.

Believing that there must be such a struggle, we initiate it. The civilized races, remember, will soon exterminate such savage errors as still persist—or maybe, on a lighter note, absorb them, if it turns out that all subspecies are interfertile (but that is not what he says). Whatever heritable traits stand behind the civilized races' greater energy, inventiveness, rapacity, and lack of self-control will certainly infect the later generations of our species. It is not certain that this will be good for us, nor that we shall not "regress." The Greeks "who stood some grades higher in intellect than any race that has ever existed" still "retrograded from a want of coherence among the many small states, from the small size of their whole country, from the practice of slavery, or from extreme sensuality, for they did not succumb until 'they were enervated and corrupt to the very core.'"[46] Let that be a lesson to us all.

One further familiar inference: the differences between men and women are to be explained as natural consequences of our evolutionary past.

> Woman seems to differ from man in mental disposition, chiefly in her greater tenderness and less selfishness. . . . Woman, owing to her maternal instincts, displays those qualities towards her infants in an eminent degree; therefore it is likely that she should often extend them towards her fellow-creatures. Man is the rival of other men; he delights in competition, and this leads to ambition which passes too easily into selfishness. These latter qualities seem to be his natural and unfortunate birthright. It is generally admitted that with woman the powers of intuition, of rapid perception, and perhaps of imitation, are more strongly marked than in man; but some, at least, of those faculties are characteristic of the lower races, and therefore of a past and lower state of civilization. The chief distinction in the intellectual powers of the two sexes is shewn by man attaining to a higher eminence, in whatever he takes up, than woman can attain—whether requiring deep thought, reason, or imagination, or merely the use of the senses and hands.[47]

Comment seems superfluous. Not only is the mental and physical superiority of male to female assured, but even the characters in which women surpass men are suddenly symptomatic of an earlier and lower state of civilization. The future lies with energy and perseverance, in which a few exceptional women might perhaps be trained, but not the "whole body of women," who must always lag behind.

In brief, there seems good reason to suspect that Stove and other, earlier critics were correct. Darwinism—by which I mean the metaphysical and ethical theory, rather than any more cautious, and partial, scientific theory—is an incitement to crime. The robber barons who took comfort from Social Darwinism did neglect the strong Darwinian reasons to believe that success is not always to the swift or strong or crafty. But Sociable Darwinism is no great improvement. If successful tribes must always be composed of people who are loyal, brave, and energetic in pursuit of tribal goals, this will bring especial comfort to another sort of robber baron, eager to be convinced that kindliness is only misplaced maternalism, and that caring for the poor, or hoping to educate women to the highest standard, or conceding land rights to a wandering savage is not just bad for his bank account, but for the nation's as well. It follows that we have every right to be perturbed if neo-Darwinian theory, in Social or Sociable form, is taught to our children as an obvious truth that only obscurantists can dare to question. Social Darwinists destroy society; Sociable ones—or National Socialists—may yet destroy the world. Neither kind, it seems, can ever quite understand what others have against them.[48]

Even more traditional moralists, of course, concede (or state) that every organism wills its own continued being and is attached to other things in some proportion to their involvement in its being. It is *natural*, the Stoics held, "for human beings to be friendly and philanthropic, to live in organized communities, to possess private property, to marry and have children."[49] It is also right, they went on to say, to recognize every human being as sharing the one nature and to strive to treat all others as we would treat our nearest kin. It is even right to recognize the world itself as something more than *our* world, structured by our needs and fancies. The wise will realize that all of us together make the world. Stoics remained more anthropocentric than seems sensible. Whereas the Platonic and the biblical traditions alike insisted that human beings were neither the most important creatures that there were nor the only reason for the world's existence, Stoics tended to suppose that everything must be "for us" and should be used at will. Even things we might at first think pests were for our good: "Bed-bugs are useful for waking us, and mice encourage us not to be untidy."[50] But even Stoics would have rejected any notion that the proper use of things was simply to satisfy our appetites (which could not ever be satisfied, since they grow with their own fulfillment).

Traditional morality, not only in the West, has rested on the notion that there are forms of life in which all human beings can find satisfaction. Ever since the Axial Age, we have supposed that human beings everywhere deserve respect and that we should not take hold of everything as if it were exclusively our own. The Spaniards whom Darwin so despised took the trouble to debate their treatment of the Indians and drew the true conclusion that they merited the same respect as any human creature.[51] Every such creature, however strange it seemed, was one for whom Christ died, and any service given them was claimed as service to God. That there were greedy and rapacious Spaniards (as there were also greedy and rapacious Aztecs) is obvious: at least they claimed neither God's nor Nature's license to be greedy and rapacious. Even those traditionalists who made much of the great divide between the Human and the merely Animal usually acknowledged that the animals were also God's creation. Darwinians, in breaking down the wall between the human and non-human, have too often implied that, being animals, we must expect to behave as we supposed that "animals" or "savages" do. Stove's comment is apt: "Human societies are almost inexhaustibly various, but there is one thing which *no* human (or even animal) society is even remotely like: namely, 'savage' life, and civilised life below the veneer, *as selfish theorists conceive it.*"[52]

My intention is not to deny that there has been evolution, nor that all living creatures here on earth are genealogically related. Even those claims go beyond the merely scientific: as Philip Gosse pointed out, all the available evidence is quite compatible with God's having begun the world, in much the shape we see, a few millennia ago.[53] That there "really was" a time when "dinosaurs ruled the world" is as metaphysical a claim as that there really was not. All science can say is that it is as if they did. I have no quarrel with that metaphysic, of a real past time, though I think it harder than some have thought to make much sense of what the world was like before there was a mammalian or human vision of it. My quarrel here, however, is with the mechanism Darwin theorized for evolution and its ethical implications. In its strictest, least-fudged form, this demands that we believe that every sort of creature is struggling for existence and for a share, by proxy, in the next generation. We are asked to believe (without the slightest evidence) that any sudden mutations from which radical new types can grow are not those that a providential force intended (as Asa Gray, for example, argued),[54] but only those that happened without reason. We are asked to believe, in turn, that only those behavior patterns that would survive in dire circumstances can be counted on: whether those patterns are those of Social or of Sociable Darwinism hardly matters. Either way the laws of justice and right reason that our moralists have preached are bogus: the future will be as Orwell's O'Brien told us—a boot stamping eternally upon a human face. Those who believe they will wear the boots may find this prospect comforting; the rest of us will not.

Virtue—as every moralist since Socrates has noticed—is not hereditary, and even Darwin usually only *hopes* that it may perhaps become so.[55] It does not follow that it is not persistent. The prophets of the past have realized that, left to ourselves, we may indeed become fat, lazy, and indifferent to the pains of others. It has been their claim that something new is always being intruded into history and the natural world, such as the radical claim that virtue is not measured by expectable, worldly triumph. They have claimed, in brief, that the world of nature is not closed, that something different interferes to remind us whence we came. They may, of course, have been mistaken: maybe their words are only mental microbes of the sort that interfere in a decent Darwinian "progress." But, as before, this claim is as metaphysical, and as value laden, as its opposite. Those of us who hold to the faith have at least this comfort—that it is not the expectably successful who have left their mark most clearly on our history. When the great, self-praising empires have all fallen, it is still the wandering Aramaean, summoned at seeming random from the nations of the Middle East, or the mendicant princeling who abandoned palace, wife, and child to seek enlightenment, who has preserved such images of international decency as we still have.

It is an axiom of sound philosophy (and of the Enlightenment) that the Truth is worth discovering and can be discovered by honest and critical inquiry. If Darwinism is substantially correct, we cannot long think that the Truth is itself worth knowing, nor that we have much chance, by whatever methods, of discovering it. Our beliefs are dictated by "the selfish genes," or else by the equally "selfish memes," and survive in the human population only if they manage to parasitize the stock. Believing that we have believed things only so that the beliefs are spread, we have already stopped believing. "The idea that one species of organism is, unlike all others, oriented not just toward its own increated prosperity but toward Truth, is as un-Darwinian as the idea that every human being has a built-in moral compass—a conscience that swings free of both social history and individual luck."[56] If Darwinism is true, we have no reason to care, nor any right to suppose that we could prove it. If it is not true, it may still have given us things to think about and theories worth pursuing.

NOTES

1. See, for example, Gwen Raverat, *Period Piece* (London: Faber, 1954), 130, recounting a rare outburst of anger when one of his sons thoughtlessly ridiculed those who were prosecuting a governor of Jamaica for the brutality with which he had suppressed a Negro rebellion.

2. Daniel Dennett, *Darwin's Dangerous Idea* (New York: Simon and Schuster, 1995): "anyone who doubts today that the variety of life on this planet was produced by a process of evolution is simply ignorant—inexcusably ignorant." As Alvin Plantinga has remarked, Dennett here goes one step beyond Richard Dawkins's claim that doubters are "ignorant, stupid or insane (or wicked, but [he'd] rather not consider that": by Dennett's rule, doubters (not even positive disbelieves) are *both* ignorant *and* wicked. See Alvin Plantinga, *Books and Culture*, May/June 1996, obtainable on the Web at URL: http://id-www.ucsb.edu/fscf/library/plantinga/dennett.html.

3. Though, in fact, things never are thus "equal": it is the entire organism that lives to breed, or to breed a little more successfully than others, and its success will very rarely rest on any single phenotypic character, let alone a single gene.

4. Peter J. Bowler's comment that "experience shows that the laws of nature work by allowing the past to control the present, not the present to be drawn toward a future goal," in *Evolution: The History of an Idea* (Berkeley: University of California Press, 1984), 213, is a little confused: final causation is not *backward* causation, and we do not discover, but stipulate, that it has no place in scientific thought.

5. And so becoming, respectively, a Manx cat or a Rex.

6. See W. E. Reif, "Evolutionary Theory in German Palaeontology," in *Dimensions of Darwinism*, ed. M. Grene (Paris: Cambridge University Press and Fondation de la Maison des Sciences de l'Homme, 1983), 173–204.

7. Reif, "Evolutionary Theory," 181.

8. Reif, "Evolutionary Theory," 15, citing O. H. Schindewolf, *Paläontologie, Entwicklungslehre und Genetik* (Berlin: Borntraeger, 1936), 59.

9. Charles Darwin, *The Descent of Man* (Princeton: Princeton University Press, 1981; facsimile of the 1871 edition), 1, 235 (my emphasis).

10. Darwin, *Descent of Man*, 1, 227.

11. Darwin, *Descent of Man*, 1, 191.

12. See "Apes and the Idea of Kindred," in The *Great Ape Project: Equality Beyond Humanity* , ed. P. Singer and P. Cavalieri (London: Fourth Estate, 1993), 113–25.

13. "Their expression was wild, startled and distrustful. They possessed hardly any arts, and like wild animals lived on what they could catch; they had no government and were merciless to every one not of their own small tribe," Darwin, *Descent of Man,* 1, 404. David Stove, *Darwinian Fairytales* (Aldershot: Avebury, 1995), 75, points out that we know, from the personal testimony of one who lived with them, that Darwin was completely wrong.

14. Olaf Stapledon, *Last and First Men* (Harmondsworth: Penguin Books, 1972; first published 1930), 277. Stapledon's assumption that marine worms would eventually produce vertebrate offspring is unjustified.

15. Stephen Jay Gould, *Wonderful Life* (New York: Norton, 1990); see my "Does the Burgess Shale Have Moral Implications?" *Inquiry* 36 (1993): 357–80.

16. Darwin, *Descent of Man*, 1, 174, citing W. R. Greg, *Fraser's Magazine* (September 1868): 318. Stove (*Darwinian Fairytales,* 46) points out that Greg was actually arguing *against* Darwin and that the article is entitled "The Failure of 'Natural Selection' in the Case of Man"!

17. Darwin, *Descent of Man,* 1, 170.

18. In so doing, of course, the Spanish were only doing what other Darwinians had seemed to praise: Walter Bagehot described how "the wild, or absolutely incoherent men were cleared away" during prehistory, adding that war then injected beneficial variability to counteract too great a genetic uniformity (Paul Crook, *Darwinism, War and History* [Cambridge: Cambridge University Press, 1994], 51, citing Walter Bagehot, *Physics and Politics* [London: Henry S. King, 1872], 147ff).

19. Darwin, *Descent of Man*, 1, 179, quoting F. Barham Zincke's "Last Winter in the United States: being table talk collected during a tour through the late Southern Confederation, the Far West, the Rocky Mountains, etc." (London: J. Murray, 1868)

20. Darwin, *Descent of Man*, 1, 172: "Malefactors are executed, or imprisoned for long periods, so that they cannot freely transmit their bad qualities. Melancholic and insane persons are confined, or commit suicide. Violent and quarrelsome persons often come to a bloody end. Restless men who will not follow any steady occupation—and this relic of barbarism is a great check to civilization—migrate to newly-settled countries, where they prove useful pioneers."

21. Darwin, *Descent of Man*, 1, 180.

22. Ibid., 1, 162.

23. Ibid., 1, 403.

24. Ibid., 1, 166 (my emphasis).

25. The point was recognized by R. C. Macfie concerning those who were rejected for military service, not because of genetic but of acquired sickness. See Crook, *Darwinism*, 169.

26. Darwin, *Descent of Man*, 1, 405; see also 101: "the virtue [of humanity], one of the noblest with which man is endowed, seems to arise incidentally from our sympathies becoming more tender and more widely diffused until they are extended to all sentient beings."

27. Darwin, *Descent of Man*, 1, 201, citing Schauffhausen, *Anthropological Review* (April 1867): 236. The belief that black men were closer to the apes, attested in Darwin's German popularizer, Haeckel, and elsewhere, is a lot closer to Darwin than his admirers think. See Alfred Kelly, *The Descent of Darwin: The Popularization of Darwin in Germany 1860–1914* (Chapel Hill: University of North Carolina Press, 1981), 117.

28. See Crook, *Darwinism*, 143, citing "Recreation and Reversion," *Pedagogical Seminary* 22 (1915): 510–20.

29. Crook, *Darwinism*, 101, citing H. G. Wells, *Anticipations* . . . (London: Chapman and Hall, 1902), 212.

30. See Raverat, *Period Piece*, 109.

31. Dawkins coined the expression "meme" but not the idea. Witness D. G. Ritchie, *Darwinism and Politics*, 2nd ed. (London: Swan Sonnenschein, 1891), 22: "The ideas which rise in the minds of men with the same tendency to variation that we find throughout nature, compete with one another for sustenance and strength." See also Edward Carpenter, *The Art of Creation*, 3rd. ed. (London: Allen & Unwin, 1916), 214ff.

32. Darwin, *Descent of Man,* 1, 161.

33. Ibid., 1, 166.

34. There is a concomitant, laughable suggestion that the "gay gene" encourages its bearer to relish sex with men, and that, since this is likely to be shared by a gay man's sisters, they will indulge more often and so have more children. This would be funny if it did not reveal such painful ignorance of mating and mothering practices.

35. Darwin, *Descent of Man*, 1, 173.

36. See Colin Turnbull, *The Mountain People* (London: Picador, 1974); cf. Stove, *Darwinian Fairytales*, 104ff.

37. Stove, *Darwinian Fairytales*, 59, quoting Charles Darwin, *The Origin of Species* (Cambridge: Harvard University Press, 1966; facsimile of 1859 edition), 61.

38. Stove, *Darwinian Fairytales*, 74.

39. Late eighteenth- and nineteenth-century attitudes toward the poor—and especially toward the Irish poor—are explored in E. S. Furniss, *The Position of the Laborer in a System of Nationalism* (Boston: Houghton Mifflin, 1920). It was frequently supposed—as it is now—that the poor were deliberately idle, having no impulse higher than that of immediate physical gratification. That the poor, and savage, are also supposed to be frantically superstitious and to live in desperate fear of spiritual foes seems, on the face of it, a little odd.

40. Laurence Braddon (1717), quoted by Furniss, *Position of the Laborer*, 78.

41. "We expect to find that no-one is prepared to sacrifice his life for any single person, but that everyone will sacrifice it for more than two brothers [or offspring], or four half-brothers, or eight first-cousins." W. D. Hamilton, "The Genetical Evolution of Social Behavior," *Journal of Theoretical Biology* 7 (1964). See Stove, *Darwinian Fairytales*, 137ff. Simon Blackburn has criticized Stove's mockery of this passage on the grounds that Hamilton was explicitly offering a mathematical model that was only approximately true of the real world ("I Think I Am a Darwinian," *Philosophy* 71

[1994]: 605–16). This is to miss Stove's points; see James Franklin, "Stove's Anti-Darwinism," *Philosophy* 72 (1997): 133–36.

42. Stove, *Darwinian Fairytales*, 213, citing E. O. Wilson, *Sociobiology: The New Synthesis* (Cambridge: Harvard University Press, 1975), 129 (submission signals); and Richard Dawkins, *The Selfish Gene* (London: Paladin Books, 1979), 110 (abductions).

43. Darwin, *Descent of Man*, 1, 180, 185: "Man tends to multiply at so rapid a rate that his offspring are necessarily exposed to a struggle for existence, and consequently to natural selection."

44. Darwin, *Descent of Man*, 1, 387 (my emphasis).

45. Suppose that some character N has an initial distribution of 1 in 10, and that organisms with that character tend to have 5 offspring who survive to breed rather than the more usual 4. In the very next generation the distribution of N will be 1 in 8.2. If the character is dominant, in the next generation it will be 1 in 6.76, and so on.

46. Darwin, *Descent of Man,* 1, 178, citing Greg, *Fraser's Magazine* (September 1868): 357.

47. Darwin, *Descent of Man*, 1, 326–27.

48. It is customary, at this point in the argument, to mention Hitler's own use of Darwinian theory to oppose the Jewish and Christian humanitarian error: "The law of selection justifies this incessant struggle by allowing the survival of the fittest. Christianity is a rebellion against natural law, a protest against nature." (*Hitler's Table-Talk*, ed. Hugh Trevor-Roper [London: Weidenfeld & Nicolson, 1963], cited by Mary Midgley, *Evolution as a Religion* [London: Methuen, 1985], 119; and Stove, *Darwinian Fairytales*, 72. See also J. L. Mackie "The Law of the Jungle," *Philosophy* 53 [1978]: 455–64.) No doubt such theories, along with many others, did provide excuses, but it is worth noting (as above) that German biologists were generally non-Darwinian and that Hitler denounced Darwinian theory as un-German (see Kelly, *Descent of Darwin*, 122: "Darwinism, after all, entailed a common primitive beginning for all men, and above all it stressed change. Acceptance of evolution by the Nazis would have been tantamount to a denial of the eternal, immutable superiority of the German race.") As I noted before, it does not seem that Darwinism has done much to dent the conviction that *the human species* is eternally and immeasurably superior to all others, so it may be that the Nazis could afford to be more Darwinist (as they occasionally were) than Kelly concedes.

49. A. A. Long and D. Sedley, eds., *The Hellenistic Philosophers* (Cambridge: Cambridge University Press, 1987), 1, 352 (57F), summarizing Cicero, *De Finibus* 3.62f.

50. So Chrysippus said, according to Plutarch, *On Stoic Self-Contradictions* 1044d: *Hellenistic Philosophers*, 1, 328 (54O).

51. "Today it is becoming increasingly evident that no other nation made so continuous or so passionate an attempt to discover what was the just treatment for the native peoples under its jurisdiction than Spaniards." Lewis Hanke, *Aristotle and the American Indians* (London: Hollis & Carter, 1959), 107; see also Anthony Pagden, *The Fall of Natural Man* (Cambridge: Cambridge University Press, 1982). Hanke also quotes "the prominent Quaker John Archdale," who claimed, in the eighteenth century, that "Providence had reserved the extermination of the Indians for the '*Spanish* Nation, and not for the *English*, who in their Natures are not so cruel'" (100).

52. Stove, *Darwinian Fairytales*, 108.

53. Philip Gosse, *Omphalos: An Attempt to Untie the Geological Knot* (London: J. van Voorst, 1857). Gosse's point was not that God could have included fossils in the rocks to test

our faith, but that the creation of any organized cosmos *automatically* included features that could be read, from inside that cosmos, as traces of a past that actually did not occur.

54. See Bowler, *Evolution,* 211, who cites Darwin's response that such guided variation would make selection superfluous, and that most observable variations were apparently quite pointless. Neither claim seems cogent.

55. Darwin, *Descent of Man,* 1, 104.

56. Richard Rorty, "Untruth and Consequences," *New Republic*, 31 July 1995, 32–36, cited by Plantinga, *Books and Culture*. I must add that I do not myself draw Rorty's conclusion; rather the reverse.

Chapter Nine

Ontology and Ethical "Foundations" in Taylor

Stephen K. White

No thinker today has done more to press broad ontological questions than Charles Taylor. He has pursued this campaign for a number of years and has been all too aware of how much his work has challenged "the current distribution of the onus of argument" in philosophy and social theory. The dominant modern philosophical perspective has privileged a portrait of the self as essentially "disengaged" from its world. For this self, what is primary is gaining epistemological purchase on, and practical control of, its world. It aims at mastering the terms of engagement. This is, of course, a kind of ontological perspective, and it has largely been assumed to be the only reasonable one. This has fostered "a kind of eclipse of ontological thinking" in contemporary moral and political theory.[1] Sometimes this has bordered on "motivated suppression" of ontological reflection, Taylor asserts, an orientation justified "because the pluralist nature of modern society makes it easier to live that way."[2] Too much emphasis on ontological fundamentals will rigidify lines of division between different ways of seeing the world and the human predicament.

   Although I agree with many of Taylor's claims about the current philosophical climate, I would suggest that he is overly pessimistic about the fate of ontological reflection. Rather than being largely eclipsed, it is actually emerging in a variety of quarters with renewed philosophical life. A growing number of thinkers have begun to conclude that the simple avoidance of ontology is a bad strategy in the face of late modern concerns.[3] The costs of a commitment—either explicit or implicit—to a "disengaged" view of the self now outweigh those unearthed when we rethink the self as part of some "richer ontology."[4] There are many paths to such an ontology, which conceptualizes the self as more constitutively embedded in the world, its other, and the beyond-human. The most interesting paths, however, are those that affirm simultaneously the necessity of recourse to fundamen-

141

tal conceptualizations *and* the necessity of admitting the contestability of such conceptualizations. Such a dual affirmation characterizes what I call "weak ontologies." Affirmation of the first necessity alone, on the other hand, characterizes traditional, strong ontologies. In short, weak ontologies take seriously the growing sense that we live in a postmetaphysical condition.[5] Accordingly, such ontologies will possess characteristics that look peculiar from the standpoint of strong ontology. For example, weak ontologies will imagine themselves as active constructions, the process of which will be understood not only in cognitive but also in aesthetic-expressive terms. We "cultivate" weak ontologies, and their resonance or lack of it for us is not a straightforward matter of cognitive truth. Further, a weak ontology will, in its most basic concepts, actively draw attention to its own contestability and historical embeddedness. And, in terms of ethical-political values, a weak ontology can provide us only with some prefiguration; it does not offer a touchstone from which determinate normative judgments are derivable.

Again, my initial, broad claim is simply that Taylor's search for a richer ontology is not an isolated one. The more crucial issue in this chapter really has to do with exactly which kind of ontology Taylor is developing. A critic who is wary of ontology might be willing to modify her strong skepticism about what I have called weak ontologies, but she is likely to think of Taylor as *not* fitting that category at all, and thus as constituting as good an object for strong skepticism as one can imagine on today's philosophical landscape. This suspicion is succinctly expressed by Isaiah Berlin; Taylor, he asserts, is "a Christian and . . . a Hegelian."[6] These commitments imply a strong ontology, that is, a view that offers some foundationalist, determinate truth about the shape and direction of self and world.

As this suspicion takes hold, it energizes a couple of interpretive prejudices that in turn allow Taylor to appear hopelessly weak from the start. The first is that Taylor's views are, well, philosophically outdated, and thus, however complex they might be, not worth much serious thought. A second stance would have us take Taylor seriously, but less for his insights than for the danger that emerges from his work. Thus Quentin Skinner warns us that Taylor has placed himself on a slippery, theistic-Hegelian slope, at the end of which lie intolerance and coercion. Skinner's critique helps to buttress that default judgment of many liberals today, which I mentioned earlier: too much talk of ontology is bad for a pluralistic society.[7]

Are these criticisms fair? Is Taylor really just offering a reiteration—albeit a very clever one—of a traditional, theistic mode of strong ontology? Or is something more novel in play, something closer to weak ontology? I think the correct answers here are, respectively, "no" and "yes." To make these claims plausible, I will show in this chapter how Taylor's project lends itself quite well to analysis in terms of the aspects of weak ontology I have delineated. It claims to tell us something deep or essential about human beings and the world, and this portrait is one that emphasizes the self's stickiness or embeddedness, its partial constitution by language and the world. And yet, in this reaching for depth, Taylor's project brings into play resources for actively attuning itself to its own limits. In addition, this is an ontology that accords a crucial place to decidedly modern insights about aesthetic-expressive experience, even as it locates itself in a theistic view of the world. The resulting perspective ends up being pretty remote from a self-certain theism whose impulse toward reconciliation exerts a subtle pull in the direction of intolerance. If Taylor is successful in distancing himself from such a traditional theistic view, then he has helped to populate our contemporary ontological and ethical landscape with a distinctive sort of creature.

THE ONTOLOGY OF ENGAGED AGENCY

The propensity of modern philosophy and social theory to begin with a disengaged self oriented toward scrutinizing its possible terms of world engagement betrays, according to Taylor, a willful neglect of how the self is always already engaged, embedded, or situated in a variety of ways. Human agency is partially, but deeply, constituted by this engagement with the world. A richer ontology is, accordingly, one that gives us a better sense of the facets of this relationship. It is only on the basis of such an elucidation of the conditions of possibility of selfhood or agency that one can adequately engage questions of epistemology, ethics, and politics.[8]

Methodologically then, Taylor deploys an argument of conceptual necessity to generate a set of existential universals. This sort of strategy for getting at depth is, of course, a rather bold one in today's philosophical climate. Its apparently apodictic quality evokes strong skepticism. Claims about agency *in general*, rather than agency in historical-cultural context, are notoriously difficult to sustain, at least if they go beyond certain uncontroversial minima. Taylor contends, nevertheless, that such a project can be fleshed out in a way that does not run roughshod over historical or cultural variation. Clearly this is an ambitious task.

In this section I begin to examine this project, both in how it construes depth and engagement ontologically and in how it admits its own contestable status. This requires, first, an analysis of what Taylor sees as the necessary features of any ontology, features implied by the very concept of agency. Second, I will elucidate his fascinating attempt in *Sources of the Self* to show how modern Western questions about identity are best explored in terms of different sets of ontological constellations that are more historically porous than the array of concepts he associates with the identity of agency as such.

Taylor's ontological reflections are best understood when one distinguishes three levels. The first includes those concepts necessary to map the "space of questions" in which human being is embedded. This level constitutes a template of "inescapable questions," as it were, onto which any specific ontological constellation must be capable of being inscribed. A second level of inquiry concerns which constellations provide insightful and perspicuous interpretations of the diverse character of modern Western identity; in short, which "fit" cogently with a historically constituted "us." Finally, a last level broaches the issue of which of the interpretively reasonable constellations is actually the best for a late-modern West. Speaking in a way that already begins to separate him from strong ontology, Taylor says of the second two levels of reflection that they involve "contestable answers to inescapable questions." It is to the level of supposedly invariable questions that I want to turn first.[9]

An agent is always already reacting to and evaluating situations that confront it and doing so against an implicit set of background commitments. The character of this background or "lifeworld" cannot be illuminated by considering it as a possible object to be comprehended in an attitude of full disengagement. Rather, the background is partially constitutive of oneself. The task of gaining clarity here must be one of trying to reconstruct, from within the agent's perspective, how this background structures one's reactions and evaluations. Taylor refers to this mode of analysis as "a phenomenological account of identity" or an internal account of "what it is to be an agent."[10]

Situations strike us. Some do so in ways that are relatively simple conceptually, such as when a high-pitched sound causes pain or a wonderfully prepared dish elicits the comment "delicious." Others, however, evoke more complex reactions—indignation, shame, remorse, admiration, condemnation, and so on. Here our capacity for ethical discrimination in its broadest sense is entwined with feeling or sentiment. This entanglement is too often seen in contemporary moral philosophy, Taylor contends, as something to be marginalized in the name of getting a clear, rational purchase on moral judgment. But this strategy merely betrays the typical effect of an attachment to the idea of disengaged agency: a desire to start serious thought from outside of engagement. From within the standpoint of engaged agency, however, the connection of discrimination and feeling is intrinsic. Indeed, "feeling is our mode of access to . . . what it is to be human."[11] When we react in this fashion, we are engaged in "strong evaluations"; that is, we find our feelings articulated by rich languages of contrastive characterization that enable us to classify the actions, persons, and motivations we encounter as better or worse, higher or lower, worthy or unworthy, right or wrong.[12]

In making such "qualitative distinctions," we draw upon, explicitly or implicitly, some "ontological account" of self and world: a "background picture" that portrays us as a certain type of creature in a certain type of world, say, creatures of God standing before divine judgment, or rational agents standing alone in a disenchanted universe. It is these pictures of our moral and "spiritual nature and predicament" that structure our moral intuitions in such a way that we "see-feel" some action as meriting a corresponding reaction. (Taylor uses "spiritual" here to include a wide range of concerns, from what constitutes a fulfilling life to the shape of one's sense of the beyond-human.) In the broadest terms, background pictures are what allow us "to make sense of our lives" morally and spiritually, to articulate them as meaningful.[13]

Although Taylor sometimes describes this orienting role in terms of a map, the analogy is actually quite limited in its usefulness. At night, we might quickly resolve our uncertainty about direction by shining a flashlight on a map. We get full illumination of the whole terrain. Background pictures, however, orient us only through incremental interpretation; we "articulate" them through language as we reflect upon our specific moral reactions. Full articulateness, like full control of our language, is an illusion.[14] Embeddedness is a condition of human being, not an optional or dispensable stance.

There is, for Taylor, no coherent way in which we can stand outside the orienting force of background pictures. Such embeddedness is constitutive of the very notion of having an identity. "Our identity is what allows us to define what is important to us and what is not." The idea of a person without a background framework altogether is the idea of a person outside our normal sphere of interlocution: in short, "pathological."[15]

Above I pointed out the central role that feeling or sentiment plays within Taylor's analysis. This emphasis extends as well to the quality of background pictures. So far, I have explicated them as something like metainterpretations, which define the space within which the specific interpretations evident in our moral reactions take form. This way of seeing Taylor's point is not incorrect, but it is one-sided. Our background picture defines what is of "incomparable" importance to us, our good. And since it does, how we stand within its space is not a matter we can regard with detached indifference. "One of the most basic aspirations of human beings," Taylor tells us, is "the need to be connected with . . . what they see as good, or of crucial importance, or of fundamental value." This means that in regard to the space offered by our background picture, we are "not . . . able to stop caring where we sit."[16]

This necessary, affective bond with what we take—however implicitly—to be "incomparably" good also throws our capacity for articulation into a new light. It is now no longer a primarily cognitive activity of working back and forth between text (situation and reaction) and context (background picture) so as to better comprehend both. Articulation, seen in affective terms, "can bring us closer to the good as a moral source, can give it power" in our lives. This empowering capacity of articulation, this ability to inflate "the lungs of the spirit," is largely missed when morality is conceived narrowly as simply a set of obligatory norms of right.[17]

Stepping back now from the ontological sketch of agency that has emerged in the last few pages, one can ask: what is the exact philosophical status Taylor claims for his arguments? Clearly, as I noted earlier, it has something of the sense of a transcendental claim: he has laid out conditions of the possibility of agency. And yet Taylor speaks only of "'transcendental conditions,'" being careful to insert scare quotes.[18] To get at just what the commitment here amounts to, consider how Taylor confronts counterarguments. The most immediately evident challenges would come not from premodern or non-Western modes of thought, many of which might be seen to fit fairly plausibly within Taylor's ontological template. Rather they come from modern Western views such as utilitarianism. This school of thought, as Taylor is well aware, would not find the idea of incomparable goods and background pictures at all necessary to its way of imagining our moral life. Agents simply label things according to the amount of pleasure they would provide and then calculate what combination would maximize their overall happiness. Accordingly, morality becomes simply a matter of determining, across agents, what arrangement yields the greatest net happiness. Taylor confronts such an account of moral agency, in which a background picture or framework is a fifth wheel, by asserting that, if we attend carefully to the utilitarian's account, we will see that he in fact "doesn't lack a framework" within which strong evaluation proceeds. In reality "he has a strong commitment to a certain ideal of rationality and benevolence. He admires people who live up to this ideal, condemns those who fail or who are too confused even to accept it, feels wrong when he himself falls below it." In effect then the utilitarian does indeed live "within a moral horizon" of the sort Taylor describes, but he cannot give any account of it within his own moral theory.[19]

In *Sources of the Self*, one of the central purposes is to reconstruct modern traditions like utilitarianism and show that they can give plausible accounts of themselves only if they invoke the language of background pictures, moral sources, and so on: in other words, if they accept the idea of an ontological space of inescapable questions. This does not mean that what such traditions might come to accept as their central moral sources would be substantively the same as for, say, a theistically based morality. Taylor's primary intention in the book is not to declare a specific, substantive ontological constellation the one true ground for modern identity, but rather to show that the *diversity* of modern identity is best understood by seeing it as a bundle of answers to questions that are constitutive of agency as such.

In the answer Taylor provides to his utilitarian opponent, one can begin to see how he wants to distinguish and yet not completely separate the necessary space of agency from its fuller and variable historical manifestations. Sometimes, however, he does seem to speak as though he can fully insulate the former sphere from the latter and give it an unshakable defense. In this vein, he maintains that the picture of agency explicitly defended by utilitarians is that of a "monster," something simply beyond the concepts that define us humans.[20] Taylor is nevertheless thoroughly aware that he has no philosophical means of establishing an absolutely incontestable boundary for us/monsters. Accordingly, he admits that his appeal to conceptual necessity is in reality always open to contest. "The question is whether one could draw a convincing portrait of a subject" for whom the moral and affective logics implied in these core concepts were "quite foreign."[21]

Although Taylor is clearly doubtful about the prospects of such a counterportrait, it would be wrong to see his statement here as a kind of rhetorical device designed to make him appear receptive to a sort of challenge to which his thought is in reality effectively closed. As I have said, weak ontology must not only state its limits but must also in some sense *actively embody the force of that statement in its own logic*. In a moment, I will show how Taylor, in fact, satisfies this requirement. But consider first a likely objection to Taylor's project. If he has indeed admitted the possible porosity of his strong conceptualization of agency as such, what do his claims about its "necessity" really amount to? Why not simply jettison this template dimension of ontology and stick with the more modest task of reconstructing those dominant ontological constellations that are embedded in modern Western thought? In trying to answer this question, one can, I think, better comprehend how this deepest level of weak ontological reflection might be understood. Clearly, its distinctiveness cannot derive from a claim about incontestable grounding. Rather, the "inescapability" encountered at this level has to be seen as constituted by the limits of imagination. More specifically, Taylor would argue that he has tracked the limits of human imagination *as he is capable of construing it*. It is against the background of such a template that we can give the best accounts of more historically specific embodiments of that imagination. In elucidating these limits, Taylor is not claiming to have discovered a level of metaphysical bedrock. Rather, he is claiming that from within the perspective of engaged, embodied agency, these limits operate for us in our moral-spiritual lives analogously to the way "up" and "down" and "here" and "there" operate for us in our physical lives.[22]

Yet Taylor is well aware that we can reimagine things. He cannot close off the possibility of reimagining some aspect of his ontological template. The template's elucidation, however, constitutes for him a declaration of limits beyond which he cannot see at present.

In *Sources of the Self*, Taylor tries to elucidate what might be called the "deep meaning of living in the modern West." He develops an interpretation of the ontological constellations that constitute the dominant answers that have emerged in the West to the questions mapped by his formal, ontological template.

In the modern world there is a diffuse, broad agreement on some fundamental "life goods": individual freedom and universal justice; benevolence, especially the avoidance of suffering; and the affirmation of ordinary life, that is, the everyday sphere of family and work. This commonality rests, however, upon "profound rifts," something that becomes apparent when these life goods are placed within the different ontological constellations around which the dominant variations in modern identity cohere. The divergences relate to the highest, or "constitutive," goods—and thus the moral sources—that animate the imperatives we attach to the foregoing life goods. The first of these constellations is the original theistic one, within which God is the constitutive good. For an adherent of this constellation, the realization of life goods is construed as enhanced participation in the "divine affirmation of the human."[23]

The second constellation emerged with the Enlightenment. Taylor calls this the "naturalism of disengaged reason." The core ideas have taken many forms: some of them, such as utilitarianism, denying completely that they in fact imply any constitutive good. Taylor, as I indicated earlier, works extremely hard to demonstrate that such a mode of self-understanding is simply not coherent. Proponents of naturalism may fix upon a highest good that is not "external to man," such as love of humanity, but such a good has the constitutive and affective qualities that God manifests within the theistic constellation. In short, it functions as a moral source, "the contemplation of which commands" one's admiration and awe. The naturalists' "reductive ontology," however, prevents them from formulating and recognizing these sources. So the sources will typically do their work from behind the scenes, structuring the rhetoric and empowering the attack on the opponents of naturalism. Thus, the force provided by these sources is present, even when explicitly denied. We find it, for example, in Jeremy Bentham's "*cri de coeur* about the love of mankind," or in "the agnostic's austere commitment to progress," or in the Sisyphean struggle to relieve suffering in a disenchanted world, captured in a figure such as Camus's Dr. Rieux in *The Plague*.[24]

The third modern ontological constellation emerges from Romanticism and continues especially in certain strands of modern art and literature. It is a reaction against both orthodox theism, with its remote, commanding God, and naturalism, which increasingly reduces the natural world to a field of matter that we engage only instrumentally. Within the third constellation, the moral source is associated with individual creativity and expression, the power to make something meaningful manifest. This source may be conceived of as in a mutually constitutive relationship with some nonanthropocentric source, in the sense that our capacity for expression allows us to attune ourselves with the impulses of nature or become empowered in construing "the order in which we are set."[25] Within this constellation, the exploration of the beyond-human takes a novel, modern form. The nonanthropocentric source is not understood as being like an object that we attempt to discover or to which we simply find access. Rather, its being is constitutively tied to our powers of expression. Thus, in this way of understanding the exploration of nonanthropocentric sources, "*Discovering . . . depends on, is interwoven with, inventing*" (emphasis added).[26]

But the creative self as source may also be conceived in a radically subjectivized sense, where it is sheer self-celebration in some form that is the highest good. Taylor clearly finds this second variant of the ontological constellation formed in the wake of Romanticism to be lacking. Such "subjectivized expressivism," he argues, roots itself in an unwarranted certainty about the world that "means not only that it is closed to any theistic perspective, but that it can't even have a place for the kind of non-anthropocentric exploration of sources" that has characterized the first variant, as it appears, for example, in the works of Rainer Maria Rilke, Marcel Proust, Thomas Mann, T. S. Eliot, or Franz Kafka.[27]

Taylor's overall claim can now be stated as the assertion that the senses of modern identity are best understood as clustering around one or more of these three ontological constellations. In one sense, this is a broadly descriptive or interpretive claim; and the length of *Sources of the Self* is a result of Taylor's trying to make it persuasive across the expanse of Western ideas. But in other senses it is normative as well. Part of what he is suggesting is that the three constellations have established a terrain of reflection on our predicament, and that perspectives that try to wall off some part of this terrain as essentially unworthy of reflection are guilty of a kind of willful inattention to the terms of our predicament. It is just such a failure that Taylor finds in the radically subjectivized variant of the third constellation. It fails to keep itself uncertainly open to the terrain of contestation about human being and world that is itself part of what we moderns are.

Here one might suspect that Taylor is really just offering us a theistic, strong ontological wolf in weak ontological sheep's clothing. But he is also critical of variants of theism that want to deny the central significance of subjective articulation of meaning and sensibility. We cannot just willfully retreat behind this part of the modern terrain of consciousness to the certainty and objectivity of a God of commands.[28] In sum then, Taylor does indeed affirm a certain openness to ontological diversity.

This degree of affirmation of contestation would, however, hardly allay all suspicion. Taylor has certainly urged attentiveness to the full space of concerns occupied by the three ontological constellations. But one has only to reflect for a moment to think of various possible objections, in the light of which Taylor seems to be limiting the contestation allowed. For example, is his ambitious interpretation of Western history correct in its conclusion that the ontological space of understanding is adequately covered by just his three constellations? Have significant voices and possibilities been shunted aside?

For Taylor, no interpretation is beyond contestation. The articulation of thought and feelings and the effort to understand the other's expressions are not secondary characteristics of our being. The work of understanding, of linguistically negotiating between the interpretations of self and other, identity and difference, is a constitutive part of what we are. Borrowing here from Hans Georg Gadamer, Taylor expresses this thought succinctly: *"Verstehen* is a *Seinsmodus."*[29] To imagine human being in this way means simultaneously that you also privilege the activity of dialogue or conversation within which we bring our interpretations to bear. There simply is no foothold outside of conversation on which to put one's weight in order to assert that I "have got it simply right against all others."[30]

But such appeals to the final court of conversation are hardly likely to convince critics without further clarity on exactly what Taylor embraces in Hegel. This entanglement, when combined with Taylor's expressed hope for "reconciliation" of the voices in the conversation of humankind, gives at least some initial cause for concern.

In Taylor's discussions of conversation and reconciliation, Gadamer rather than G. W. F. Hegel is the leading figure. In this sense, there is no question of Taylor believing that, say, intercultural conversations have some unifying, necessary *telos*.[31] There is rather, only the idea of an omega point, as it were, when all times and cultures of humanity would have been able to exchange and come to an undistortive horizon for all of them. But even this would still be only de facto universal. If it turned out that one culture had been left out by mistake, the process would have to start again. The only possible ideal of objectivity in this domain is that of inclusiveness. The inclusive perspective is never attained de jure. You only get there de facto, when everybody is on board. And even then the perspective is in principle limited in relation to another possible understanding which might have arisen. But all this doesn't mean that there is no gain, no overcoming of ethnocentrism. On the contrary; it is overcome in inclusiveness.[32]

This Gadamerian ideal is, in effect, an ideal of possibility: the possibility of reconciliation between what seems at first to be irremediably in opposition or incommensurable. There are no guarantees, however, no necessity of progress. What this ideal primarily gives us is simply the motivation to "try and see" what progress can be made.[33]

Taylor does realize that the dominant conversations of Western modernity have often been carried on with a false, universalist self-understanding. But that, in itself, is not enough to warrant the view that, on principle, one should affirm a thorough relativism or incommensurability of different forms of life. Taylor has, it seems to me, two grounds for refusing to accept such a perspective. First, he can point to historical instances where apparently irreconcilable orientations have reconceived themselves. "For a long time our ancestors couldn't conceive how to reconcile popular rule and public order. Now the most law-abiding societies are democratic."[34] A few historical examples like this are, however, a fairly slim reed on which to rest the full weight of his ideal of the possibility of reconciliation. The real burden of argument must fall somewhere else, and that spot is his understanding of language and articulation. Taylor has not, to my knowledge, used this understanding to mount exactly the kind of argument I will present below, but I think it is suggested by the claims he has made.

Taylor is perfectly willing to admit that we may run up against irreconcilables or incommensurability in the mutual confrontation of forms of life, moral sources, and so on. The claim to know that such an outcome is inescapable *from the start,* however, betrays an implausible comprehension of the orientation of self to lifeworld. By "lifeworld," I mean broadly the unthought of our thought, the implicit of our explicit, the unconscious background of our conscious foreground. "Background" in this sense has a broader reach than the notion explored earlier of "background picture"; the latter is one aspect of the former. Now the claim to know categorically that, say, one's form of life is irreconcilable with another would ultimately have to rest on a couple of other claims, both of which are implausible. First, it would have to rest on the assertion that one's form of life was in some sense fully available to oneself in all its implications and complexity. But since one's form of life is inextricably entangled with the language that interprets one's lifeworld in general, to claim that one has an exhaustive grasp of the former's boundaries and possibilities is thus also to claim that one has such a grasp of one's language and lifeworld. This is at root an astounding image of mastery. It is as if a person who is frustrated that she keeps missing things in the background of her visual field, because she is concentrating earnestly on something in the foreground, might simply decide to solve her problem once and for all by "foregrounding" everything.

For Taylor, linguistic articulation of that which is part of the inarticulate background that is one's lifeworld is always a partial achievement. We make something manifest, but it remains located against an enduring background, which may be different now. The relationship of this linguistic manifestness to its background is represented by Taylor with the image of a web that is touched in one spot. A specific expression that makes something linguistically explicit cannot help but resonate through the background of that which is left implicit, the way the touching of a web resonates throughout the entire structure of filaments.[35]

The claim to possess a level of explicitness about one's form of life, moral source, and so on, sufficient to know its precise boundaries and thus to declare its irreconcilability with others from the start, also runs afoul of another characteristic of articulation. This is the fact that the activity of articulation, especially when it concerns our moral and spiritual life, has a potentially transformative or transvaluative effect:

> Much of our motivation—our desires, aspirations, evaluation—is not simply given. We give it formulation in words or images. Indeed by the fact that we are linguistic animals our desires and aspirations cannot but be articulated in one way or another. . . . But this kind of formulation does not leave its object unchanged. To give a certain articulation is to shape our sense of what we desire or what we hold important in a certain way.[36]

In expressing our thoughts and feelings, we are always engaged in an at least potentially transformative activity. Rephrasing this more precisely for present concerns, one would say that the very activity of articulating those things that are morally and spiritually crucial to one's form of life unavoidably puts one in a position of seeing/feeling them in new contexts and with new possibilities.[37] The clear implication of this is that any confident announcement of irreconcilability at the start must be seen as betraying a willful blindness to the possibility of new avenues of reconcilability opening up in the mutual articulation of conversation. Such an argument does not, of course, establish that reconciliation will emerge in any given case. It merely shows that the affirmation of irreconcilability, which often advertises itself as the ripe fruit of a renunciation of Western gestures of mastery, must in fact root itself in its own inconspicuous gesture of mastery.

Taylor does not explicitly identify this ethical failing of the rigid proponent of irreconcilability, but it is related to the way he describes how agents can be said to be "responsible for our evaluations." In our moral evaluations, we "strive to be faithful" to our "deepest unstructured sense" of what is of decisive importance: say, that "a certain mode of life [is] higher than others . . . or . . . that belonging to this community is essential to my identity."[38] But, as we saw above, this striving to keep one's bearing in moral space cannot be done honestly by simply holding tight to the highest object of one aspirations. Honest striving, and hence acceptance of responsibility for one's evaluations, is realized only in a stance of careful attentiveness to possible shifts in the meaning such objects carry for us.

If this is indeed the philosophical sense of Taylor's orientation to conversation and reconciliation, then it would seem to have very little in the way of Hegel in it. And yet some vestige of him does remain. Taylor affirms the idea of human "potentialities" that can be realized in history. Even this notion is hedged with significant qualifications: there is no unitary set of potentialities; no unitary direction of unfolding; and no unfolding of potentialities that is pure gain; rather, there is always gain and loss. Finally, the realization of a given potential, which allows one to speak of some gain and progress, is a story that is told for a civilizational "locality," in the sense that for modern Western identity, "The Greeks and we are in one 'locality.'"[39]

Although Taylor would want to defend a number of gains of this sort, such as a universalistic notion of rights, in the present context one gain is particularly worthy of note. The account he provides of articulation and conversation is of a potentiality realized or at least partially realized. The normative status that he accords this model results from its capturing our capacity to better grasp our character as language animals, to better understand and employ the capacity we have as such creatures. The crucial, initial enhancement of insight into this potential, as Taylor frequently stresses, came with Romanticism and its new account of expressive meaning. Although many today reject the details of various Romantic theories, Taylor would claim that at some level "we have all in fact become followers of the expressive view" that "has brought language more and more to centre stage . . . as the indispensable medium without which our typically human capacities, emotions, relations would not be." And, as this quality of the medium has moved to center stage, so also has the increasing awareness that our relation to it is not one of controller-controlled. One reason for our intense fascination with language in the twentieth century is that we can't seem to unravel fully the open, uncertain, mysterious quality of our engagement with it.[40] Taylor's foregrounding of this quality in his accounts of articulation and conversation guarantees that his ontological insights, whether relating to templates or full constellations, signal their own limits and contain their own sense of contestedness; in short, they offer themselves as "weak" in my sense.

Ironically, then, the vestige of Hegelianism that attaches to Taylor's use of potentiality here is the vehicle for deflating more robust figures of thought that emerge from that legacy and, at the same time, more closed to the challenge of otherness. Insofar as Taylor has a problem with blindness to this challenge, to the possibility of contestation, it is not so much a question of there being any crucial shortcoming in his ideal of conversation as it is that he is sometimes too unconcerned about how, in practice, conversation has hegemonic silences or is drawn into certain channels by the simple power of predominant discursive formations. In this regard, Taylor should perhaps temper his well-known antipathy for thinkers such as Michel Foucault and Jacques Derrida. He may be right about some of the philosophical shortcomings of postmodern thought, but he has perhaps overlooked the way in which certain disruptive modes of reflection, such as genealogy and deconstruction, might provide leavening strategies that could find a reasonable place within his own model of conversation.

THEISM AND THE AESTHETIC EXPRESSIVE DIMENSION

Up to this point, all of Taylor's claims that I have examined can plausibly be interpreted in a weak ontological fashion. Things become more complex when one directly confronts his affirmation of theism. Readers of *Sources of the Self* are likely to end up somewhat concerned about the tension that seems necessarily to arise between Taylor's portrait and affirmation of the *diversity* of modern moral sources, on the one hand, and his belief, stressed at the book's conclusion, that *one* such source, the Christian God of *agape*, is the only "adequate" alternative, on the other.[41] Although Taylor emphasizes that he is uncertain about his ability to make this belief convincing, it is difficult for the reader not to begin to feel that the earlier talk of diversity is somehow drained of its force.[42] The strong ontological trump card may still be held close to the vest, but its potential to sweep the game seems palpable.

In this section, I want to explore some reasons for resisting such a reading of Taylor. Toward this end, I will examine more closely his presentation of the third modern ontological constellation that arises out of the expressivism of the Romantics. Although Taylor ultimately sides with the first, theistic constellation, the precise meaning of this affirmation has to be taken in light of that other affirmation I noted earlier that "we have all become followers of the expressive view."[43] The historical articulation of this view—or, better, constellation of views—from the late eighteenth century until today has brought to full consciousness an aesthetic-expressive potentiality of human being that theism cannot simply deny.[44] A theism that grapples seriously with this issue will have no trump card to play vis-à-vis weak ontologies. There are no trump cards in this game.

The rich historical tale that Taylor relates about the emergence and varied development of the expressivist constellation is one of the most fascinating aspects of *Sources of the Self.* But this interpretive story is interwoven with judgments of greater or lesser adequacy in ontological terms. Adequacy here refers, first, to fit with the general template of moral sources and to openness to the diversity of sources that defines modernity. A stronger sense of adequacy, however, also comes into play. At issue is not which ontological constellation is minimally acceptable, but rather which can demonstrate its superiority over the other acceptable competitors. Here Taylor tries to show how the most defensible position today is one that integrates certain elements of expressivism with theism. It is important to keep these different senses of adequacy separate to understand just what Taylor's theism implies philosophically.

What Taylor calls the "Expressivist Turn" emerges as several different insights coalesce in the German Sturm und Drang writers and continue to develop through English and German Romanticism. Collectively these insights begin to constitute a conceptual constellation distinguishable both from orthodox Christianity and the disengaged rationalism of the radical Enlightenment. In relation to the former, there emerges a growing attachment to nature as an order "conducing to the life and happiness of the sentient creatures which it contains."[45] Increasingly, a sense develops that this order is a moral source in itself, whose power need no longer be conceptualized in terms of the Creator within Christianity. In tandem with this growing affinity for nature, there emerges the sense that it is through the feelings or aesthetic sensibility—as much as or more than through reason alone—that one becomes attuned to this new source.[46] Our affective and aesthetic capacities give us access to "an inner impulse or conviction which tells us of the importance of our own natural fulfillment and of solidarity with our fellow creatures in theirs. This is the voice of nature within us." And it is this impulse of nature that comes to play the role of a "substitute for [the] grace" of the God of Christianity. Not surprisingly, for proponents of expressivism, contact with this source was threatened by a posture of cold, disengaged reason.[47]

To think in terms of such an inner voice or impulse is simultaneously to bring expression to the center of human being. In "articulating what we find within us," we also make something manifest, bring something of nature to expression. Two distinctive qualities characterize this novel sense of expression. First, that which is brought to expression is not something that "was already fully formulated beforehand"; rather its very character is partially constituted by the expression. Second, this curious quality of creating/discovering pertains both to that "élan running through the world" and to the being who is articulating it.[48]

This expressivist turn, which finds its moral source in the goodness of nature, goes through a variety of transformations in the nineteenth and twentieth centuries. As Taylor picks his way through this array of modifications, his primary concern is focused around two ontological axes, in terms of which he measures continuity and change: first, in a given manifestation of expressivism, *what is* it exactly that is *being expressed*; and, second, is the expressivism still tied to a moral source, and is that source still conceived as *good*? In elucidating these issues, I want to start with what Taylor sees as the most challenging deviations that appear in the expressivist constellation and then consider the continuities he finds. It is within the currents of the latter that he discerns alternatives worthy of affirmation today.

From the very start, the expressivist emphasis on inwardness and the creative imagination sets up the conditions for later tension between the idea of an external order as the moral source, on the one hand, and the idea that the human self alone can become the pure center and measure of all that is around it, on the other. This is most clearly seen in that drift in much modernist art and literature through which aesthetic sensibility and its created objects come to claim for themselves an autotelic status. The "what" of expression collapses thereby into *self*-expression, and, correspondingly, the moral source becomes identified with the "powers of the self."[49]

A parallel deviation from the original forms of expressivism occurs as the assumption of the goodness of nature begins to come into question. Arthur Schopenhauer is a pivotal figure here for Taylor; after him the way is open to a new range of views—from Friedrich Nietzsche to Joseph Conrad—in which the "great current of nature" is reconceived as "vast, unfathomable, alien and amoral. . . ."[50] This shift allows for new expressivist options in which the source is still external or beyond human, but it is no longer a moral one, at least in as straightforward a sense as in theism or the original variants of expressivism.

Along with these deviations from the initial commitments of expressivism, there have also been continuities. Here Taylor is especially concerned to show how, in certain strands of modernist literature and poetry, the central idea of an "epiphany" has been retained. Taylor uses this term to capture the "notion of a work of art as the locus of a manifestation which brings us into the presence of something which is otherwise inaccessible, and which is of the highest moral or spiritual significance; a manifestation moreover, which also defines or completes something, even as it reveals."[51]

Although Taylor wants to persuade us of expressivist continuity through this epiphanic experience, he is well aware that this kind of experience has been reconceptualized substantially in the twentieth century. He refers to the earlier Romantic conception as an "epiphany of being" in the sense that through artistic expression the goodness of being was to be intensely experienced. This is largely replaced in the twentieth century by the idea of an "epiphany of interspaces" or a "framing epiphany." Here the sense of being or nature as intrinsically and clearly characterized by good purpose has fallen away; accordingly, the epiphanic experience can no longer plausibly be comprehended as *expressing* such *purpose*. But that does not reduce the experience to a radically subjectivized one: "the great works of modernism," Taylor asserts, "resist our understanding them in a subjectivized fashion, as mere expressions of feeling or as ways of ordering the emotions."[52] Such works are rather concerned with some "transaction between ourselves and the world," some fashion in which the aesthetic object creates a frame or space that brings to presence some "forces" or qualities of "the order in which we are set." What such works keep open then is the exploration of the beyond-human, the domain of external moral sources. Taylor sees such exploration at work in modern figures as diverse as Mann, Rilke, Ezra Pound, and D. H. Lawrence.[53]

Thus, the distinctiveness of the framing epiphany is manifested in its bringing something beyond human to presence and yet no longer being fully expressive in the older sense, since the aesthetic experience does not clearly express some larger purpose. Moreover, this epiphany still gives a pronounced role to subjective expression, for now the "moral or spiritual order of things must come to us indexed to a personal vision" that is articulated in language or other symbolic forms. In other words, "the search for moral sources *outside* the subject" proceeds only "through languages that resonate *within* him or her. . . ."[54]

Clearly what attracts Taylor to those writers, philosophers, and poets who share this idea of epiphany is how they make central to human being moments of intense mutual vivification between an intensified subjectivity and sources external to it. Expressivism always emphasized the peculiar process of creating/discovering, as I noted earlier; but now the role of creativity is even more enhanced. Our expressive powers increasingly become essential to the "efficacy" of external sources. This extends finally to the very idea of "transfiguration" or "transmutation," the notion that aesthetic sensibility can be engaged to help redeem in some way a "despiritualized reality."[55] This conviction has, of course, taken a variety of forms. Some bind themselves to the theistic constellation of Christianity, such as Fyodor Dostoyevsky or Rilke; others stay radically at a distance, as is the case with Nietzsche's notion of affirming the world. Despite these differences, however, their emphases on transfiguration are responses to that "crisis of affirmation" that has arisen as conviction of the innate goodness of things has waned in the nineteenth and twentieth centuries. In these responses, we see "the development of a human analogue to God's seeing things as good: a seeing which also helps effect what it sees."[56]

I will return shortly to this specific question of the affirmation of the goodness of being. For the moment, however, I want to reengage the question with which I started this section: what exactly does Taylor, as a proponent of theism, find to affirm within expressivism? The answer takes us back to the idea of a realized human potentiality for linguistic or symbolic articulation. In effect, Taylor is saying that our modern experience of expressivism offers certain insights that theism today must integrate. Accordingly, theists must understand that there is simply no immaculately uncontextualized "nugget of transcendent truth." In general, "our sense of the certainty or problematicity of God is relative to our sense of moral sources." What this means more specifically in relation to the expressivist constellation is that God as a moral source is now inextricably entangled with subjective articulation. Referring to this "interweaving of the subjective and transcendent," Taylor says that theology is "indexed" to "languages of personal resonance."[57]

Given this acceptance of a core element from expressivism, it becomes difficult to see how Taylor's theism could interpret itself as capable of deploying a strong ontological trump card. No religious tradition or individual belief can legitimately carry such force into the space of Taylorean articulation and conversation. There is no royal route that cuts through others; there is only the work of mutual interpretation and articulation of moral sources, in the context of which my arguments may or may not finally resonate with you.

Thus, the suspicious secular reader of Taylor must, it seems to me, take him at his word in *Sources of the Self*. His claim is that the "major point" of the book is to elucidate our modern predicament as one in which three ontological constellations compete with one another, *and* in which resolutions of this predicament that try to succeed by conjuring away its constitutive terms are failures from the start. Such failures may come in the form of a utilitarianism that denies the very idea of moral sources or in the form of a theism that finds its full bearings solely from some immaculately authoritative commands of God.[58] Each betrays a kind of willful blindness that marks it as inadequate in the sense either of ignoring "inescapable" ontological issues or of failing to do justice to the full range of problems and potentialities that are entangled with modern identity.

Understood in this fashion, the primary normative point of *Sources of the Self* is not that theism is best, but rather that certain ontological qualities and a certain range of sensitivity are necessary components in arguments about the modern self and its predicament. One could also say of such a claim that it broadly supports the idea of weak ontology. By this I mean that Taylor's claims about the three ontological constellations and how each must understand itself and its respective others accord reasonably well with the criteria I have laid out for weak ontological reflection. For my purposes, the especially interesting contribution Taylor makes is to delineate a theism that is no longer explicitly or implicitly tied to strong ontological claims. He shows persuasively that, regardless of whether one embraces theism or is thoroughly secular, the space of late modern conversation is such that no one can play strong ontological trump cards with any legitimacy.

None of this means, however, that Taylor forgoes arguments aimed at defending one specific ontological constellation as the best. These arguments are crucial to him. Their force and urgency emerge from their role as basic articulations of the theistic moral source he affirms. But within the weak-ontological, conversational space of modernity, this force and urgency are perverted if they are understood as pure evidence of truth. Their proper role in this context has to do with motivation: inspiring one to a love of, and care for, conversational engagement and the commitment to interpretive work that it requires.

If we turn to the specific, substantive arguments that Taylor articulates in support of his own weak ontology, the paramount concern revolves around the *goodness* of moral sources. Here I first want to consider how Taylor squares off against at least some variants of the second modern ontological tradition, that rooted in the Enlightenment; more specifically, what arguments does he marshal against utilitarianism and Deweyan pragmatism?[59] After briefly surveying these contests, I will turn back to the relationship of Taylor's theism to the expressivist ontological tradition. As I have shown, he draws deeply from this tradition; yet it is also from this direction that he sees the most disturbing challenge emerging, more specifically in the form of Nietzsche.

Utilitarianism does not really enter the contest over which is the most adequate ontology. As shown earlier, it does not meet the first set of criteria of adequacy for philosophical frameworks Taylor establishes; in short, it does not even fit onto the ontological template. It typically draws upon a moral source, but it does so implicitly, in a fashion that cannot be comprehended within the utilitarian framework that source empowers (as noted earlier in this chapter). But one could certainly ask here: how might things change if that source were to be made more explicit? Taylor clearly finds the immediate prospects of such a shift to be dim. That is because the source that utilitarianism implicitly trades upon is entangled in the radical Enlightenment's thorough rejection of religion in the name of "doing justice to the innocence of natural desire." Such an affirmation would make for a utilitarianism that is adequate to Taylor's ontological template, but how would its claim to be the best ontological account look? It would, Taylor asserts, remain deeply flawed. How can we sustain a simple faith in the goodness of natural desire today "in the face of our post-Schopenhauerian understanding of the murkier depths of human motivation?"[60]

An especially interesting challenge to Taylor from within the second ontological constellation has been articulated by Richard Rorty. He accepts Taylor's account of the inextricability of the concepts of agency and moral source. But he sketches an alternative view, the source of which is not external yet has a greater capacity to empower than the bare idea of the rational, autonomous self. Specifically, we can affirm John Dewey's ideal of radical social imagination and hope, interpreting it now as a moral source. This scheme would, Rorty argues, fit quite plausibly both on Taylor's ontological template and into that second modern constellation, naturalism. This option would be an ontologically "*non*-reductive naturalism."[61] Central here would be the notion that we come to receive inspiration and empowerment as we articulate a vision we have collectively imagined of a "Social Democratic Future."[62] This source in no sense "reflects" something like *the* human predicament; rather, it is grounded solely in the exercise of our capacity to hope, imagine, and will.

Rorty's reflections here touch upon an extremely important point, namely, how do we decide what exactly counts as an acceptable weak ontology? Is Rorty mistaken about the Deweyan position fitting onto the weak ontological template? Or is he correct, thereby revealing that Taylor's arguments concerning external moral sources are actually structured more by his advocacy of theism than by his interpretive efforts to illuminate the boundaries of all that could plausibly count as weak ontology? In response to Rorty's challenge, Taylor attempts to explain exactly why the Deweyan alternative does not really count as an acceptable ontology. The reason is that its would-be moral source is reducible finally to a collective human projection. The ideal is in no way rooted in an "order in which we are set," in other words, one not entirely of our choosing. Taylor clarifies this problem with Rorty's position by contrasting it with another that is radically secular and antimetaphysical but that would nevertheless fit the ontological template. Here he refers us again to Camus's Dr. Rieux in *The Plague*, in which we are presented with an ethic that preserves

> a moment of the recognition of something which is not made or decided by human beings, and which shows a certain way of being to be good and admirable. This may be nothing beyond the disenchanted universe which is the human predicament along with the human potentiality to respond the way Dr. Rieux does. But we recognize

that *we have created neither this world nor this range of human capacities.* What remains open to us is to respond to this or not. But here we experience the choice not as one in which we might confer on this predicament its inspiring character, but rather it is a matter of whether we see it as truly moving. If we find ourselves forced to concede that it is, then there is no further role for the will beyond that of letting ourselves be moved by it.[63]

As Taylor sketches how the foregoing would count as weak ontology and Rorty's alternative would not, he helps to illuminate an issue related to any sort of talk of criteria in such matters. In both my general remarks at the start of this chapter, as well as in Taylor's arguments in *Sources of the Self,* the very sense of ontological reflection today is entangled with historical-interpretive judgments about the costs of the culture of modern subjectivity; more specifically, the effects of its disengagement from, and instrumental objectification of, its world. This means that what is allowed to count as a weak ontology cannot be divorced entirely from a pragmatic judgment as to whether a given alternative—say, Rorty's—generates enough critical distance from modern subjectivity and its typical blindnesses. Rorty shows a very precise sensitivity to this issue. Although he would like to think that his Deweyan perspective could generate such critical distance without an external moral source, he is honest enough to admit that the broad heritage of socialist thought is deeply entangled in instrumentalism. In regard to this pragmatic judgment of adequate distance, he concludes: Taylor "may be right."[64] This admission is rather remarkable from someone who is renowned for countering any talk of transcendence with therapeutic advice to stop scratching what are really just imaginary itches. Rorty is not, of course, giving away the whole game to Taylor just yet; what he is doing, though, is recognizing just how distinctive and defensible an ontological position Taylor has developed. Rorty has thus, unlike many others, listened very carefully and not been drawn to inappropriate assessments by simple labels like "Christian and Hegelian."

Taylor does not really elaborate upon exactly why the Deweyan option comes up short, but his dissatisfaction would likely come down to two reservations. The Deweyan has hope, love for humanity, and the will to transform society. For Taylor, however, that sort of love, which is chosen in a radical sense, will likely be too fickle or qualified to match a love for humanity that patterns itself after God's unqualified *agape* for His or Her creation. Taylor's second reservation would be directed against the transformatory aspect of a Deweyan vision. Here the concern would not be that all social transformation in pursuit of modern life goods is to be condemned; Taylor's perspective would, in fact, lend support to such efforts. His suspicion rather is that visions of transformation entwined with a disengaged conception of subjectivity are precisely part of what is problematic in Western modernity. Only a moral-political vision linked to the articulation of an external moral source will provide the vivification of finitude and experience of humility necessary for generating an *ethos* in which transformative social projects will not produce monsters.

The threat of monsters is perhaps the appropriate point at which to turn back to the challenge of Nietzsche. Nietzscheans (or at least some of them) affirm a source external to human being, but it is an *amoral* source. For them, the heart of things is an unfathomable, purposeless, "presencing" of life. What unsettles Taylor most deeply about such an ontological configuration is that Nietzsche joins it with a rejection of the modern life goods of benevolence and justice, something he sees as necessary to wean us from a costly moral rigorism that too often follows from ethical commitment, especially when it is powered by a conviction that one is fulfilling God's purposes. Although, as I indicated earlier, Taylor initially admires Nietzsche's emphasis on affirming and transfiguring the world, he ultimately finds it to be unsatisfactory, since it has lost any footing in a commitment to doing good to others; in effect, the affirmation of the world is ethically idle. Consequently, Nietzsche offers us a "cruel dilemma": affirmation without benevolence or benevolence with moral rigorism.[65] Taylor, of course, wants to convince us that we need not accept these terms of choice.

If Nietzsche does indeed present us with precisely the dilemma Taylor attributes to him, then a certain kind of theism looks accordingly more attractive. But the really fascinating question here is whether one can develop a weak ontology that might accept something like Nietzsche's external, amoral source and yet find a way of articulating it in a more life good-friendly fashion. If one developed an ethical orientation consonant with such an interpretation of sources, then it would constitute a powerful competitor on Taylor's own terms.

It is difficult to read the conclusion of *Sources of the Self* and not feel that Taylor deeply discounts the likelihood of such a challenge being successful. Arguments for this discounting are not really made explicit there, but a high degree of confidence seems present. The reasons behind this confidence become somewhat clearer in a later essay. There he argues that thinkers like Nietzsche and Foucault represent a kind of "immanent counter-Enlightenment." This description is meant to capture two features of their legacy. First, they question, as we have seen, the Enlightenment's assertion of the primacy of human flourishing expressed in the affirmation of benevolence and justice. Second, this primacy is not decentered by transcendence in the theistic sense, but rather by an *immanent* transcendence in which the "locus of death" comes to provide "in some sense a privileged perspective, the paradigm gathering point for life." Although this urge to immanent transcendence has taken a variety of forms, Nietzsche and the neo-Nietzscheans seem to be Taylor's main antagonists.[66] In *Sources of the Self*, these antagonists were indicted only on the count of having disengaged from central modern life goods. Here, however, Taylor expands the charges. When an emphasis is laid upon human finitude, and this is not in turn connected to a source that is good but rather amoral, the result is a peculiar "fascination with death and suffering" that finally cannot "escape the draw towards violence." This draw may manifest itself in different ways. Nietzsche expresses it through his attachment to a pre-Socratic kind of warrior ethic, within which risking death is the paradigm experience of life; Foucault expresses it in his fascination with transgression and "limit" experiences.[67]

Now we can see the heart of Taylor's concern when it comes to a weak ontology's affirmation of external sources that are understood in amoral terms. In one sense, they serve a curious positive role for theism today, because they are a perpetual embarrassment to the legacy of the radically secular Enlightenment: they testify to "an ineradicable bent to respond to something beyond life."[68] They are, however, also profoundly dangerous, because construing this "bent" so brings also a fascination with violence.

It is hard not to read this as a fatal judgment. Others certainly have made similar pronouncements before. But is Taylor really entitled to make this determination with such apparent finality? Here it is instructive to turn to his own response to critics who assail Christianity and other religions for their history of intolerance and violence. Such critics, Taylor replies, "take the self-destructive consequences of a spiritual aspiration as a refutation of this aspiration." The fact that a theistic moral source has involved violence historically does not necessarily invalidate it, especially when the alternative of a "stripped-down secular outlook" with no opening to external sources involves its own sort of self-mutilation: "stifling the response in us to some of the deepest and most powerful spiritual aspirations that humans have conceived." Since either alternative thus bears its own heavy burden, there is no easy choice. The theistic view can be embraced only with a deep sense of the challenge of overcoming "the terrible record of its adherents in history."[69]

But having situated his commitment to theism in this fashion, can Taylor so categorically pass judgment on those who would embrace some variant of a Nietzschean external source? I don't think so. His concern with this tradition's "draw" toward violence has to be construed as a challenge to it, not a final sentence. Taylor stands to the Nietzscheans as his secular critics stand to him. The door thus remains open to the possibility of a successful weak ontological competitor to Taylor's theism that affirms an external but amoral source.

NOTES

Earlier versions of this chapter were presented to a seminar of the Dutch National Research Group on The Ethics of Care at the University for Humanist Studies, Utrecht, May 1997, and at the 1997 Annual Meeting of the American Political Science Association, Washington D.C., August–September 1997. I would like to thank Simon Critchley and Joep Dohman for their critical comments on those occasions as well as Karsten Harries for his reactions to this version.

The following abbreviations are used for referring to Taylor's books:
HAL   *Human Agency and Language. Philosophical Papers I* (Cambridge: Cambridge University Press, 1985).
PA   *Philosophical Arguments* (Cambridge: Harvard University Press, 1995).
PAH   *Philosophy and the Human Sciences. Philosophical Papers II* (Cambridge: Cambridge University Press, 1985).
PAP   *Philosophy in the Age of Pluralism*. Edited by James Tully. (Cambridge: Cambridge University Press, 1994).

POR   "The Politics of Recognition," in *Multiculturalism: Examining the Politics of Recognition*. Edited and introduced by Amy Gutmann. (Princeton: Princeton University Press, 1994).

RS   *Reconciling the Solitudes: Essays on Canadian Federalism and Nationalism*. Edited by Guy Laforest. (Montreal and Kingston: McGill: Queen's University Press, 1993).

S   *Sources of the Self: The Making of Modern Identity* (Cambridge: Harvard University Press, 1989).

   1. "Cross-Purposes: The Liberal Communitarian Debate," *PA*, 185.

   2. *S*, 10.

   3. For a discussion of this drift in current political theory, see my "Weak Ontology and Liberal Political Reflection," *Political Theory* (August 1997): 502–23; and my *Sustaining Affirmation: The Strengths of Weak Ontology in Political Theory* (Princeton: Princeton University Press, 2000).

   4. "Explanation and Practical Reason," *PA*, 39, and *S*, 21. Taylor sometimes uses the term "philosophical anthropology," rather than "ontology," to describe his project. Given the traditional connotations of the latter terms, this seems appropriate. But Taylor is himself not entirely satisfied with the former term. I think that my notion of weak ontology would be largely appropriate for the kind and level of philosophical reflection he has in mind; see *S*, 514–15. He speaks, for example, of the "ontology of human life: what kinds of things you invoke in talking about human beings in the different things we do: describing, deliberating, judging . . . "; "Rorty in the Epistemological Tradition," in *Reading Rorty*, ed. Alan R. Malachowski (Oxford: Blackwell, 1990), 261.

   5. For the distinction between "weak" and "strong" ontology, see my forthcoming *Affirmation in Contemporary Political Theory*. Gianni Vattimo has used the term "weak ontology" or, more familiarly, "weak thinking," to characterize a possible direction for postmetaphysical thought. While I am moving in what I think is a similar direction, I am unsure whether or not he would find the specific claims that I gather under the rubric of "weak ontology" compatible with his own line of thought. See Gianni Vattimo, *The End of Modernity: Nihilism and Hermeneutics in Postmodern Culture*, tr. Jon R. Snyder (Baltimore: Johns Hopkins University Press, 1998), 85–86.

   6. Isaiah Berlin, "Introduction," *PAP*, 1.

   7. See Quentin Skinner, "Who Are 'We'? Ambiguities of the Modern Self," in "Symposium on Charles Taylor's *Sources of the Self*," *Inquiry* 34 (1991): 133–53. In this chapter, I will not be directly confronting the issue of pluralist politics. On this topic, see my forthcoming *Affirmation in Contemporary Political Theory*.

   8. "Preface," *PA*, viiff.

   9. *S*, 41, 529.

   10. *S*, ix, 29, 32.

   11. "Self-Interpreting Animals," *HAL*, 6; and *S*, 8.

   12. "Human Agency," *HAL*, 15–23; *S*, 4.

   13. *S*, 3–8, 18, 74. Taylor uses the term "see-feel" in "Self-Interpreting Animals," *HAL*, 70.

   14. "Human Agency," *HAL*, 35ff.; "Self-Interpreting Animal," *HAL*, 62ff.; and *S*, 8, 18, 77–80.

   15. *S*, 27, 30–31.

   16. *S*, 42, 44.

   17. *S*, 92–94, 520.

18. *S,* 32.
19. *S,* 31.
20. *S,* 32.
21. "What Is Human Agency?" *HAL,* 28.
22. "The Validity of Transcendental Arguments," *PA,* 30.
23. *S,* 495, 521.
24. *S,* 93–94, 324–25, 331–39, 496.
25. *S,* 496, 510.
26. *S,* 18.
27. *S,* 490, 506–8, 510.
28. *S,* 512.
29. *S,* 72, 233–34; "Heidegger, Language and Ecology," *PA,* 118.
30. "Charles Taylor Replies," *PAP,* 230.
31. James Tully, "Preface," *PAP,* xiv–v.
32. "Comparison, History, Truth," *PA,* 151.
33. "Explanation and Practical Reason," *PA,* 55.
34. "Charles Taylor Replies," *PAP,* 214.
35. "Language and Human Nature," *HAL,* 231.
36. "What Is Human Agency?" *HAL,* 36.
37. "Heidegger, Language and Ecology," *PA,* 107–9.
38. "What Is Human Agency?" *HAL,* 35, 38, 40–41.
39. "Comparison, History, Truth," *PA,* 151, 159–64.
40. "Language and Human Nature," *HAL,* 235–36. In speaking here of language, Taylor includes other symbolic forms as well, such as music and dance.
41. *S,* 10, 432, 516–21.
42. *S,* 10–11, 499.
43. *S,* 235–36.
44. *S,* 312–13, 491–93.
45. *S,* 315.
46. *S,* 282–84, 294–302.
47. *S,* 369–70, 411.
48. *S,* 373–75.
49. *S,* 490.
50. *S,* 417, 441ff.
51. *S,* 419. Taylor says that he both borrows from James Joyce's use of this term and modifies it.
52. *S,* 474–76, 490–491.
53. *S,* 477, 482, 510.
54. *S,* 428, 510.
55. *S,* 446, 482.
56. *S,* 448–49. The relevant biblical reference is to Genesis I.
57. *S,* 312, 491–92, 512–13; and "Reply to Commentators," in "Symposium on *Sources of the Self,*" *Philosophy and Phenomenological Research* 54 (March 1994): 211.
58. *S,* 312, 512, 520.
59. I leave aside here some important arguments that procedural liberals would make to the effect that ontology is unnecessary for taking up matters of justice. I engage this question in my *Affirmation in Contemporary Political Theory.*

60. *S*, 516–18; "Cross-Purposes," *PA*, 186ff., 202.

61. Richard Rorty, "Taylor on Self-Celebration and Gratitude," in "Symposium on *Sources of the Self*," *Philosophy and Phenomenological Research* 54 (March 1994): 197–201. For Taylor's critique of naturalism's "reductive ontology," see *S*, 337, 495.

62. Rorty, "Taylor on Self-Celebration and Gratitude," in "Symposium," 200.

63. Taylor, "Reply to Commentators," in "Symposium," 212.

64. Rorty, "Taylor on Self-Celebration and Gratitude," in "Symposium," 200.

65. *S*, 455.

66. "The Immanent Counter-Enlightenment." Paper presented at Castelgandolfo Colloquium VII, August 1996, 7–12. Taylor mentions here various thinkers who fall into this category: Sartre, Camus, Derrida, Mallarmé, as well as Heidegger, at least as manifested in his early analysis of "*Sein-zum-Tode*."

67. Taylor, "Immanent Counter-Enlightenment," 12, 15.

68. Ibid., 14.

69. *S*, 519–21.

Part Three

Instilling
Ethics Today

Chapter Ten

Are We Living in an Ethical Age?

Louis A. Ruprecht Jr.

As a sort of preliminary to my own tentative remarks, I want to comment on the larger structure of this book and thus to hang my own remarks on this structural framework that it so helpfully provides. In the first segment of our collective thinking, we address the question of the sources for contemporary moral reflection. I notice a priority given to political and social thought, which seems easy enough to understand.[1] "Ethics," after all, is what we do whenever we try to organize ourselves in groups, and to help those groups cohere. *Ta erôtika* is a Greek term denoting the relation (namely, the erotic relation) that two, and only two, persons can have together. Eros makes only a semblance of sense in groups. *Ta êthika*, by contrast, involves how humans relate in groups of three or more. The two ideas were related in ancient Greek moral speculation.[2] And numbers, of course, were signally important to a great deal of early Greek thinking—not only among the Pythagoreans.[3] In the pithy, oft-quoted words of Paul Ramsey, "Justice is what . . . love does when confronted by two or more neighbors."[4] Ethics then, as this aphorism makes clear, finds itself always in the challenging presence of more than one neighbor.

I notice an interesting constellation of thinkers who count as sources for this volume—Greeks (Aristotle), Romans (Cicero), and modern Europeans (Jean-Jacques Rousseau and Immanuel Kant). I also notice the absence of Plato until later—more on that lacuna shortly. Now, these moral "sources" tell a well-known tale, a tale Europeans began telling in the nineteenth century, I suspect: the story of the "ancients and the moderns," with the "medievals" standing in some uncertain, and largely disarticulated, relation between the two. In all likelihood, the name "postmodern" is intended to broadcast the fact that *some* contemporary thinkers can no longer recognize themselves in this story—as ancient, or as medieval, or as modern. They no longer wish to narrate their moral reflection in that way. Finding other, alternative narrations seems to be one of the premier challenges before us on the contemporary intellectual scene, evident nowhere more clearly, perhaps, than in the newfound prominence of "ethics" in the curriculum and in the culture.

And so we move to the much more devilish challenge of discarding foundations. Here our primary attention needs to be directed to Friedrich Nietzsche, and so he appears as a prominent voice, if not the most prominent voice, still, in contemporary moral debate (however interesting, and even anticipatory, Niccolò Machiavelli may prove to be). Nietzsche, of course, presents us with a profound intellectual challenge—to uncover, as honestly as we may, what he calls the *pudenda origo*, or the "dirty origins,"[5] of every moral ideal, and so to aspire to a moral language, and a moral standpoint, somehow "beyond [the traditional language of] good and evil." I will return to that idea as well.

These two ideas then, taken together, may help to inform the nature of moral debate today. We have, so we think, a *tradition* of moral enquiry—a narrative taking us all the way "from the ancients to the moderns"—and that is precisely the tradition, and the story, we are calling into question. In the 1950s, when Superman spoke in defense of "truth, justice, and the American way," everyone cheered; when Christopher Reeve said these same words on film some thirty years later, audiences either chuckled nervously or sat in stony silence.

If we do not want to think about ethics in the old ways, then what *new* ways present themselves? With this question before us, we turn to the vast topic of ethics and expression today. I will say less about this topic, largely because it is so well examined in this book. I wish simply to mark two things implicit in the earlier and later examinations. First and foremost, it is interesting that a great deal of ethical attention has been devoted to the arts, especially to the grand, even monumental, metaphor of architecture. It is not only a system builder, such as Hegel, who is an architect. Presumably we all are, speaking morally. To use another memorable Nietzschean metaphor, we must learn "to philosophize with a hammer"—not in order to bludgeon and destroy, but rather to sound out idols, as if with a tuning fork. Nietzsche himself pointed importantly toward making explicit connections between aesthetic and ethical theory, as had Kant before him. Of more immediate concern to my present purposes, though, it seems to me to have been the comparative "thinness" of contemporary attempts to find new philosophical (rather than artistic) ways of talking about "ethics" that really forces the question I address here: Are we living in an ethical age?

A COMIC VIEW OF THE MATTER

Now, how in the world am I to address such a vast question? I want to tackle two related aspects of it. First and foremost: what do we mean by this pesky word "ethical"? And second, what do we think is so special about our own "age"? To address these enormous topics, I want to lay claim to two additional "sources" that can—if properly and carefully used—help to illuminate some of the territory before us. One of these resources is *comedy*[6]—which was a powerful tool for political and social critique in sunny old Athens—and the other is *irony*[7]—which was one of the things that probably got Nietzsche ignored in his own day and almost certainly got Socrates killed, so I will try to be especially careful with that one.

To comedy, then. Fans of the original *Saturday Night Live* crew may well remember the following scene in the 1980 film *Caddyshack*. We are seated in the office of Judge Smales (Ted Knight) in the Bushwood Country Club, where we find him dressing down an upstart young caddy named Danny (Michael O'Keefe), who has recently been caught, in flagrante delicto, with Smales's young niece, who is visiting for the summer.

As it turns out, Smales is not out to scold; he is out to keep things quiet. He wants to maintain the appearance, the semblance, of moral order—regardless of the reality in which he lives. What he really wants is to keep the caddy quiet. Smales has a handsome bribe—in the guise of a college scholarship—to offer in return. But none of this is spoken, at least not at the outset. Instead, what *is* discussed, however wildly and improbably, is *ethics*.

> *Smales:* You know, despite what happened yesterday, I . . . I'm still convinced you have many fine qualities. I think you can still become a gentleman someday, if you understand and abide by the rules of decent society. Danny, Danny, there's a lot of, uh, well, *badness* in the world today. I see it in court every day. I've sentenced boys younger than you to the gas chamber. Didn't want to do it; felt I *owed* it to them. The most important decision you can make right now is what do you stand for, Danny: goodness or badness?
> *Danny:* I know I've made some mistakes in the past; I'm willing to make up for that. . . . I wanna be *good*.
> *Smales:* Good. Good. *Very* good. [laughs]

The conversation continues interminably, and concludes:

> *Smales:* You know, I . . . I know how hard it is for young people today, and I want to help. Well, just ask my grandson, Spaulding; he and I are regular pals. . . . Are you my pal, Mr. Scholarship Winner? [They shake hands]
> *Danny:* Yes, sir, I'm your pal.
> *Smales:* How about a Fresca? [Smales tussles Danny's hair]

This is reminiscent of that excruciating scene from another film, *Catch 22,* where the soldier who wishes to escape from the irrationality of the war may leave any time he wishes to do so—*so long as he likes his colleagues first*. Danny is offered what he believes he wants—scholarship money and the status that may come with it—but he, too, must like his colleague first, must, in fact, become Smales's "pal." It is this transaction that Nietzsche decries, the selling of one's soul for a mess of moral pottage. "Goodness" and "badness" are offered to the ambitious young caddy like pieces of money and a death sentence. Guess which one he picks? Well, unsurprisingly, he picks "the good," despite the fact that no one has defined the term. Apparently, no one needs to.

And this is precisely what Nietzsche worried about in his own ironic way. Scratch beneath the surface of every moral ideal, he argued, and you will find this same subtle suasion, moral language itself serving as a veiled, or not-so-veiled, bribe and threat. The teachers of virtue, Nietzsche quips, use the same tactics as their enemies do.[8] Plato was not above lying; he just called his lies "noble."[9] Such are the "dirty origins" of morality. We are taught to do *this* and not *that*, simply because others have named *this* for us as "good." They have made it what we want.

The young caddy in the film is not a moral agent at all; he is infantilized, infantilized by the very language that is allegedly offered to liberate him, the moral language that is supposed to be "for his own good." What he is finally after, we soon see, is simply money and status—or, in the telling image from the film, "membership in the club." Here again, Nietzsche is ironically premonitory: He, too, knows that the traditional rhetoric of morality too often infantilizes rather than empowers.

What I worry about is the ways in which some of our own self-satisfied language of "ethics" may tend to infantilize our students in some of these same ways. It offers them membership in another club, one as elite and tantalizing, in its own way, as the one lying in plain view of the Bushwood caddyshack.

AN IRONIC VIEW OF THE MATTER

Let me turn from comedy to irony to make this point a little more substantively. The irony is largely directed at myself and my status as an "ethicist." And *self*-irony, I think, is quite possibly the only thing that keeps irony close to its political purpose. *Irony*, in any case, is the rhetorical tool that Plato and Nietzsche share, if they share anything at all. My own larger intellectual purpose, which animates this chapter as well as most of my own work in "ethics," represents an attempt to dramatize what it is that Plato and Nietzsche share, although ultimately I feel even more instructed by Plato than I have been by Nietzsche.[10]

When I first undertook my own doctoral training, in 1986, I was housed in a "Graduate Division of Religion" and had a declared concentration in something called "Ethics and Society." When people asked me what I studied, I could technically say *either* "ethics" or "religion." The disciplines were related, but theoretically separable—just as Nietzsche insisted they were. Nietzsche offers us, in his last creative year (1888),[11] one of the most intriguing diagnoses of modern European "ethical culture" with which I am familiar. It comes from *Twilight of the Idols*, that marvelous summary statement of his mature thought and its own daunting moral trajectory. And it comes from a long chapter bearing the title "*Streifzüge eines Unzeitgemässen*" (perhaps best translated, if a bit too freely, as

"Attacks of an Unmodern Freedom Fighter"), an absolutely masterful sketch of nineteenth-century European culture and Nietzsche's problematic relation to it. He says: *"Sie sind den christlichen Gott los und glauben nun um so mehr die christliche Moral festhalten zu müssen: das ist eine* englische *Folgerichtigkeit."* (They have gotten rid of the Christian God, and so they cling all the more tightly to Christian morality. That's *English* consistency for you.)[12]

We can actually and cogently preside over the death of every classical theological idea we have ever had (and here Darwin, the consummate Englishman, becomes singularly relevant to his purposes[13])—about Providence, about justice and its relation to the natural order, even about the soul's immortality—and still cling to the same moral standards, all the while.

Nietzsche often refers to morality as a *mask*, a mask worn by frightened or disenchanted or resentful persons. But he intensifies this image later in his career. Morality, he suggests then, may be what we *use* to mask the horror of what he calls "the death of God," to hide the prospect of traditional religion's failure from our eyes. On the one hand, if we can talk reasonably about "ethics," then perhaps our beliefs are not in the disarray we fear they may be. Perhaps our foundations *are* still stable and secure. On the other hand (and this is the entire point of Nietzsche's other great book from 1888, *The AntiChristian*: Here is what Jesus said. Here is what the Church did. The two do not fit together very well.

"Goodness," Judge Smales insisted, was what Danny needed to embrace if he wished to succeed in polite society. He never told Danny what this "goodness" involved. Ethics, I was told in graduate school, was similarly a matter of the gravest importance. "We need more of it in this society," I was told. But what in the world did people think "it" was?

AN EIRENIC VIEW OF THE MATTER

Answering that complex question requires a change of venue. It seems to me that if we want to understand the North American preoccupation with "ethics" in the 1990s, we need to attend to what has been happening at our major universities. Most young people go to college in this country now, and they learn, among other things, how to *argue* there. At Emory University, where I learned how to argue, we shared the dawning and widespread public sentiment that "ethics" was something we "needed more of." We oversaw the creation of a new office—we called it "The Ethics Center," but its official title is the somewhat more ponderous "Center for Ethics in Public Policy and the Professions."

Such "Ethics Centers" are popping up all over the place: from Harvard and Princeton to Duke, to Emory and Georgia State and Georgia Tech—all three of them in Atlanta, a city that perhaps "needs more of it"—and now even including the U.S. Naval Academy and all three other national service academies, which have been required to install an "ethics component" in their curriculum, thereby removing the very last elective the midshipmen and cadets had in their entire four-year curriculum. There is an instructive, entirely Nietzschean, parable in that mandate. Ethics will not make you free.

We do not realize nearly often enough how unusual a book such as ours was only a decade ago, when I was first laboring to become an "ethicist," and just how prominent such books now are. That is the larger development in our culture that I am trying to begin to comprehend—the newfound prominence of "the ethical."

Our "Ethics Center" was an office in search of self-definition, but some initiatives were pretty clear early on. Above all, the Ethics Center was responsible for defining an academic concentration, of sorts, by tracking every course offered anywhere in the college that had an "ethical" component (whatever we thought that meant). You cannot major in ethics at Emory, not yet, but I suspect that one day within the next five years or so you *will* be able to (a committee was formed to explore the possibility last year).

Now, the list of ethics courses we drew up was an instructive one, and I would like to pause here to reflect upon it briefly. As nearly as I can tell, what counted as "ethics" courses at Emory University comprised two distinct groups. On the one hand, we teach "ethics" classes that present a series of "hard cases," exploring the issues of gay sexuality, abortion, the death penalty, nuclear disarmament—and, more recently, the urgent moral questions raised by physician-assisted suicide and human cloning. On the other hand, we teach courses on what we might call the "self-evident," courses in which we discuss things like rape, racism, torture, genocide, and how to combat them. Put very simply, some "ethics" courses are designed to address areas of profound moral uncertainty, whereas others are directed to those issues about which we feel *most* certain. Both kinds of courses earn the name of "ethics."

Here, then, is one tentative observation about my students' four years of college and the so-called "ethical" training we provide them: Our students are being trained with coherent and even admirable intellectual goals, *yet they are designed to be discrepant.* Students are taught to see at least two sides to every moral issue—except for the ones where they do not. Students are taught to "tolerate" things—except the intolerable. Except intolerance. It has been argued that this is the ultimate fate of political liberalism, by the way.[14] And, while I do not agree finally with that diagnosis, it is possible to read certain political and cultural landmarks in this country in precisely this way.

This issue came into singular focus during the Chinese diplomatic visit to the United States in 1996, and was replayed when President Bill Clinton visited China the following year. *We* kept talking about universal "human rights." *They* kept talking about "cultural differences" and "national sovereignty," using Western language to silence the West quite effectively. The only argument left to the administration seemed to be the rather vague idea of "being on the wrong side of history." And that is where the conversation consistently stalled. For my part, I found it all quite unsatisfying *and* disturbing. Such cross-cultural discussion—if discussion it be—begins to look like an intractable moral argument, and no amount of theory *or* classroom conditioning will make it more easily resolvable, unless we arbitrarily decide to silence one side or another. This is all rather uncomfortable news for those of us who, according to Nietzsche, cling all the more tightly to a morality when we know that it can no longer be firmly grounded. And so I ask my original question again, but with a new twist. Not "What is ethics?" this time, but rather, "Why am I being *congratulated* for teaching it?" It seems to be more trouble than it is worth.

A PLATONIC VIEW OF THE MATTER

Now I would like to suggest a somewhat different approach to the purposes of an "ethics" classroom, one closer, I think, to the *Greek* notion of what "ethics" entails.[15] Let me first reiterate the main point, which I have been rather long in making. In the past several years, "ethics"—very much like "goodness" itself—has become a hot topic. And I have suggested one working hypothesis to help explain this dramatic development.

The diagnosis, be sure to recall, is Nietzsche's. We cling all the more tightly to the language of "ethics" at precisely the moment when we suspect that this language cannot be fully grounded. We claim most loudly that we are a "Christian nation" in the very moment when we most clearly are not so, culturally speaking, anymore. We do away with God, Nietzsche quips, and then cling all the more tightly to that same God's morality.

That may or may not be "English consistency," but it is pretty clearly a response to an apocalyptic perception—the perception that things are falling apart and that our moral center cannot hold. New beasts, blond or otherwise, forever slink toward Bethlehem to be born. Note that the operative assumptions behind Nietzsche's analysis are twofold. The first is that things have come apart—and we do not want to face up to the fact. But Nietzsche also assumes later in his career that once things did hold together—in what he repeatedly calls "the tragic age" of the Greeks. I am deeply suspicious of that second claim.[16]

So, I return to the storied Socratic question: What is it? What is ethics? My hypothesis goes something like this: Every society, like every language, has its buzzwords. Buzzwords do not *need* to be grounded. Once they are invoked, the moral argument has for all intents and purposes been made. Speak of "rights," or of "democracy," or of "the separation of church and state," at least in North America, and the argument pretty well *has* been made. "Good" and "evil," as Nietzsche insisted with his astonishing clarity (and brutal honesty), are two particularly salient examples of such buzzwords, especially, he went on to argue, in the post-Enlightenment *modern* world. Many others would, I think, agree to that diagnosis—if not to Nietzsche's rather jarring proposals for a cure. His cure, we recall, sometimes seems to be simply the "discarding of foundations" altogether.

My work begins with the hunch—and it is really only a hunch—that one of the essential buzzwords in this culture is "religion." "Tolerance" and "multicultural" are two others, and I think that "modern" has recently become one, too. Now I wish to add "ethics" to this august list. It is not that these words mean nothing but rather that they are *supersaturated* with meaning. They do not mean too *little*; we almost ask them to mean too *much*. At the end of the day, "ethics" somehow has been conceived as being in the business of perplexity—even when we know it is not or else wish it not to be. The distinctively modern retrieval of "the ethical" is part of a much larger modern fixation upon the apparent groundlessness of moral appeals and the enduring problem of securing universalizable moral judgments. We worry about this at the United Nations and in the World Court, and we worry about it in the increasingly *multi*cultural college classroom.

I would like to suggest that the tradition of Greek moral thinking was far more concerned with the inescapable phenomenon of *moral failure* than it was with establishing *moral certainty*. Greek-speakers in this period were far more comfortable than we seem to be with the idea of *moral intuition* as a necessary first step in a moral argument, with the idea that we know what we should do far more often than we do not. "Hard cases," as the constitutional lawyers so often remind us, "make bad law."

The Greeks did not deny the existence of moral perplexity; they simply were not obsessed with it. Nor were they obsessed with finding universal consensus. *We*, the modern ones, seem to be obsessed with it—as Nietzsche himself was. He remained far more "modern" than he believed himself to be, in my judgment.[17]

Let me use an example from my own classroom. I recently asked my students to tell me what they thought the notorious Socratic maxim—"virtue is knowledge"[18]—might mean. Not surprisingly, they began to reflect on the ways in which this claim, if true, would mean that virtue is the same thing for all rational persons. That is to say, virtue is universalizable. That is just the way we are all trained to think about "ethics."

It took a lot of digging (and a lot of pushing, to be honest) to get them to take seriously the idea that Plato's interest was in moral failure, not in moral certainty. The implication, for Socrates, seems to be that, if virtue is a kind of knowledge, then it may—just may—be teachable. Yet even that is the wrong metaphor. Virtue may be *learnable*, not teachable.[19] It does have a cognitive component. But the focus on *teaching* implies that the decisive activity is the *teacher's*, whereas a focus on *learning* admits that the decisive moral activity is the *student's*. No Ethics Center, no book, no teacher can make you virtuous. All we can hope to do is to nurture the process of moral development. Moral development is not the matter of a semester but rather of a lifetime. The premier Platonic metaphor for the moral life is that of a journey, a journey with no clear end in view.

Any approach that denies this infantilizes our students, requiring them to aspire to forms of "goodness" with veiled threats and without telling them why such a thing is worthy of their aspiration. Clearly, this focus—on failure, rather than on certainty—makes a big difference, and not only if you're Bill Bennett. It implies that moral improvement is indeed a possibility, however slight. No one can claim immunity from it because they are just vicious "by nature."

Now this Greek concern with moral failure was an explicitly psychological concern as well. Nietzsche is nowhere more misleading than when he claims to be the first moral philosopher who was also a psychologist.[20] He knows well that Plato saw himself as one, too. After all, it was Plato's realization—not Socrates', I do not think—that we will need to attend to the nature of the human soul[21] if we are to understand how a person with perfectly clear moral intuitions can violate them so dramatically with his or her very next breath. The following statement does seem deeply irrational: "I can't believe that I am about to ———."

"How can we know the good and not do it?" Socrates wonders with bewilderment, in one dialogue after another. Plato's answer was a *psychological* one, an attempt to say what it is about the human soul, and what it is in the nature of human *desire,* that creates this paradox and this precise problem.

I am unconvinced that the question—"Do we live in an ethical age?"—would have made much sense to a fifth-century Athenian. Most likely, the reply would have been something like the following: "Well, we all agree on a number of things that you should and shouldn't do, and we all seem to fail to live up to those standards pretty regularly. That's why we go to court so often. On top of that, there are a number of other things that we *think* we all agree on—what words like 'truth' and 'justice' and 'the Athenian way' mean—but the sophists and philosophers sure seem to have demonstrated that we don't agree about those things at all. So, I guess I really don't know *how* to answer your question. Can you tell me more about what you mean by an 'ethical age'?"

Now, this apparent "dead end" is what Plato called an *aporia.* It is important to add that an *aporia* is not simply the experience of argument, nor of agreeing to disagree. That, in Plato's view, is a rather *un*interesting event, philosophically speaking. An *aporia,* by contrast, is the experience you have when the thing you have always thought, and the language you have always used to communicate it, has proven inadequate, and you do not yet see your way clear to a new way of thinking or of speaking. That experience, the very one Socrates seemed so expert at inducing with his questions, is philosophically fertile and can prove to be quite interesting.

We have been led to confront the inadequacy of one of our buzzwords, it seems to me—"ethics" itself—and we do not clearly see yet how to enrich the meaning of the term. Perhaps the great challenge before our Ethics Centers today is to refuse to take Judge Smales's easy way out, to refuse to retreat into vacuous generalities and vague appeals to "goodness," and to refuse, even more emphatically, to infantilize our students in the process.

The Greeks did not *interrogate* "the ethical" theoretically so much as they attempted to *display* it. A great many self-styled "postmodernists" (Emmanuel Levinas is perhaps the most popular contemporary example) speak in some of these same ways.[22] Put in a more philosophical idiom, they saw practices as embodying forms of knowledge and were so bold as to claim that "theory" was itself a special form of practice. This is one reason a whole range of ancient Greek moral philosophers have a way of seeming stunningly full of life to us, largely because they talked in some of these intriguing and instructive other ways. Very much as Nietzsche, in his better moments, admitted that they did.

NOTES

I believe that the most important moral gesture for me to make initially is the public expression of thanks to the organizers of the two-day Olmsted Symposium on "Instilling Ethics," which was held at Yale University February 27–28, 1998. That conference proved to be a rich and varied (and, now, quite moveable) intellectual feast. I am honored to have been considered worthy of participation in such an event, and I owe a special debt of gratitude to Professor Norma Thompson for extending the initial invitation to me.

1. Bringing modern political theory into dialogue with the classical and Hellenistic tradition has become a major preoccupation, certainly since the enormously influential work of Leo Strauss in North American social theory.

See, for example, J. Peter Euben, *Corrupting the Youth: Political Education, Democratic Culture, and Political Theory* (Princeton: Princeton University Press, 1997), and J. Peter Euben, *Greek Tragedy and Political Theory* (Berkeley: University of California Press, 1991).

For an intriguing use of Herodotus to a similar purpose, see Norma Thompson, "Public or Private? An Artemisian Answer," *Arion*, 3rd ser., 7.2 (1999): 49–63.

2. I have devoted a short book to this constellation of ideas by focusing on Plato's erotic language in the Middle Period Dialogues. See my *Symposia: Plato, the Erotic, and Moral Value* (Albany: State University of New York Press, 1999).

3. See Kenneth Sylvan Guthrie, ed., *The Pythagorean Sourcebook and Library: An Anthology of Ancient Writings Which Relate to Pythagoras and Pythagorean Philosophy* (Grand Rapids, Mich.: Phanes Press, 1987).

4. Paul Ramsey, *Basic Christian Ethics* (Chicago: University of Chicago Press, 1950), 243, also see 42–45. Ramsey makes the claim specific to Christian love, but I believe, unlike Ramsey, that the Christian notion is derivative from the Platonic one (*contra* Ramsey's claim at 106–7).

5. Friedrich Nietzsche, *Daybreak*, 42. In every case, I have consulted Massimo Montinari and Giorgio Colli's *Friedrich Nietzsche: Sämtliche Werke, Kritische Studienausgabe in 15 Bänden* (Berlin: de Gruyter, 1967-1977), III, 49–50 (hereafter referred to as *KSA*).

6. J. Peter Euben has also made an eloquent case for recovering comedy as a significant source of political reflection, ancient or modern. See his "When There Are Grey Skies: Aristophanes' *Clouds* and the Political Education of Democratic Citizens," *South Atlantic Quarterly* 95. 4 (1996): 881–918.

7. The most eloquent contemporary spokesperson for the virtues of political irony was Gregory Vlastos. See his *Socrates: Ironist and Moral Philosopher* (Cambridge: Cambridge University Press, 1991).

More recently, Alexander Nehemas (Vlastos' student) has extended these same ideas to the Platonic corpus in *The Art of Living: Socratic Reflections from Plato to Foucalt* (Berkeley: University of California Press, 1998), and *Virtues of Authenticity: Essays on Plato and Socrates* (Princeton: Princeton University Press, 1999).

8. Friedrich Nietzsche, *Will to Power*, 304–29; *KSA* XII, 264, 273–83, 376, 415–16, 421–22, 426, 437–39, 472, 476–77, 504–5, 511–12, 515–19; XIII, 169, 289, 491–92.

9. The charter text is, of course, *Republic* 389 b–c.

10. I lay this methodological point out in my *Symposia: Plato, the Erotic, and Moral Value*, 1–20, and I will summarize here in shorter form what I discuss at greater length there.

11. For a lovely sketch of that last year, see Lesley Chamberlain, *Nietzsche in Turin: An Intimate Biography* (New York: Picador USA, 1996).

12. Friedrich Nietzsche, *Twilight of the Idols*, "Attacks of an Untimely Warrior," 5; *KSA* VI, 113–14.

13. See Nietzsche's telling critique entitled "Anti-Darwin," in *Twilight of the Idols*, "Attacks of an Unmodern Freedom Fighter," 14, *KSA* VI, 120–21.

14. The charter text for this indictment of liberalism is Alasdair MacIntyre's *After Virtue*, 2nd ed. (Notre Dame: University of Notre Dame Press, 1984). For a critical assessment of that critique, see my *Afterwords: Hellenism, Modernism and the Myth of Decadence* (Albany: State University of New York Press, 1996), 91–123.

15. I develop this point in greater detail in the preface to my *Symposia: Plato, the Erotic, and Moral Value*.

16. I develop this argument in some detail in my *Afterwords*, 23–63.

17. Nietzsche, *Ecce Homo*, "Why I Am So Clever," 4; *KSA* VI, 286–87.

18. *Meno* 70c, 87c.

19. I owe this important distinction to Joseph Cropsey, *Plato's World: Man's Place in the Cosmos* (Chicago: University of Chicago Press, 1995), 151–53.

20. Nietzsche, *Ecce Homo*, "Why I Am a Destiny," 6; *KSA* VI, 370–71.

21. *Phaedrus* 246a–57a, as well as the appendix to my *Symposia: Plato, the Erotic, and Moral Value*, 127–40.

22. For more on these developments, see my "So You Do Theory, Do You?" in *Philosophy Today* 42.4 (1998): 439–47.

Chapter Eleven

Ethics Reform: A Study in Failure

Glenn Harlan Reynolds

In 1969, Yale held a conference on the subject "What is happening to morality today?" Yale law professor Alexander Bickel's answer was: it threatens to engulf us. According to Bickel, the legal order had heaved and groaned for years under a prodigality of moral causes and, if not broken, it is badly bent. Bickel prescribed a cooling-down of moral ardor, and an increased attention to technical aspects of law and procedure.[1]

We have followed Bickel's advice with a vengeance. The results suggest that Bickel—and the rest of us—would have done well to heed the cautionary observation of Bickel's colleague, Grant Gilmore: "In Heaven, there will be no law, and the lion will lie down with the lamb. . . . In Hell there will be nothing *but*, law and due process will be meticulously observed."[2]

As I study the newspaper headlines, it seems to me that, in following Bickel's prescription we have come much closer to Gilmore's idea of Hell than to Bickel's or Gilmore's version of Heaven. Louis Ruprecht talks about learning from failure. The post-Watergate ethics explosion should teach us a great deal.

There can be no doubt that we *have* followed Bickel's advice. After Richard Nixon and Watergate, conventional morality, already in fairly bad repute, was seen as ineffectual: it had failed to restrain Nixon, after all, and steadily mounting revelations about misconduct by the CIA, FBI, and other governmental agencies—as well as the deceptions involved in the Vietnam War—suggested that it was not restraining anyone else much either. It was time for a new approach, a legal and procedural war on immorality in government and the distrust it engendered. The changes brought on by this war are known in political ethics circles as "the Big Bang," for afterward everything was different.

The centerpiece of the federal war against public distrust was the Ethics in Government Act of 1978. The law established the Office of Government Ethics, created a special prosecutor's office (today's Office of Independent Counsel), imposed financial disclosure obligations on high-level executive branch officials, and instituted a variety of related reforms. The Ethics Act was accompanied by legislation broadening the public's right to information under the Freedom of Information Act; federal privacy legislation; a law providing public financing for presidential elections; a statute requiring presidents to notify Congress of covert actions by the United States; the Foreign Corrupt Practices Act of 1977; the Civil Service Reform Act of 1978, granting official protection for whistle-blowers; and the Inspector General Act, which created a dozen new inspectors general, who were required to make independent reports to Congress.

A score of states adopted ethics reform measures similar to the Ethics in Government Act. State ethics agencies, boards, and commissions sprang up. Stung by the highly publicized fact that many of the Watergate principals were lawyers (including President Nixon, Attorneys General John Mitchell and Richard Kleindienst, White House Special Counselor Chuck Colson, White House Counselor John Dean, White House Counselor John Ehrlichman, Gordon Liddy of the Committee to Re-Elect the President, acting FBI Director Patrick Gray, "Plumber" Egil [Bud] Krogh, CREEP Deputy Director Robert Mardian, and Nixon's personal lawyer, Herbert Kalmbach), the American Bar Association for the first time required accredited law schools to teach at least one ethics course. The ABA also recognized legal ethics as a practice specialty, transmitted the names of attorneys involved in Watergate to state bar groups, and began drafting new model ethics rules. Commercial arbitrators, prosecutors, legal assistants, and even law libraries adopted ethics codes.

Other professions reacted similarly. Within months of Nixon's resignation, the Board of the American Society of Newspaper Editors replaced its 50-year-old Canons of Journalism with "A Statement of Principles" intended to preserve, protect, and strengthen the bond of trust between American journalists and the American people. The American Medical Association's Judicial Council recommended that the AMA's ethics code likewise be revised. Centers for legal ethics, business ethics, government ethics, and medical ethics were born. The Big Bang, in short, led to the largest and most pervasive government and professional ethics reform effort undertaken in American history and to the creation of the modern Ethics Establishment.

America's approach to Vietnam was distinguished by both the massive use of firepower and the self-imposed constraints of limited war. On the one hand, the United States dropped on North Vietnam triple the bomb tonnage released on Europe, Asia, and Africa during World War II.[3] On the other hand, it refrained for years from pursuing North Vietnamese soldiers when they retreated to their Cambodian sanctuaries.

America's response to the domestic credibility crisis has borne similar markings and, unfortunately, similar results. We have bombarded major breaches of trust as well as slight improprieties with some of the largest weapons in our arsenal: federal, state, and local government ethics bureaucracies; increasingly complex and pervasive professional society regulations; specially retained independent criminal investigators and prosecutors; ever-expanding federal criminal-ethics laws; elaborate, often sensational, legislative oversight hearings; and relentless and intensive media scrutiny. At the same time, we curiously have refused to attack certain persistent problems at their source.

The result has been a sharp and indisputable drop in public trust from the disturbingly low points of Vietnam and Watergate. This failure may not be as dramatic as television footage of American helicopters pulling away from the rooftop of the U.S. embassy in Saigon while the North Vietnamese made final preparations to enter the city, or of President Nixon's helicopter banking away from the White House lawn one last time after Nixon had flashed his signature "V for victory." But the defeat is just as real. And given our talents and resources as a nation, it is in certain ways just as troubling.

Time was, people understood what would be criminally wrong about a defendant's alleged misconduct in a high-profile prosecution. This is no longer so. From Iran-Contra to Whitewater, people have been left confused, not enlightened. Too often cases lack coherence. And any positive message that might be communicated is frequently drowned out by charges that the prosecution does not represent the rule of law but mere politics disguised as law. ("Don't your mommy and daddy know I'm a convicted felon?" one subject of a recent corruption case asked a friendly high school student. The not atypical reply: "My folks don't care. They said it's just politics."[4])

One might have thought that the increased civil regulation of ethics (and greater attention to the ethics of public officials) would have made it less necessary to use *criminal* laws to enforce *ethical* behavior. In fact, the opposite has proved true. The increase in federal prosecutions for breaches of ethical standards after the Big Bang lives up to the name: the Big Bang is commonly described as an explosion, followed by a period of inflation—exactly the phenomena we have seen in the definition of conduct prosecutable as a federal crime.[5] In the original Big Bang, the temperature of the universe declined as its size increased. In the same way, the moral heat associated with ethical violations has cooled as the volume of behavior encompassed by the ethical universe has grown. The term *inflation*, of course, is more commonly used to describe the devaluing of a currency even as its supply is increased. But whichever metaphor one chooses, it is clear that by so expanding the universe of federal crimes, we have dissipated one of our most precious resources for moral instruction.

At the same time, perhaps trying to get more educational bang for our diminishing bucks, we have increasingly used the criminal law for symbolic gestures (making flag burning a crime or enacting a mandatory death sentence for killing a federal poultry inspector). These pronouncements are calculated to give the appearance of toughness on crime. But what they have done is further devalue the criminal law's moral currency, as well as divert us from seeking hard solutions to difficult social problems. Moreover, as we have become more accustomed to approaching problems from the standpoint of how they *appear*, we've tended to develop appearance-oriented solutions, like the War on Drugs, which eschew cost-effective and achievable goals in favor of imagery and special effects.

SETTING THE STAGE

Public-corruption prosecutions exploded soon after Watergate, when newly installed President Gerald Ford directed federal prosecutors to target political corruption at the state and local levels[6] and the Justice Department established its Public Integrity Section. Jimmy Carter nonetheless attacked Ford during the 1976 presidential debates for not adequately addressing white-collar crime.[7] Once elected, President Carter intensified the federal effort to prosecute government officials.

In 1970, before Watergate, federal prosecutors indicted forty-five federal, state, and local officials. By 1980, when President Carter left office, this annual figure had increased about tenfold (to 442); by 1990, it had increased more than twentyfold (to 968).[8] The concentrated federal digging into official misconduct initially uncovered activities (such as bribery and extortion) that were rich in criminality. It became increasingly difficult over time, however, to extract pure criminal ore from the mine. The prosecutorial machinery nonetheless continued to drill, justifying the cost of deeper exploration with more exotic criminal theories for assaying various samples of unethical behavior.

We began expending our criminal resources in this profligate way just as social research was underscoring the need for frugality. People obey the criminal law less from fear of sanction than because of its moral legitimacy.[9] Since the power to stigmatize and concentrate public blame is a scarce resource, Columbia University law professor John Coffee and others have argued that the criminal law must use that power sparingly if it is to perform its socializing role as a system for moral education. Unfortunately, the more complicated and detailed our civil regulation of ethics has become, the more we have delegitimized civil ethics rules and diluted their educational benefits, and the more we have felt we needed the criminal law to teach right from wrong. The criminal law, we learned in Watergate, can be a powerful moral stimulant. But, like true stimulants, its effects have been diminishing with overuse.

As columnist Maureen Dowd writes in the *New York Times,* public hostility to the government has reached levels that would have shocked most Americans at the height of Vietnam and Watergate. One spontaneous display of feeling came at previews of the movie *Independence Day,* in which: "The White House is shown quietly at night when suddenly it explodes into a big orange fireball. It is detonated by space aliens, not Republicans. In movie houses everywhere, audiences wildly cheer the preview when they see the White House vaporized."[10] Dowd is not unsympathetic. She goes on to say: "It figures. This city has not only alienated aliens, but earthlings, too. It is said that people get the governments they deserve, but can we possibly be bad enough to deserve this one? . . . It's exhausting listening to all their convoluted excuses and backtracking and lawyerly rationales and demands for executive privilege."[11]

Nor are such sentiments limited to spontaneous demonstrations. Poll after poll demonstrates that they are widespread and deeply felt. In 1964, Americans trusted the government to do the right thing 76 percent of the time. By 1995, they trusted the government to do the right thing 25 percent of the time.[12] When asked, "Do you think elected leaders in Washington are really interested in solving the nation's biggest problems, or do you think that they are just interested in *appearing* to solve them," 65 percent answered "Only want to appear to solve them."[13] In the same poll, 54 percent said that they thought the "overall level of ethics and honesty in politics" had fallen over the previous ten years; only 12 percent thought it had risen.[14]

Indeed, the problem has gone beyond simple withdrawal and disaffection, with a surprisingly large number of Americans—some number it in the hundreds of thousands—openly arming themselves against the possibility of outright revolution and entertaining all sorts of farfetched conspiracy theories about the plans of government officials to deprive them of their constitutional rights.[15] Nor can these Americans be entirely dismissed: a recent *Los Angeles Times* poll showed 16 percent of all Americans described themselves as "sympathetic" to such views, with 3 percent describing themselves as "very sympathetic."[16] Obviously, trust in government has not grown. While there has always been what Richard Hofstadter called a "paranoid style" in American politics,[17] there is no question but that it has reached a new high.

How can this be? After all, many argue that American government has never been cleaner, and in a sense this is true. Campaign finance, formerly the domain (literally) of briefcases full of cash, is now heavily regulated, with Federal Election Commission filings for presidential candidates running in the tens of thousands of pages. Many unethical practices have been criminalized. And a vast array of laws bar not only the substance but also the appearance of impropriety. If asked, the political reformers of twenty or thirty years ago would undoubtedly have predicted (in fact, they *did* predict) that such a situation would produce widespread confidence in government, not its reverse.

THE ETHICS ESTABLISHMENT

One of the most important results of the Big Bang was the creation of an Ethics Establishment: a complex of interlocking organizations and institutions revolving around questions of political ethics and scandal. One reason for the public's decline in confidence in government officials *and* their ethical watchdogs may be that the Ethics Establishment—designed to police conflicts of interest in others—

possessed a number of serious and unacknowledged conflicts of interest itself. Though unacknowledged, these conflicts were not unapparent, and the public eventually caught on.

The Press

Robert Redford now reports that he feels guilty about his role in the Watergate movie *All the President's Men*. The reason, he says, is that the movie inspired an entire generation of journalists to aspire to bring down a president. Redford may be giving himself too much credit, but there is something to what he says. The fact is that the press, the most visible component of the Ethics Establishment, has a lot to gain from keeping the fires of scandal burning. In a recent example, television punditry was a depressed market until the Monica Lewinsky scandal broke. Suddenly, people were watching talking-head shows. To benefit from governmental wrongdoing while appearing to censure it is hypocrisy, and the public has noticed. Similarly, to denounce cover-ups and obstruction of justice while protecting the identities of those who leak confidential information is, to say the least, inconsistent. Trust in the press has suffered accordingly. How things came to such a pass is a classic example of pride coming before a fall.

From small towns to college campuses to Washington itself, once investigative journalism became the path to fame (and occasionally fortune), journalists began looking for scandals to uncover to a degree never dreamed of by the "muckrakers" of decades gone by. The post-Watergate ethics reforms made their jobs much easier. Though Robert Woodward and Carl Bernstein were "outsiders" to the mainstream Washington journalistic establishment, their reporting had been hard-fought traditional journalism. The facts that they documented involved slush funds, illegal break-ins, abuse of intelligence agency resources, and more. Even in Tennessee Governor Ray Blanton's case (dramatized in its own movie, *Marie,* which gave Fred Thompson's acting career its start), the crimes involved were traditional, involving bribes for liquor licenses and criminal pardons, and so were the methods of discovering and reporting them. Such journalism was hard work.

But thanks to the rise of post-Watergate appearance ethics, the work of journalists became much easier. Suddenly the "appearance" of impropriety, or of a conflict of interest, was enough. Such appearances were far easier to uncover than the sort of things involved in Watergate, making the path to journalistic success easier.

Of course, such ease came at a price. When the Watergate story broke, it was something unparalleled in American history: rampant and serious abuse of power, meticulously documented by the press, and unconvincingly denied by the administration. Later scandals, based on appearances, had less resonance. In part, of course, that was because few could equal the importance of Watergate. But it was also because the scandal currency had been debased. With appearance ethics making scandals easy to create, more were created. Although the supply of scandal increased, demand, by all appearances, did not. Such matters were grist for hearings and investigations, but not, it seems, for moral outrage.

The Independent Counsel

The Independent Counsel is supposed to be a solution to conflicts of interest. But an Independent Counsel, more than other prosecutors, makes or breaks his or her reputation by bringing the accused to book. Ordinary prosecutors can plead caseload pressures, limited staff and budgets, and so on to explain why they do not prosecute a case. The Independent Counsel has no such excuses. Prosecutorial discretion is viewed as a protection of liberty because it allows prosecutors, in the interest of justice, to decline to prosecute some crimes. The Independent Counsel, however, is in this regard less independent than ordinary prosecutors. Furthermore, the appointment of an Independent Counsel often serves to turn moral or political questions (was it *right* to do X?) into dry, legal questions (was it *legal* to do X?). This often has the effect of letting real wrongdoers off the hook even as those largely blameless are hounded for years over purely technical matters.

The Bureaucrats

Nothing in Washington is real unless there is a bureaucracy dedicated to it, and the ethics world is no exception. But the rules that bureaucrats have come up with often do not match well with most people's sense of justice. This, too, has served to discredit the entire enterprise.

The day-to-day encounters of most federal employees with the ethics laws begin and end with the regulations promulgated by these ethics bureaucrats. For example, a federal employee who was given a free ticket after his flight was delayed five hours while he was on official travel was told that the ticket belonged to the federal government. The employee argued that he was being compensated for the airline's poor performance: the government concluded instead that the ticket was "promotional" because it was intended to "enhance a company's image or customer service" and hence was government property. The employee argued that since the government would have allowed him to keep the ticket if he had gotten it in exchange for giving up his seat voluntarily on an overcrowded flight, he should be allowed to keep a ticket given to him in exchange for suffering a lengthy delay. The government responded that "payment for voluntarily relinquishing a seat, however, is unique in that it advances the government's regulatory policy requiring airlines to encourage volunteers to give up their seats on oversold flights." The government went on to note that "the Federal Travel Regulation explicitly prohibits employees from keeping compensation when an airline involuntarily bumps them from a flight," and that "an involuntary delay is more analogous to an involuntary bump than the excepted circumstances."[18]

Even the government's chief ethics officer couldn't make sense of a 1989 congressional ban on outside income. Office of Government Ethics Director Steven Potts said the law—the "Honoraria Prohibition" of the 1989 Ethics Reform Act—was "not sensible" and undermined respect for legitimate restrictions on federal workers. Peter Crane, a Nuclear Regulatory Commission lawyer, who writes about Romanov-era Russian history in his spare time, also complained about the law's absurdity. For the sake of appearances, Crane explained, the law forbade federal workers from accepting pay for writing articles or giving speeches even on topics unrelated to their work:

> No other form of moonlighting (selling real estate, repairing cars) [is] banned, just writing and speech. . . . It bans articles but not books, nonfiction but not fiction, and individual speeches but not a series of speeches.

The regulations implementing the law read like *1984* updated by Monty Python. In a January 1991 Federal Register notice, the Office of Government Ethics declared that a federal worker can legally accept pay for a "comic monologue"—unless, that is, the government decides that the talk was actually an "amusing speech," in which case the federal worker could be fined $10,000 and drummed out of the government.[19]

The National Treasury Employees Union quickly challenged the provision in court. The federal workers began piling up predictable legal victories on First Amendment grounds, including in the Supreme Court.[20] Many people wondered why Congress ever went down this rocky path to virtually certain court disapproval. Crane had the answer:

> The answer lies in the now largely forgotten history of Congress's attempt to pass a long overdue pay raise in the late 1980s. A first pay increase, hurried through Congress, was scuttled after talk show hosts and Ralph Nader mobilized intense public opposition. At about the same time, questions were raised in the media about House speaker Jim Wright's book deal and about honoraria to senators for token appearances.
>
> Congress's answer was to reenact the pay raise, but this time with an "ethics reform" attached: In return for higher pay, Congress would forswear "honoraria" for speeches and articles. In the name of "uniformity," the ban would apply to the whole federal government. Senior government executives also got a large pay raise.
>
> Uniformity quickly went out the window, however, because senators (historically the recipients of many more honoraria than representatives) voted to reject the pay raise and keep their honoraria. The statute also included an exemption for writing books. Thus the two kinds of abuse that gave rise to the law—a book deal and payments to senators—remained unaffected by the new law. For Congress, it was a perfect solution. House members got a pay raise but could proudly tell their constituents they had renounced their outside earnings. Senators got to keep their outside earnings but could proclaim that they had refused the offer of a pay raise.
>
> On the other hand, the several million federal workers who were not senior executives had their right to outside earnings curtailed but got no raise to make up for it. That meant the mailroom clerk in my agency who supplemented her modest salary

by writing articles about horse shows had her outside income—and with it, a hobby that had given her joy—taken away. But a senior executive whose moonlighting did not include writing articles or giving speeches could continue to earn outside income, on top of the hefty new pay raise.[21]

It is fair to say that this world of regulatory ethics *is* rather complicated, and that the "ethics" label we place on these sorts of reforms is hardly proof of where the public interest—or the moral interest—actually may reside. Indeed, the "public interest" groups in the *National Treasury Employees Union* case were on opposite sides of the issue: Common Cause supported the honoraria ban as "part of a careful and deliberate choice by Congress to guard against conflicts of interest and the appearance of impropriety."[22] Public Citizen and People for the American Way, however, sided with First Amendment groups and the federal employees.[23]

The Interest Groups

The post-Watergate era saw the blossoming of numerous public interest groups that were supposed to create ethical behavior in government. Yet such groups themselves had a problem. Their primary fund-raising system was direct mail, a medium that rewards press attention, exaggerated claims, and personal attacks. They thus had an incentive to create scandals where there were none and to support legislative initiatives that produced many opportunities for photo-ops, congressional testimony, talk-show appearances, and so on. Our post-Watergate ethical regime certainly fits that description. Unfortunately, over time these groups' stances of rectitude became harder and harder to swallow. Feminist groups defended Robert Packwood for a long time despite claims of sexual harassment against him because they valued his pro-choice stance. Clarence Thomas received very different treatment. More recently, feminist groups seem to have placed politics over principle in defending President Clinton from charges of sexual harassment. It soon became obvious that good government groups, in fact, had partisan agendas and that their devotion to those agendas frequently overrode their devotion to good government.

The Hill

Although Congress had traditionally avoided calling attention to executive branch improprieties (much less its own), in the wake of Watergate and the Ethics in Government Act all that changed, for it could not escape notice that many members of Congress had gained enormous stature and influence with both the public and their peers as a result of Watergate. Senator Sam Ervin, previously a little-regarded opponent of desegregation, emerged from the Watergate hearings a hero, perhaps even an icon. Peter Rodino, chair of the House Judiciary Committee, became a household name. Senator Howard Baker (later Senate Minority Leader and White House Chief of Staff) got his start at national prominence with his question "What did the President know and when did he know it?" And many lesser lights, such as New York Congresswoman Elizabeth Holtzman, Texas Representative Barbara Jordan, and Maine's freshman Representative William Cohen, first entered the national stage as a result of Watergate hearings.

While Watergate was hardly the first time that members of Congress used televised hearings to gain national stature (the subversion hearings chaired by Joseph McCarthy and the organized crime hearings chaired by Estes Kefauver of the 1950s were precedents), it was a much more dramatic event. And, coming as it did just before the explosion in appearance ethics, it set in motion a powerful tendency for such hearings to become the norm, rather than the exception, in the conduct of government business. This tendency was exacerbated by two related phenomena. One was the weakening of the traditional party system. Without that system, politicians who wanted to advance had to do so largely through publicity seeking. Another was the rise of "public affairs" journalism: political talking-head shows, newsletters, cable TV networks such as CSPAN and NET, and so on. All of these outlets needed new material on a constant basis and rewarded those who fed them with fame, and often fortune. Add to this (as either a symptom or a cause) a massive expansion of congressional staffs, providing the necessary legwork for more hearings and press conferences, as well as revolving-door career paths between the Hill and the other institutions of the Ethics Establishment, and the stage was set for an explosion of ethics scandals, real or invented. There were plenty of both.

The Consultants

After Watergate, ethics rules were enacted that rivaled the complexity of the Internal Revenue Code. Such technicalities, however, called for expertise to match them, and in very short order there developed an entire industry built around compliance with ethics rules. Like most such things, it featured newsletters, conferences, and, most especially, high-priced consultants.

The consultants offered advice, much of it useful in the narrow sense. Those entering government service were often encountering the complexities of post-Watergate ethics laws for the first time. Since those laws often involved disclosures and forms that most individuals found daunting and difficult to decipher, they naturally turned to professional help, just as so many Americans turn to accountants and tax lawyers at tax time each year. (One Washington lawyer even claims a specialty in "ethics and congressional spouses."[24]) Americans expect taxes to be complicated. They might be forgiven for wondering why matters of right and wrong have to be equally difficult. The instrumental answer, of course, is that failing to treat ethics laws with the same kind of respect as tax laws can produce equally unpleasant results.

Hiring *government* ethics consultants offers another benefit, which accounts for much of their appeal. Many of those consulting on ethics matters have special expertise gained while serving on the staff (or occasionally as members) of House or Senate committees that draft ethics laws or on the staff of special prosecutors or Independent Counsels enforcing them. The hiring such individuals serves not only as a source of advice but also of insurance: because of their experience, these individuals carry weight with their successors in such positions, who cannot help but imagine themselves out there earning high consulting fees later on. What better source of insulation against ethics charges than to be able to say, "I hired a leading expert in the field, a former Watergate special prosecutor, who told me I had no problems"?

Such individuals are often called upon to advise legislators on the drafting of new ethics rules. With their encyclopedic knowledge of the minutiae of existing rules—and the likelihood of future consulting work at least in the back of their minds—the advice offered by these consultants is, not surprisingly, often to make rules that further complicate matters. With luck, the consultants can then testify at congressional hearings on the new rules, further underscoring their expertise.

The Iron Triangle

Indeed, the combination of revolving-door career paths and political favor trading among all of these institutions has created a true "establishment" in the political ethics world. Although the term *Iron Triangle* was coined to describe the relationship between the Pentagon, its contractors, and its allies in Congress,[25] it is just as applicable here. Sometimes also called "issue networks," these loose but powerful assemblages have several key characteristics. One is that they act in their own (shared) interests, not necessarily in the public interest. Another is that they resist reform. A third characteristic is that they are poorly understood by the public. And a fourth is that they are seldom reported on by journalists because journalists are often too involved in the horse trading that goes on to be objective.

All of these characteristics are true of the Ethics Establishment. The relationship between ethics bureaucrats—whether permanent or ad hoc, like Independent Counsels—and Congress and interest groups is marked by constant interaction and trading of favors. Congressional staffers get "dirt" from interest groups who, for example, oppose the confirmation of a particular judge or the implementation of a particular policy. They then leak the information to journalists and hold hearings that generate more news and afford interest groups an opportunity to testify and otherwise get their message out. Journalists investigating the scandals get still more leaks from government officials close to the scandal, often in exchange for not linking those officials to what went wrong or occasionally in exchange for defending those officials in columns or on political talk shows. All of this provides interest groups with opportunities for publicity and direct mail fundraising. And when the scandal is over, often new legislation is introduced in response, adding yet another layer of legal requirements (often quite technical ones) that increase the opportunity for more such events in the future. As John Milton wrote,

"Chaos Umpire sits/And by decision more embroils the fray/By which he Reigns."[26] It is clear that such a regime serves the interests of all the players. What is not clear is that it does anything to promote ethical behavior.

THE RESULTS

None of the foregoing is to say that the individuals involved have, or ever had, evil intent. As appearance rules themselves are supposed to recognize, however, even those with pure intent can have their judgment distorted by conflicts of interest. And the Ethics Establishment itself possesses a huge unacknowledged conflict of interest: the kinds of rules that benefit the Ethics Establishment are not the kinds of rules that promote ethical behavior. With this in mind it should come as no surprise that appearance rules, and the tangle of technical regulations that go with them, have done nothing to curtail scandal.

To the contrary, these rules and regulations—like the new House "gift" rules, which were praised by groups like Common Cause at the time—have simply added more fuel to the fire. Thus, lobbyist Ann Eppard's "gifts" of overnight lodging to Congressman Bud Shuster of Pennsylvania prompted the Government Accountability Project to demand a criminal investigation and Common Cause to seek a House ethics committee investigation, while a bevy of ethics experts publicly debated the fine points of a "hospitality" exception to the House rules. (The short answer: so long as they were having sex, it was okay.[27]) Similarly, a conservative "public interest" group responded to House Minority Whip David Bonior's lodging of about one hundred ethical charges against Speaker Newt Gingrich by demanding a House ethics committee investigation of Bonior's alleged misuse of staff and funds to write his own book. As a result of these sorts of charges and countercharges, the number of ethics complaints filed in the House of Representatives in the past several years has been skyrocketing, far outpacing staff resources.[28]

The post-Watergate approach has failed. Perhaps the real surprise would have been the adoption of elaborate ethical rules and regulations that *did* curtail scandal. Such surprises were not to be had. As a cynic might have predicted, the products of the Ethics Establishment did far more for the welfare of the Ethics Establishment than for the promotion of ethics. By the 1990s, even the Ethics Establishment itself was admitting the problem:

At no time in the history of our country has government ethics been more intensively scrutinized and extensively regulated.

Yet something is wrong. The more zealous the effort to identify and legislate against wrongful conduct, the more elusive the goal of achieving ethical behavior has become. Each reform initiative has added another layer of regulation. The result is a complex and formidable rule structure, whose rationale is increasingly obscure and whose operation is increasingly arcane. Ethics is in danger of becoming an elaborate legalistic ritual, in which the application of multipart tests substitutes for the internalization of values, and the establishment of multilevel clearance processes replaces the development of a supportive institutional culture. For government employees who must negotiate this ritual, the result is frustration and alienation. For citizens who hear all the ethics fanfare but nonetheless see government "as usual," the result is disillusionment and cynicism.[29]

The diagnosis is correct. The Ethics Establishment has produced rules, regulations, and fanfare galore. But the average citizen, while not familiar with the intricacies of the rules, can plainly see that the ethics emperor wears no clothes: government is not appreciably more ethical than it was. Nonetheless, the damage is spreading, as the Ethics Establishment now reaches far beyond the governmental context into a variety of other institutions. Unfortunately, the results have been no better.

WHAT TO DO

The analysis above might seem overkill—the equivalent of a physician coming upon someone who has been hit by a train and spending several days and many thousands of dollars before concluding solemnly that he's dead, Jim. Although the failure of the post-Watergate reforms is virtually beyond dispute, the reasons for the failure have received less attention. Following are a few thoughts on what we can learn from the failures described above.

The first lesson is that *conflicts of interest are not an aberration: they are the norm.* Few of us have only one role in life, and the different roles we fill are almost certain to conflict at times. Presidents are heads of government *and* heads of political organizations. Citizens are members of the polity *and* members of organized interest groups. Bureaucrats are employees of the government *and* turf protectors. Journalists are exposers of secrets *and* protectors of unidentified sources. Any system that ignores this fact—or treats it as inherently wrongful— is doomed to saturation.

Which leads us to the second lesson, which is that *condemnation (moral or legal) is a scarce resource.* All currencies, including the moral and legal varieties, are subject to loss of value through inflation. To conserve that value, we must exercise self-control. If the scandal printing presses run twenty-four hours a day, the value of scandal will soon be reduced to the value of the paper it is printed on, if that.

Which brings us to a third lesson: *we must choose our targets carefully.* Lots of bad conduct inevitably goes unpunished, just as many good works go unrewarded. In a perfect world that would not be so, but we do not live in a perfect world. If there is one single lesson from this rather depressing century, it is that trying to make this world perfect is unlikely to make things better. As (yet another) Yale law professor, Art Leff, noted: "In complex processes . . . a move in the right direction is not necessarily the right move. To pick a simple illustration, if I am on a desert island, subsisting solely on coconuts and oysters and beginning to hate it a lot, and across the bay from me there is another island, lush and fertile, I do not improve my position in life by swimming half way across."[30]

Leff wrote these words in 1974, as the Watergate wave broke; they should have been heeded as the response to Watergate was crafted. Instead of trying to make the world perfect (when he signed the Ethics in Government Act, Jimmy Carter promised that the act would not only make public officials honest, it would keep them honest), we should recognize that in an imperfect world it may take most of our effort just to keep things from getting worse. We must focus in on the kinds of behavior that are truly wrongful and not allow ourselves to be distracted by technical issues or mere potential wrongdoing.

I realize, of course, that the chief flaw in these prescriptions is that they require self-discipline on the part of ethics regulators, public officials, and the polity. The post-Watergate reforms did not. They sought to replace self-discipline with rules: rules to constrain the behavior of officials and rules to ensure that accusations of misbehavior were investigated, even if the investigators had their doubts about the value of such an endeavor. One thing we have learned from failure is that such an approach is, well, doomed to fail. And that is the fourth lesson: *character matters.*

People used to know this. When I was in law school, I had some reason (I have forgotten what it was) to look at some letters of recommendation written many decades ago. One thing that struck me and continues to strike me was how different those letters were from the letters people write today. The old letters invariably spent a lot of time on the character of the person being recommended, with particular attention to the recommendee's honesty. Letters today seldom mention that topic or, if they do, mention it only in a pro forma way. Nowadays they spend much more time talking about how smart the person is.

It's important to be smart, of course, but as Jurgen discovered in James Branch Cabell's novel of the same name, cleverness was not at the top of things and never had been.[31] Our modern society tends to value cleverness above all else. As a result, we tend to elevate people who are, above all else, clever. We should not be surprised if, at the end of the day, we find society being run by people who are rather more clever than they are brave, honest, or loyal. If we want something different, we will have to value something different.

How to go about that is a topic for another chapter, and another day. But here are a few thoughts. First, the signals that we send have a lot to do with the way people behave. If we constantly play up cleverness, while pooh-poohing honesty, integrity, and so on, then many people will come to the conclusion that cleverness is what matters. Second, I believe that ethical behavior is taught by example more than by instruction. Do as I say, not as I do, is a poor formula for instilling values. Such values are not very well instilled these days. Ask yourself: when was the last time you heard of a public figure foregoing some important advantage because doing so would violate his or her moral beliefs? Yet it is by such examples that we teach ethical behavior: to our children, to each other, and ultimately to ourselves.

NOTES

1. Recounted in Alexander Bickel, *The Morality of Consent* (New Haven: Yale University Press, 1975), 199–20.

2. Grant Gilmore, *The Ages of American Law* (New Haven: Yale University Press, 1975), 111.

3. Stanley Karnow, *Vietnam: A History* (New York: Penguin Books, 1988), 415.

4. James B. Stewart, "The Illegal Loan," *New Yorker*, 15 July 1996, 36–37.

5. For example, Kathleen Brickey, "Corporate Criminal Liability: A Primer for Corporate Counsel," *Business Lawyer* 40 (1994): 12; John C. Coffee Jr., "From Tort to Crime: Some Reflections on the Criminalization of Fiduciary Breaches and the Problematic Line Between Law and Ethics," *American Criminal Law Review* 19 (1981): 117, 119–26.

6. Geraldine Szott Moohr, "Mail Fraud and the Intangible Rights Doctrine: Someone to Watch Over Us," *Harvard Journal on Legislation* 31 (1993): 164 n. 40.

7. "The Key Points," *Newsweek*, 4 October 1976, 38.

8. Moohr, "Mail Fraud," 154 n. 6.

9. See, for example, John C. Coffee Jr., "Does Unlawful Mean Criminal? Reflections on the Disappearing Tort/Crime Distinction in American Law," *Boston University Law Review* 71 (1991): 193, 194 n. 3 [citing, for example, Tom R. Tyler, Why People Obey The Law (New Haven: Yale University Press, 1990)]

10. Maureen Dowd, "The Gang That Couldn't File Straight," *Austin-American Statesman*, 14 June 1996, A15.

11. Dowd, "The Gang," A15.

12. *Washington Post*, 28 January 1996, A1.

13. Daniel Balz and Richard Morin, "A Tide of Pessimism and Powerlessness Rises," *Washington Post*, 3 November 1991, A1 (emphasis added).

14. Balz and Morin, "Tide of Pessimism."

15. See, generally, Richard Serrano, "Militias: Ranks Are Swelling," *Los Angeles Times*, 18 April 1996, A1.

16. Serrano, "Militias," A1.

17. Richard Hofstadter, "The Paranoid Style in American Politics" in *"The Paranoid Style of American Politics" and Other Essays* (New York: Alfred A. Knopf, 1965), 3–41.

18. D. Davis, Complimentary Airline Ticket. Official Travel, B-257704, 14 November 1994. Federal employees could read about this edifying decision in *Government Ethics Newsgram*, summer 1995, 7. The same publication also told them about such details as the application of criminal conflict of interest statutes to high school students who work for the government in the summer (a6) and the availability of a special video that follows three SGEs (Special Government Employees) through many of the ethical hurdles they face in the course of their government service (7).

19. Peter Crane, "Let My People Write," *Washington Post*, 8 February 1994, A19.

20. *United States v. National Treasury Employees Union*, 115 S.Ct. 1003 (1995).

21. Crane, "Let My People Write."

22. Brief of Amicus Curiae Common Cause in Support of Petitioners (No. 93-1170) (10 June 1994).

23. Brief of Amicus Curiae of Public Citizen, Inc. in Support of Respondent (29 July 1994); Brief of Amicus Curiae Freedom to Read Foundation, Association of American

Publishers, Inc., People for the American Way, Pen American Center and the National Writers Union in Support of Respondents (28 July 1994).

24. Ruth Marcus and Walter Pimus, "Enid Waldhotz: Savvy Politician or Duped Wife?" *Washington Post*, 26 November 1995, A1.

25. See Gordon Adams, *The Iron Triangle* (New York: Counsel of Economic Priorities, 1981). The term has spread to cover the relationship among special interests, bureaucrats, and congressional overseers in a variety of fields. See, for example, William Kristol, "Term Limitations: Breaking up the Iron Triangle," *Harvard Journal of Law and Public Policy* 16 (1993): 95; Harold McDougall, "Lawyering and the Public Interest in the 1990s," *Fordham Law Review* 60 (1991): 1.

26. John Milton, *Paradise Lost* (London: S. Simons, 1667), book 2, lines 907–9.

27. No, really. The House rules contain an exception for gifts provided on the basis of personal friendship. If Eppard and Shuster were actually sleeping together, they would have had an airtight argument that the gift of overnight lodging was intimately bound up with their personal friendship. For more on this, see Peter W. Morgan and Glenn H. Reynolds, The *Appearance of Impropriety: How the Ethics Wars Have Undermined American Government, Business, and Society* (New York: Free Press, 1997), 31–33.

28. Eliza Newlin Carney, "Uneasy Empires," *National Journal*, 18 May 1996, 20.

29. American Bar Association on Government Standards, C. Farina, reporter. "Keeping Faith: Government Ethics and Government Ethics Regulation," *Administrative Law Review* 45 (1993): 287, 290.

30. Arthur Leff, "Economic Analysis of Law: Some Realism about Nominalism," *Virginia Law Review* 60 (1974): 451, 476.

31. James Branch Cabell, *Jurgen* (Mineola, N.Y.: Dover, 1978), 292. In the novel, Jurgen has just met Koschei the Deathless, who made things as they are. Though immensely powerful (Koschei created God and Heaven to satisfy Jurgen's grandmother), Koschei is not particularly bright. This fact went far toward explaining a host of matters that had long troubled Jurgen.

Chapter Twelve

Architecture as Ethical Conduct

Carroll William Westfall

If architecture were a private art, it might be possible to argue that it stands outside ethics. Ethics in this sense is embodied in activity (*praxis*) of a public nature. It is not a condition or state but an attribute of an individual's character, an attribute that can be judged only when the individual is engaged in actions that affect others within a community, that is, public actions in a city.

Architecture's public nature is indubitable. To practice it requires the engagement in public of a number of people from designers to brick masons, from bankers to government officials, from owners to users, all working together to accomplish a common end. Furthermore, the product of their enterprise will have an effect not only on those who produced it but also on others, both when it is new and as it becomes old.

And architecture is an art, that is, a practice undertaken by a person with the proper gifts who makes choices guided by a knowledge and rational understanding of the rules appropriate to that art. In the traditional understanding of things, architecture is a liberal art, that is, an art of a free person and, therefore, of a person who is accountable for how he practices that art. Its practice therefore has its analogy in *prohairesis*, that is, the "customs and habits that form our characters [and] promote the capacity for thinking and speaking in a distinctively and specifically human way," a practice possible only in a political community.[1] Architecture is the art that produces buildings and other material things both larger and smaller, as large as public forums and cities, as small as furniture and kitchen utensils. Their production requires extensive collaboration among a broad range of skilled people. These people may be divided into three categories. One is the architect, who brings theory and practice together to produce a design and direct the work that produces the building. The second is the patron (now called client), who engages the architect, specifying what he is to do and then paying for it. And the third is the army of workmen who take the direction of the architect and the payment of the patron. Among these, the architect is generally held most responsible for the result of their collaboration. The remarks here will focus on the architect, with the understanding that the others are complicit with him to one extent or another.

Buildings—particularly the large, complex structures associated with the practice of public architecture today but also those prominent in our understanding of the history of architecture—are, quite obviously, important parts of the contingent world. They are material objects illustrating highly complex methods of construction, seemingly built to last for a long period, and intended to serve definite, often quite specific, purposes. The major buildings informing our understanding of architecture are often so enormously complicated that it is difficult to imagine how they might have been other than they are. The contingent and utilitarian seem to define the very substance of building. And we have articulated explanations covering these contingent conditions. We all know that architecture illustrates how form follows function, as Louis Sullivan said. We have learned, following a doctrine formulated by Eugène-Emmanuel Viollet-le-Duc in Europe and translated into American terms most famously by Frank Lloyd Wright, that a building's forms arise naturally from the materials in which it is built. And we have been persuaded by a long line of historians and heroic modernist architects such as Le Corbusier and Ludwig Mies van der Rohe that each epoch demands and receives its own architecture.

These modernist positions and others like them that reached maturity in the 1920s have in common the absolute rejection of tradition as a guide to current practice.[2] Although revolutionary, they have been framed within a tripartite schema articulated two millennia ago by the Augustan architect Vitruvius.[3] Every architect and architecture student knows that a building must satisfy the three criteria of commodity, firmness, and delight. In current thought they are considered separate and isolated criteria. Commodity is satisfied if the building serves the purpose of those immediately responsible for its construction, and that is more likely the patron, that is, the client or owner, than the architect. Only in the most extreme cases of public memorials and such things are the sentiments of the larger, general public given much play. Firmness, or structural stability, is present if the building does not collapse. And delight, or the visual pleasure we receive from a building, is present if the observer discovers that it is; the judgment is that of the observer, and it is valid only for himself, not for others.

This is a fairly recent interpretation of the three criteria. Commodity became linked with functionalism in the wake of the Napoleonic reform of architectural education and in architecture's response to the changed demands the industrial and commercial revolutions made on building. The interpretation of firmness grew out of the architects' absorption of Newtonian mechanics and the concomitant expansion of mathematics as a way to understand change in the material world and thus of the structural properties of materials and building technologies.

Delight has undergone a series of shifts. In the late seventeenth century, in response to René Descartes' natural science and mathematics, Claude Perrault explained that beauty must be thought of as residing in mere custom and personal inclination rather than in the visible presence of universal qualities linked ultimately to other universals such as goodness and truth.[4] Then, following the line first laid down by Giambattista Vico, beauty came to be thought of as particular to certain ages and cultures, an idea replaced by the idea that history itself somehow brought into existence the architecture demanded by any particular age.[5] Meanwhile, beauty was displaced by the sublime, which was soon joined by various brands of Romanticism's historicism. When the Hegelian and Marxian world supporting this architecture failed to deliver on its promises, the resulting vacuum in the aesthetics of delight was filled by a variety of intellectual positions, all of them indebted to a nihilism traceable to Friedrich Nietzsche. In the subsequent anarchy, architecture became generally accepted as a private indulgence or personal expression unbound by rules, unshackled by tradition, and unconnected to public accountability.[6]

The current interpretation of the three criteria is shot through with a kind of soft determinism, that is, with a general acceptance that the architect is somehow bound by contingencies and therefore not really responsible for much of what goes into what he builds. The client determines what commodity must satisfy, and the engineer and the building codes he helped frame handle issues of firmness. This leaves the architect with determining "how the building looks," and according to the current zeitgeist the building's formal qualities are supposed to be the projection of the architect's personal vision, which itself is an extension of his inner impulses or his response to current stylistic imperatives. Either way, the building's appearance resides beyond the reach of public judgment. As the architect sees things, honoring his artistic sensibility stands superior to responding to claims of citizenship or to the aesthetic position of fellow citizens. There is no *prohairesis* here.

This stance is clearly muddleheaded, if not wrong. Indeed, whatever the architect designs must be useful and must be paid for, but an analysis of the purposes and of the budget does not lead inexorably to the building's design. So, too, as he practices his art, the architect is deeply immersed in the contingencies of nature, whose laws are beyond his control, but those laws do not make him an automaton when designing the structural and material qualities of the building. Similarly, formal characteristics peculiar to any particular time and place, the equivalent in architecture to the *endoxa*, or the respected ethical and political beliefs or values of any human community, always mark the work of any person practicing architecture then and there. Each architect does have a unique talent resulting in personal interpretations of that aesthetic *endoxa*. But to say that either of these determines the architect's choices, choices that manifest his *prohairesis*, or his rational reflection as a free person on the connection between things like beauty in general and beauty in this particular thing, is to deprive him of the very status of free person he requires to practice his art.

This soft determinism and the related recent interpretations of the Vitruvian trilogy have shattered the connections architecture has had with other arts and civil activities and disrupted the trilogy's traditional interpretation. But current theory to the contrary notwithstanding, architecture is still the most public among the visual arts, those who practice it are still responsible for what they produce, and the trilogy is still one of the best matrices for understanding the art of architecture. In the balance of this chapter I will use an extended discussion of the three criteria as the basis for understanding the practice of architecture as ethical conduct.[7]

Putting the three criteria in a different order and expanding their reach will provide a framework for understanding the practice of architecture as ethical conduct, as an embodiment of *prohairesis*. Commodity is reformulated to address the building's contribution to the larger, civil, public purposes it serves and only secondarily to account for the immediate functional needs that brought it into being.[8] Commodity therefore moves from first position, a threshold a building must satisfy, to last, the consummation of architecture's contribution to civil society. Here it is renamed the civil aspect of architecture. Firmness remains in the middle but can be renamed the architectonic, a term that refers to the material means by which a building combines its civil ends with the formal demands of the art of architecture. Finally, the formal demands replace delight and move to the front. In this scheme, architecture is an art that begins with formal concerns that can be rendered in material to serve civil purposes. To put it another way: the formal (what we see), the architectonic (how we build), and the civil (why we build) constitute three related aspects of architecture, each with its own demands. The art of the architect resides in finding the proportionate balance and proper coordination and integration of the three within contingent conditions and universal standards appropriate to each of the three.

This formulation opens up the work of the architect to public scrutiny and makes the public his collaborator. In the best of all possible worlds, this scrutiny takes the form of the good-spirited collaboration of expert and amateur, of architect and public. It requires that the architect respect the public and that the public have a basic grounding in the art of architecture. To be successful, the architect must not consider himself part of an avant-garde leading a public of philistines and thinking of his art as a way of reforming public taste. Nor can he be the leading edge of the zeitgeist whose full realization is being delayed by the benighted public whose spirit will be reformed by his designs. Neither can he consider architecture the extension of a technology that only experts can comprehend, or as the best formal solution to distinct, contingent functional problems about which a nonexpert public cannot have an informed opinion.

These positions do not assume a common interest and common knowledge shared by architect and public, but just such a commonality must be present if an interchange between amateur and professional is to flourish. Both need to be immersed in the same formal, architectonic, and civil tradition.

In essaying these terms, we may begin where the art of architecture does, with the forms. The formal asks: What do we see and how are we to judge it? The formal properties of something new and original, the result of a private artistic intuition, something never before seen and therefore unique, cannot be assessed. There simply are no standards available for comparison. For judgment to take place, there must be a commonality.

There must also be the ability to understand that things could be other than they are. Something said to be "determined" by the contingent conditions of the functions it is to serve or of the technology used to build it will not be changed in response to formal criteria; in a world dominated by functional and technological considerations, efficiency replaces civility, while the judgments of the public, which can be based on nothing better than "mere taste," lack the authority to trump the architectonic. Certainly a public that thinks it is inadequately versed in the technical aspects of building will be loath to suggest that things might be other than the way the expert architect or engineer says they must be. But once the public discovers that the functional serves the civil (and not the other way around) and that the architectonic qualities may be modified to reach a certain formal end, its members can work with the architect in getting the three into a proper relationship with one another.

Not that everyone will see things the same way. Different points of view will seek to dominate one or another of the three, and the result will be a proportionality between the points of view wrought through public discussion.

The toughest view to dislodge from a putative primacy will be the one that puts first and foremost the architect's interest in the formal. It makes sense to think that the formal is the be-all and end-all of architecture, because architecture is first of all a sensate, visual art. The current understanding, the one foremost in discussions of the most prominent public buildings, where the role of the architect is taken most seriously, is that there can be no public consensus on what constitutes beautiful form, that beauty is not the issue anyway, and, therefore, that whatever the architect and his peers and supporters are promoting is the very thing the public ought to accept.

The older position held that producing a beautiful building whose beauty is accessible to all is the aim of the formal aspects of the architect's art. Establishing a rapprochement between the new and old positions is hindered by a modernist misreading of how beauty is understood to reside in a building. One example will suffice. It became accepted in the twentieth century among the architects who still thought beauty was an attribute of architecture that it could be invested in a design by using pure geometric forms and harmonic mathematical proportions extracted from "platonic" universals.[9] The "platonic" forms and proportions were thought to be beautiful and apprehensible in themselves, and when they were imposed on something in a building—say, the dimensions of a window or the rhythm of a building's fenestration—the result must necessarily be something beautiful. Furthermore, the universality overrode any local particularities; what was beautiful in Denmark was equally beautiful in Brazil. The belief in a world-pervading "International Style" eclipsed the older recognition that people live in communities, each with its particular *endoxa* within which they practice their *prohairesis*.

This recent belief was promulgated at the expense of the traditional thought about, and practice of, architecture that facilitates, indeed encourages, useful and meaningful links outside the art of architecture. For example, in the traditional understanding, regular geometric forms and harmonic proportions have no existence outside their presence in something; they are always the forms and proportions of something—a column, a door, a window. The term Vitruvius used is *symmetria*. Furthermore, these building components are assembled to produce something larger, which is itself formal and proportionate—a temple, a church, a dwelling. Vitruvius referred to this as *eurythemia*, which he also linked to what we call typology.[10] In addition, the forms and proportions of the parts of buildings and of whole buildings are ways of linking the parts or whole of a building with other things that have identifiable, formative geometric forms and mathematical proportions—the order of the universe and its *phusis,* which architecture and the other arts imitate through *mimesis*—the sounds that give pleasure to the ear; the form and figure of man; the differences between different examples of things of the same class. For example, among the three orders of columns or buildings, the Doric is the virile male, the Ionic the matronly female, the Corinthian the virginal, chaste maiden.[11] Then, too, there are certain ways the components forming a building of a certain type are composed. A church looks like a church, a house like a house, and so on. The type of building it is can be identified, and the distinctiveness of any particular example of that building type can be assessed and understood.

This traditional understanding of architecture made it possible, in the early years of our republic—for example, in the words and works of Thomas Jefferson—for a distinctly American architecture to be invented for civil buildings ranging from capitols to the residences of citizens. These were buildings that did two things at the same time. They proclaimed the continuity between the new nation and the predecessors with which it wanted to be compared. And they made clear the distinctiveness of the new republic formed in response to new ideas, new knowledge, and new, unique contingent circumstances. Jefferson's use of this tradition, one that survives and is in vivid play today in the reviving interest in traditional architecture,[12] illustrates the balance this tradition in architecture struck between the formal and the other two terms. Beyond *symmetria* and *eurythemia* and authoritative over them is the quality of *decor* or the appropriateness of, and subordination of, the formal and the architectonic to the civil ends the building is to serve. This proportionate balance is wrought through the open engagement of expert and amateur, of architect and public, in spirited discussion about the way the physical realm they share and in which they live will be formed.

Fundamental to this way of thinking about the formal properties of architecture is a body of knowledge that can be taught and learned by expert and amateur alike. That knowledge consists of the forms of buildings and their parts. It includes the means used to build them, and it reaches out to the variety of purposes buildings can serve and the variety of buildings that can serve similar purposes. The architect needs to have a broader and deeper command of this body of knowledge than the general citizen does, but what he knows exists in common with what the public knows or can know. The forms he works with originate within that body of knowledge, and his manipulation of those forms is assessed against the backdrop of that tradition. Having that knowledge in common makes possible the discussion between the expert architect and the inexpert public about what is the same and what is different, about what is valuable and what needs changing, in the formal, visible parts of a building.

So much for the formal. The architectonic aspect of building, which refers to the actual material construction of a building, raises other issues. This aspect would seem to lie within the realm of contingencies responsive only to the expertise of the architect. But here too there is a large area for interaction between the architect and the public he serves. The choice of materials and the manner of siting, constructing, servicing, and accessing a building have ecological ramifications. The labor called for in construction raises social questions: What role will organized labor play? What choices will be made about the relative roles of machine technology and handicraft? Are we better served by building something cheap that soon needs replacement or something more expensive that will last longer? These are issues of public policy, which the expertise of the architect and his engineering consultants is inadequate to answer alone. They are also beyond the sole authority of the architect's client and building owner.

The civil aspects of architecture now become dominant. What civil ends is this building to serve, and how is it to serve them? Some examples:

What contribution to the public good is made when a public institution sponsors the construction of a building that is more about current architectural fashion and esoteric theories of interest only to an artistic avant-garde than about the identity, ideals, and intentions of the institution as these are embodied in architectural form, a building whose forms the public, and perhaps even its sponsors, find baffling and perhaps even jarring and ill-suited to its surroundings?

What kind of civil justice is implicit in putting a hotel that requires many low-paid service workers in a location far removed from areas where people earning low wages can afford to live and that requires the heavy initial and operating expenses of an automobile to reach it?

What relationship between citizens of different economic means is implied when dwellings are built without grace or beauty because they are built with a subsidy from the public purse and intended for people of limited means?

What is made manifest by a parking garage in a city's center or on a university campus that degrades what one sees but whose appearance is excused because it does accommodate the requisite number of cars? Such a building makes manifest that those who built it think of it, first of all, as a piece of transportation equipment and secondarily (if at all) as a civic building, a building that could just as well have been designed as a civic building contributing to the grace and beauty of a realm dedicated to promoting the public good but still a building in which one can park cars.

And, finally, what sense of city building and promotion of a common good is implied when residential areas are laid out with a greater emphasis on moving cars than on making beautiful streets that promote civil interactions between the people who live there? Such residential areas are based on a subdivision form and land-use pattern that segregates people according to income and that forces everyone living there to drive or—if too young, too infirm, too old, or too poor to have a car—to be driven by someone else for every activity outside the house, including going to work, attending church or school, seeking playmates or a quart of milk, or even visiting a neighbor who lives across the back-lot line.

In each case the decisions of people involved in producing a building, decisions that could have been made otherwise, have affected the public good. Because buildings constitute the public art of architecture, any case involving building and rebuilding in our cities, towns, and rural areas raises questions about the ethical content of the activity. The forum that is the natural home of judgments about the interplay between public and personal, between communal and individual, is the city, the cockpit of the ethical life, the locus of the life of citizenship. In this forum everyone brings two skills to bear, one the skill exemplified by the statesman seeking the greatest good for the community, the other that of the expert in some art, in this case the art of the architect.

Briefly put, an architect is a citizen, architecture is city building, and the basis for judging the architect and his building activity must be how well it contributes to the beauty and justice of the city. The architect's task is to strike the best proportionate balance between the three, often conflicting, demands of his art, the formal, the architectonic, and the civil. He seeks to produce forms that provoke delight through their *symmetria*, *eurythemia*, and *decor*. He seeks an architectonic substance that is appropriately economical and durable and a fitting partner in the material world from which it has been produced and within which it will endure. Most importantly, he seeks to build the beautiful city that assists citizens in attaining the justice to which any good civil society aspires. This is too difficult a task to do alone. He needs the help of those who have contributed to the tradition on which he can draw, and he needs the counsel of his fellow citizens, who can guide him even as he educates them about what his art has been able to produce and what it can attain.

If there is to be a useful collaboration between an inexpert citizenry and an architect who commands the specialized expertise of a very difficult art, there must be both an abundant fund of goodwill and a common ground of knowledge. The goodwill is an attribute of citizenship. The common knowledge, as mentioned earlier, consists of the forms of buildings and their parts, of the means used to build them, and of the variety of purposes they can serve. This is the equivalent in architecture to the common possession of any citizenry that knows the stories of the founders, heroes, and events that have shaped its past and provides ballast for navigating in the civil affairs of the present.

The correlation between the practice of architecture and the practice of citizenship has been understood since the Greeks discovered the notion in the seventh and sixth centuries B.C.[13] At that time, both the art of architecture and that of citizenship became the subject of conscious reflection, of what Aristotle would call *prohairesis*, and people began to take seriously the freedom they had to indulge in that reflection and the responsibilities for ethical conduct that freedom entailed. Ever since then, it has been recognized that whether the topic is the form of a building or the form of a regime's constitution, or whether an act that has an effect on the public good is that of an expert practicing the art of architecture or of an amateur practicing his more general art of citizenship, that form and that act are subject to a judgment about the goodness or lack thereof according to the standards of ethical conduct, judgments that seek to balance universal claims against the *endoxa* of the community. Indeed, confronting that judgment is the very essence of the life of a free individual living in a community. Without a community composed of individuals seeking to live justly together, there is no freedom; without free individuals seeking their moral perfection together, there is no community.

All mature, morally healthy members of a community have the capacity to participate in the most portentous activities of their community. Indeed, the doctrines undergirding the regime of the United States declare that all mature, morally healthy people, no matter their communal affiliation, have that right as an unalienable endowment by nature and nature's God. Nature has constructed us such that each individual has the capacity to judge what is true and not true and to assess what is good and not good. In our regime, within our *endoxa,* we apply that idea within some basic constitutional provisions. In one of these, randomly selected individuals are considered competent to serve on juries charged with judging truth and falsity. Justice is a different matter; juries judge truth, a prerequisite to justice, while courts seek justice, not truth. In another provision, all people are eligible as voters to judge good and bad character. This does not mean that anybody can be a lawyer or judge or an election official or candidate.[14] Nor are truth and the *ethos* of a person's character put raw before the public for judgment. A complicated apparatus within the justice system serves up cases for judgment by juries, and a similarly complicated procedure prepares for elections. But the final arbiter of the substance of the matter is the judgment rendered by the public.

The parallel to architecture is in the recognition that beauty is to architecture what truth is to a legal system and goodness is to standards of civil conduct. Beauty, truth, and goodness are not the full extent of it, but they are the nub. Extending the principles that recognize the role of citizens on juries and at elections to the role they might play in the practice of architecture makes it clear that all citizens are eligible to judge whether or not beauty is present in a work of architecture. This is not to say that anybody can be an architect. All may judge the presence or absence of beauty; only the architect can provide it and correct deficiencies.

Matters touching on the physical form our buildings and cities ought to take need to be prepared for presentation to the public, and the public's response then needs to be translated into something buildable. Parts of such a system are present, although in disconnected and fragmentary form. Among them is the array of zoning and building codes, design guidelines and historic preservation ordinances, and special commissions charged with protecting the public interest in easily identified, highly charged parts of the physical realm such as the national parks and the federal properties in the District of Columbia. These forums usually work poorly and often produce results we deplore, because they are structured as adversarial proceedings and because decisions are based on the narrow, "objective" grounds of protecting the general health, safety, and welfare of the community. The standards in play are the standards of commodity and firmness. There is no role for the criteria of delight, much less those of *decor*. Expediency and safety, not beauty and civility, are the issues under review. As a result, these proceedings fail to operate as forums for open discussion between people of goodwill who are seeking to build beautiful and just buildings and cities. They therefore fail to embrace what tradition has long known and taught, namely, that first and foremost, the practice of architecture is a form of ethical conduct, and beauty is the form of the ethical content of buildings in a city.

NOTES

1. Quoting Stephen G. Salkever's text from his presentation at a February 1998 symposium; the term *endoxa* used below derives from the same source.

2. A useful collection of modernist manifestos is in *Programs and Manifestoes on 20th-Century Architecture*, ed. Ulrich Conrads, tr. Michael Bulloch (Cambridge: MIT Press, 1970).

3. The material is presented in Vitruvius, *De architectura,* I, iv, 2. The terms are *firmitas, utilitas*, and *venustas*. The translation of Frank Granger (Loeb Classical Library, 1933) presents them as strength, utility, and grace; Morris Hicky Morgan (Cambridge: Harvard University Press, 1914) uses durability, convenience, and beauty. Note, however, as discussed below, that these three criteria are mere thresholds to the full doctrine, not the full doctrine in itself.

4. See Claude Perrault, *Ordonnance for the Five Kinds of Columns after the Method of the Ancients,* tr. Indra Kagis McEwen, Texts and Documents series, Getty Center for the History of Art and the Humanities (Chicago: University of Chicago Press, 1993), with the useful introduction by Alberto Pérez-Gómez.

5. See David Watkin, *Morality and Architecture* (Oxford: Clarendon Press: 1977).

6. "Today, everyone [practicing architecture] is free to follow a personal path and muse . . . there are no longer any rules; it hardly matters what philosophy drives the design or what vocabulary is being used." Ada Louise Huxtable, "The New Architecture," *New York Review*, 6 April 1995, 21. For a survey of current positions see Kate Nesbitt, *Theorizing a New Agenda for Architecture: An Anthology of Architectural Theory 1965–1995* (New York: Princeton Architectural Press, 1996).

7. The best discussion of the three criteria and especially of the larger framework of which they are a part is in Herman Geertman, "Theoria e attualità della progettistica

architettonica di Vitruvio," *Le Projet de Vitruve*, Actes du collogue international organisé par l'École française de Rome, 26–27 March 1993 (Rome: Collection de l'École française de Rome 192, 1994), 7–30; I touch on the same material in "Architecture and Democracy, Democracy and Architecture," in *Democracy and the Arts*, ed. Arthur M. Melzer, Jerry Weinberger, and M. Richard Zinman (Ithaca: Cornell University Press, 1999).

8. Any great work of architecture outlives its immediate functional requirements and acquires new uses that allow it to continue to serve the regime that maintains it. For example, the Pantheon in Rome was built as a throne room or temple. It survived for 1,300 years as a Christian church, and it is now a sepulcher for the first two kings of Italy, a major tourist attraction, and, incidentally, still a church. Virtually any older college or university has its counterpart—for example, the chapels of sectarian colleges were not torn down when chapel attendance ceased being compulsory. Similarly, any number of American cities have railroad stations that are now more important as shopping malls than as train stations—if trains even visit them anymore.

9. See, for example, Colin Rowe, "The Mathematics of the Ideal Villa," in *"The Mathematics of the Ideal Villa" and Other Essays* (Cambridge: MIT Press, 1976), 1–27; for a discussion of this concept in recent historiography, see Alina A. Payne, "Rudolf Wittkower and Architectural Principles in the Age of Modernism," *Journal of the Society of Architectural Historians* 53 (1994): 322–42.

10. I use the term here not in its modernist sense, that is, as the designation of a building based primarily on its function or immediate use, but in the broader sense outlined in my chapter 4 of C. W. Westfall and Robert Jan Van Pelt, *Architectural Principles in the Age of Historicism* (New Haven: Yale University Press, 1991; paperback ed., 1993).

11. For some recent studies, see George Hersey, *The Lost Meaning of Classical Architecture: Speculations on Ornament from Vitruvius to Venturi* (Cambridge: MIT Press, 1988); and John Onians, *Bearers of Meaning: The Classical Orders in Antiquity, the Middle Ages, and the Renaissance* (Princeton: Princeton University Press, 1988).

12. This resurgence of interest in traditional architecture is evident in the publication of several periodicals. See, for example, *A & C International*, edited by Ivo Tagliaventi and Gabriele Tagliaventi, which began publication in 1995, and *The Classicist*, which began publication in 1994 under the sponsorship of the Institute for the Study of Classical Architecture. A parallel publication including the other visual arts is the *American Arts Quarterly* published by the Newington-Cropsey Foundation Cultural Studies Center; a publication serving the building trades is *Traditional Architecture*, formerly *Old House Journal*, published by Clem Lebine.

13. See the provocative essay by Indra Kagis McEwen, *Socrates' Ancestor: An Essay on Architectural Beginnings* (Cambridge: MIT Press, 1994).

14. Note that the U.S. Constitution puts restrictions on qualifications for office; see Article 1, § 2, 3; and Article 2, § 1.

Chapter Thirteen

The Reality of Information Objects

Michael J. Fischer

The widespread use of computers to store and transmit information is revolutionizing our society. Computers calculate whether or not we can obtain credit and how much taxes we pay. They enable us to communicate rapidly with people across the globe. They are gradually supplanting virtually all of our prior information systems: publications such as newspapers, books, magazines, scholarly journals, and catalogs; communication systems such as mail systems and telephone; commerce systems such as retail sales establishments; and entertainment systems such as music recordings, television, and games. These far-reaching effects are causing our time to be dubbed the "Information Age."

Information systems deal with digital data grouped together into meaningful entities. I call these *information objects*. Even though in reality these objects are simply long strings of zeros and ones in the computer's memory banks, we like to imagine that they have an independent existence, like the physical objects they replace. We imagine the computer really contains reports, documents, messages, file boxes, and trashcans that can be moved about, examined, and manipulated. We are encouraged to think that way by the icons on the screen and by the metaphors with which we interact with the machine.

Nevertheless, information objects behave very differently from their physical counterparts, as we shall see. As a result, different rules of conduct may be needed in cyberspace than the ones our society has developed for dealing with the physical world. In this chapter, I explore some of those differences and trace how they affect the ethics that people apply to information objects.

CHARACTERISTICS OF INFORMATION OBJECTS

Information objects have striking properties that distinguish them from physical objects.

1. They are incoherent and spatially diffuse.
2. They are easily and undetectably replicated.
3. They are easily and undetectably modified.
4. They are inherently insecure.

Incoherence

Information objects lack the fundamental coherence property of physical objects. A physical object can be in only one place at a time. If it is moved to another location, all trace of its being in the previous location is lost.

By way of contrast, information objects have a diffuse quality. They do not have a well-defined location in space but exist as a confluence of digital data from many possibly different and dynamically changing physical locations. They don't move through space in the ordinary way; rather, they are teleported to a new location, where the original is reconstructed. After the move, the object is in both places, and both copies will persist for some period of time or until explicitly destroyed.

Replication

Physical objects can be replicated only with difficulty. A toaster returned to the store assures the clerk that the toaster was not kept at home. Possession of a stock certificate shows ownership of the stated number of shares.

Information objects, on the other hand, can be easily replicated again and again. Indeed, replication is essential in the normal use of information objects. This is clear when accessing physically remote data, but it also occurs when simply viewing a file from a local disk. The possessor of an information object has no way of knowing how many times it has been replicated en route to its current location, how many of those replicas are still in existence, or who now possesses them.

For example, the simple act of mouse-clicking a web link and having another page appear causes copies of the new page to be created in many places along the route from the server on which the page originates to the computer on which it is being viewed. These copies exist on computer disks and computer memories, in switches and routers and gateways on the transmission path between source and destination, and even as electromagnetic fields on the wires and radio links that comprise the underlying communications media. Most of these copies are short-lived under normal operations, but there is nothing inherent in the technology that prevents them from being preserved or further replicated. A phone tap replicates the electromagnetic signal traversing the wire. An ethernet "sniffer" can watch data packets traversing a computer network and replicate any or all that it finds interesting—for example, those that appear to contain credit card numbers.

Modification

Surreptitious modifications of physical objects are often difficult to effect and difficult to disguise. A sealed envelope assures us that the letter inside has not been seen or altered while in transit. Information objects, however, are as easily modified as they are replicated. A forged object is indistinguishable from the original. A rogue gateway computer, not satisfied to merely replicate the e-mail that passes through it, can modify it as it sees fit, and the eventual recipient will be none the wiser.

Insecurity

Physical objects are commonly secured by locking them up, thereby preventing physical access to them. This one act preserves both the privacy and the integrity of the object. For objects such as passports that cannot be locked up and where privacy is not an issue, the object can be constructed so that undetectable modification and forgery become quite difficult.

Information objects, by way of contrast, are inherently insecure. Their privacy is difficult to maintain by virtue of their easy replicability. Indeed, the most obvious approach to maintaining privacy of an information object is to embed it in a physical object such as a floppy disk and then apply the usual precautions for maintaining the privacy of the physical object. But even this is problematical if any use of the information object is contemplated, for simply accessing it results in the construction of replicas. To maintain privacy after use, all replicas must be secured or destroyed.

Similarly, the integrity of information objects is difficult to maintain by virtue of their easy modifiability. Maintaining integrity of an information object requires both preserving the integrity of the physical objects on which it resides and ensuring that it is not altered during replication. One must generally take on faith that the computer and network produce authentic replicas, for there is no generally effective means of verifying that they have done so.

INTELLECTUAL PROPERTY RIGHTS

The fundamental properties of information objects—incoherence, replicability, modifiability, and insecurity—render inapplicable many of the ethical and legal principles that govern our use of physical objects and thus require that we rethink them. For example, consider the commandment "Thou shalt not steal" (Exodus 20:15).[1] This derives from a general ethical principle that one person should not derive personal gain at the expense of another. If you steal someone's food, then they cannot eat it. If you steal someone's horse, then they cannot ride it. These are obvious consequences of the coherence of physical objects.

We apply this same principle to information objects to derive a prohibition against piracy (unauthorized copying). However, the underlying ethical justification no longer holds: replicating an information object does not deprive the owner of its use. Indeed, the original continues to exist as if nothing had happened. Because the owner of the replica—really the owner of the medium on which the information object resides—is not harmed, many people view information piracy as a less serious breach of ethical behavior than theft of physical property.

This is not to say that information piracy is ethical, but one must invoke more subtle reasoning to justify its prohibition. For example, one could assert that the creator of the information object suffers a loss of sales on which his livelihood depends. Clearly a different ethical principle is being invoked in this argument: that a person has a right to the fruits of his labors. But this principle is only indirectly linked to the act of copying, for who is to say whether or not the act of copying actually prevented a sale that would have otherwise taken place?

Indeed, to address this situation, we have invented the legal concept of "intellectual property" to distinguish the information object from its many manifestations in physical media. The creator of an information object initially owns the intellectual property. A purchaser obtains a replica of the information object but owns only the right to use it. Both the intellectual property and the right to use it can be bought and sold like other forms of property.

If information objects behave strangely in comparison with physical objects, intellectual property is stranger still. Its nature derives from the fabric of laws and contracts from which it is created, and ethical questions concerning it cannot be divorced from the legal ones. As a kind of "property," it is far removed from the basal experience with physical property on which our ethical principles rest. It is not surprising that many view intellectual property rights primarily as legal rather than ethical issues.

PRIVACY

Privacy of physical objects from governmental intrusion is protected by Fourth Amendment guarantees against unreasonable search and seizure.[2] For privacy of physical objects from nongovernmental intrusion, the legal system effectively supplements physical security measures, resulting in a reasonably high level of privacy for ordinary citizens.

For information objects, more or less the same constitutional and legal guarantees apply, but because of the nature of information objects, these guarantees are far less effective in achieving their goals. An illegal search of "persons, houses, papers, and effects" is likely to be noticed and witnessed, either while it takes place or after the fact. Successfully hiding such an event can be quite difficult, as President Richard Nixon discovered to his dismay.

An information object, on the other hand, can be secretly replicated by someone with suitable access to the computer on which it resides, leaving behind no trace of the security breach. The very networks that permit global communication of digital data also permit breaking into computers worldwide. To compromise privacy, it is sufficient to penetrate just one computer or tap into just one network segment that happens to contain a replica of the information object at some point in time. Even the Pentagon is unable to secure the computers it uses for nonclassified data against break-ins.[3]

Legal sanctions against unauthorized access to information objects lose their effectiveness as deterrents because of the difficulty of tracing the replicas, the difficulty of connecting actions in cyberspace with the individuals responsible for them, and the difficulty of obtaining irrefutable evidence linking an individual with a crime. Replication of information objects occurs so often and at so many locations that it is difficult to prevent or detect unauthorized replication. The usual way of linking a thief to a crime is to find stolen property in his possession. But what does it mean to "possess" an information object? Is it enough to find it on a computer he owns? What if someone else put it there? And even if the person did put it there, what evidence would convince a jury of that fact?

One is forced to conclude that citizens do not enjoy the same level of privacy of information objects as they get with physical objects. Information objects are inherently insecure without an additional tool: cryptography.

CRYPTOGRAPHY

Cryptography changes the very nature of information objects. It can instill in them unique identities, prevent undetected modifications, and ensure a much greater degree of privacy. But cryptography is not a cure-all. Its utility depends on the assumed ability to keep cryptographic keys secret over long periods of time. One can view cryptography as a means of transferring the fundamental properties of information objects onto the corresponding cryptographic keys. The problems of controlling replication, modification, and privacy of information objects are transformed to the problem of maintaining those same properties for the keys themselves. The latter problem is somewhat easier because the keys are shorter and can remain in the local environment, but key maintenance is still a formidable problem.

What Is Cryptography?

A cryptosystem replaces an information object by a scrambled object that, ideally, is meaningless to anyone not possessing a suitable secret decryption key. The scrambled object may be passed around cyberspace and freely replicated. The scrambled object is unscrambled by the intended recipient with the use of a secret *decryption key*, which she is assumed to possess. However, others coming into possession of the scrambled object cannot learn anything from it, nor read it, nor undetectably alter its contents, unless they also somehow acquire the decryption key. The original object now appears in useful form in only two locations, the source and the destination of its travels, but not at intermediate points along the way. This greatly reduces its exposure to tampering and eavesdropping.

Although cryptography tends to tame the wild properties of information objects, it still does not succeed in making them behave like physical objects. An encrypted object can be captured during transmission and stored. Later, if the key is discovered, the object can be unscrambled to obtain the original information object. As long as the privacy of the key is maintained, the object remains secure. Once the key is compromised, however, not only can it no longer be used, but also the security of everything ever encrypted with that key in the past is compromised.

We can think of the cryptographic key as a kind of surrogate for the information object that it encrypts. The problem of protecting the privacy of a large information object that travels around the network is replaced by the more tractable problem of protecting the privacy of a relatively small decryption key that need never leave the recipient's computer. But it is important to note that the need for maintaining privacy does not go away; it just shifts from the information objects to the keys.

Politics of Cryptography

A major debate is going on concerning the civilian use of cryptography in the United States. Currently, cryptography is viewed as a munition, and export of cryptographic hardware and software is controlled by the international traffic in arms regulations (ITAR). Recent policy has been to permit export of mass-market encryption software after a one-time review only if the keys are at most 40 bits long.[4] Such systems are cryptographically weak and can be compromised in a relatively short amount of time. For example, the RSA Laboratories challenge problem RC5-32/12/5,[5] which required breaking a message encrypted using a 12-round RC5 algorithm with a 40-bit key, was solved on the Berkeley Network of Workstations cluster in just three-and-a-half hours.[6]

The effect of the export ban on strong cryptography has been to slow its widespread adoption by the civilian sector. While unrestricted use of strong cryptography by Americans is completely legal, companies are reluctant to make it available in their products, since the market for such products is restricted to the United States. However, there is no restriction against *importing* cryptographic products, so those same products, if developed overseas, may be distributed worldwide. This obviously puts the American computer industry at a major competitive disadvantage and has made the computer industry an influential opponent of cryptographic export restrictions.

Meanwhile, the government is trying to come to grips with the dilemma of its need for surveillance and society's opposing need for privacy. Law enforcement agencies would like to be able to intercept and read any information object with court authorization. They view this as the logical extension of their current right to wiretaps of telephones and cite the usefulness of wiretaps in terrorist and drug investigations for justification. Cryptography obviously makes their job more difficult, so law enforcement agencies come down on the side of opposing the use of unregulated cryptography.[7]

Civil libertarians put high value on personal privacy and so take the opposite side in support of unrestricted use of cryptography.[8]

The constituency in this debate whose importance has only recently been recognized is society at large, the users of these systems, who are left vulnerable to espionage, fraud, terrorist actions, and other attacks on their privacy, their intellectual property, and their well-being.[9] While law enforcement attempts to reduce crime through deterrence, public use of cryptography reduces crime by lessening opportunity. Even though locked doors may make police investigations of burglaries more difficult, they also make the burglaries themselves more difficult. Obviously, law enforcement and crime prevention are not unrelated, and finding the right balance is a difficult issue.

Key Recovery

In an effort to reach a compromise position that allows use of cryptography while still permitting authorized wiretaps, the government is proposing adoption of *key recovery* technology.[10] Each user is required to register his key with the government, where it is placed in escrow. Upon court order, the escrow agencies will release the key to law enforcement agencies, allowing scrambled information objects that have been intercepted to be unscrambled by the same means as employed by the legitimate receiver.

To protect the privacy of the law-abiding citizen's key, it is not stored intact. Instead, it is split into two pieces called "shares," which are then stored separately at two different escrow sites. Neither share alone allows the key to be recovered, but when both shares are brought together, the key can be recovered. The idea is that both escrow agencies will release their shares to law enforcement agencies under proper warrant, but a security breach at one escrow agency is not enough to compromise privacy of the user's keys.

But now we have come full circle, almost. Maintaining the secrecy of keys is no longer under the control of the user, and information about the keys is no longer confined to the user's local site. Instead, we are entrusting to the escrow agencies the job of maintaining the secrecy of the shares of our keys.

The escrow agencies will face formidable problems. To preserve the privacy of the shares they hold, they will need to restrict access from the outside, yet to carry out their task of cataloging and preserving hundreds of millions of keys per year or more will require a high level of automation. To keep from losing the shares entrusted to them, they will, internally at least, need to make their own replicas, if only for backup purposes. The many employees of such organizations, the many necessary replicas of the shares, the ineffectiveness of legal sanctions, and the tenuousness of ethical prohibitions against passive snooping all lead one to conclude that the task of running a truly secure escrow agency is well nigh impossible.

CONCLUSION

Cyberspace differs in fundamental ways from the familiar physical world. Information objects in particular have peculiar properties not shared by physical objects. Coming to grips with this strange new landscape will require us to rethink the associated ethical issues and force us to go back to the underlying ethical principles for guidance.

NOTES

1. Holy Bible, King James version, available at http://www.hti.umich.edu/relig/kjv and at http://etext.virginia.edu/kjv.browse.html. From the Oxford Text Archive.

2. Constitution of the United States, amendments. Available at http://www.house.gov/Constitution/Amend.html.

3. Associated Press, "Pentagon Says Its Computers Were Hacked," *New York Times*, CyberTimes edition, February 25, 1998. From web site http://www.nytimes.com/.

4. Code of Federal Regulations, Title 15, chap. VII, § 742.15. Available at http://frwebgate.access.gpo.gov/cgi-bin/get-cfr.cgi?TITLE=15&PART=742&SECTION=15&TYPE=PDF&YEAR=1998.

5. The RSA Data Security secret-key contests. Web page http://www.rsa.com/rsalabs/97challenge/html/secret-key.html (January 1997). RSA Laboratories, a division of RSA Data Security.

6. Ian Goldberg, "Cracking Crypto Keys on the NOW Cluster." Web page http://www.isaac.cs.berkeley.edu./isaac/crypto.challenge.html (January 1997).

7. Louis J. Freeh, Director, Federal Bureau of Investigation. "The Impact of Encryption on Public Safety." Statement before the Permanent Select Committee on Intelligence, U.S. House of Representatives. Web page http://www.fbi.gov/archives/congress/encrypt4.htm (September 9, 1997).

8. Joint statement, American Civil Liberties Union, Electronic Frontier Foundation, Electronic Privacy Information Center. Web page http://www.privacy.org/ipc/acp-statement.html (March 4, 1998).

9. The Clinton administration's policy on critical infrastructure protection: Presidential Decision Directive 63. Web page http://www.whitehouse.gov/Search/Query-PressReleases.html (May 22, 1998); Kenneth W. Dam and Herbert S. Lin, eds., *Cryptography's Role in Securing the Information Society* (Washington, D.C.: National Academy Press, 1996).

10. See note 4.

Chapter Fourteen

Full Circle: The Inherent Tension in Ethics from Plato to Plato

Stephanie A. Nelson

The question of individual thought as the critical element in ethics has been an enduring feature of Western thought. The problem was by no means unknown to the ancient world. Plato, Aristotle, and Cicero, each in his own way, recognized the impossibility of a purely rule-based ethics, acknowledging that an ethical system that neglects the central human faculty, the necessity of individual thought and judgment, is no ethics at all. On the other hand, ancient thinkers also were aware of the limitations of purely individual thought, seeing the necessity for guidance, for an overall formulation of ethical principles, for a developed character, and for a social system, before the individual can begin to exercise the intellectual capability that, alone, can make a human being ethical.

But there is a problem here. If ethics depends on individual judgment, there seems to be no guarantee that society can formulate any overall sense of right and wrong. On the other hand, if society is to dictate a uniform ethical code, individual ethical behavior seems to be reduced to training, obedience, or punishment — the ethics of a well-schooled puppy, not that of a human being.

This tension is profoundly treated by Plato. In the *Republic*, the dialogue that is in some strange sense "continued" or even "put into action" in his late dialogue the *Timaeus*, Plato creates an ideal state. This ideal state is constructed as a macrocosm for the ideal soul. As a just soul is one in which reason, the spirited element, and the appetites all play their appropriate role and so work in harmony, the just state is one in which the rulers, those who enforce the rules, and the producers likewise each play their appropriate role. But in the construction a problem arises. The ideal soul, it seems, could not exist within its greater counterpart, the ideal state. The ethics of the Craftsmen and the Auxiliaries has come to depend not on their own understanding, but on that of the Rulers, while the Rulers themselves have had their ultimate goal diverted from the Good, to the good of the state. Put simply, if the "reason" of the state is functioning well, there is nothing for the "reason" of the citizens to do.

The problem is brought out by Plato himself at the very end of the dialogue. The first soul to make its choice in the Myth of Er is one that lived "in a well-ordered state, participating in virtue by habit, without philosophy" (619b). As such the soul, who bears a rather striking resemblance to the portrait of Cephalus that opened the dialogue, has lived a life in which all of his actions were ethical, without the necessity of determining for himself what that might mean. He immediately chooses the greatest tyranny available. And many others like him did the same (619b). Like Cephalus, these souls never stayed to listen to the dialogue of the *Republic*; they received their understanding only by proxy—and that turns out to be utterly inadequate.

In the *Republic* there is, however, a promise of a possibility that *with* philosophy a soul may become truly ethical, and thereby truly unified, though it be only in regard to the *politeia* "laid up as a pattern in heaven for him who desires to see and, seeing, to establish himself its citizen" (592b). In the *Timaeus*, the possibility becomes far more dim. The ideal state of the *Timaeus* seems to have all the characteristics of the Republic, except the philosopher-king. The disjoining of thought and politics that this implies seems mirrored in a complete division in the cosmos, which is now portrayed as made up of two irreconcilable elements, "necessity" (*ananke*) and "thought" (*noos*). The tension between the element in us that can recognize the good and the element in us that can recognize only the satisfaction of our desires is mirrored in the cosmos. As such it now seems absolute. The best we can hope for is not the unity of the soul within an ideal Republic, but, with philosophy for the soul and gymnastic for the body (a combination that in the *Republic* had soon given way to studies directed purely at the spirited and rational elements of the soul), an uneasy truce between the two.

As David Grene has pointed out, the mythical nature of this vision also speaks deeply to our understanding of what ethics is. In the *Republic* the myth fills out the *logos*. In the *Timaeus* the *logos* is myth. All that there can be, Plato tells us, is a likely story. While in the divided line of the *Republic* the realms of Being and Becoming were joined on a continuum, in the myth of the *Timaeus* the very fact of language makes a world outside of time utterly inaccessible to us.

In the *Republic* the city is a macrocosm of the soul of man. The *Timaeus* reaches further. Here the macrocosm of the city and of the human soul is the soul of the cosmos itself. And as the soul of the world has an irrational as well as a rational element, so must the soul of man. But to see the deeper significance here, we must turn the statement around. As the soul of man has an irrational element so, indelibly, does the cosmos itself, forever limiting, if not mocking, our attempts to find unity within ourselves or with the world in which we live. This sense also informs Plato's last dialogue, the *Laws*, where behind the political and philosophical speculation lies always the possibility that human beings are merely puppets, dangled for the amusement of the gods, and philosophy itself no more than an old man's amusement in the sunshine.

The wild cosmic vision of the *Timaeus* is thus inherently connected to the vision of who man is, and so the vision of man's ethical place. As Grene has explained, there is no ethical vision without a cosmic vision, no separation of the "form" and the "content" of our ethical natures. Who we are ethically is also where we fit within the cosmos. To define us Plato has had to define all of reality. This is the reason why art and poetry are, for Plato, necessarily a part of "philosophic" analysis. Words must reach beyond the merely descriptive, to catch at something just beyond their grasp before they can be true to the vision upon which our ethical life depends. There is only a likely story. But as that is true, it is also true that words acknowledging themselves as simply words approach a reality far more than simply representative.

Plato's move in the *Timaeus*, from an ethics based on a vision of the *polis* to a view of ethics grounded in a mythical vision of the cosmos, seems to set the stage for the foundations of Western thought. Here the critical question seems to be a tension: between thought and habit, between a creative and a rule-based morality, between an ethics that is innovative and personal and one that is universal and external. In the *Timaeus* this is the division between necessity and thought— between what we do because we must and what we do because we understand. The *Timaeus* grounds this question precisely by giving it a mythic dimension. Not "what must we do and how must we do it?" but "where and how far can we fit within the cosmos?" has become the essential question of ethics.

Aristotle's ethical project reflects the significant historical change that has occurred since Plato's time, change represented by Aristotle's student, Alexander, and the radical transformation, emerging at the time of the *Ethics*, from a *polis*-based society to an imperial society. Aristotle's ethical project is not the instilling of rules, but the gradual development of the individual's ability to question the *endoxa* of the community after his or her own ethical character has been formed by that *endoxa*. Aristotle's "catalogue" of the classic virtues, such as courage and temperance, to the more subtle, such as friendliness or tact, may simply be a progression from the virtues based more clearly on habit to those more clearly intellectual. From here Aristotle's final revelation follows naturally: virtue is not based on habit, although habit must be a component, but on practical reason. Aristotle sees the necessity of *combining* an ethics based on habit with one based on individual thought.

There is an additional complexity. However we are to understand the progression of virtues in Aristotle, they clearly lead to his discussion of not one but two kinds of reason, the practical and the theoretical. This distinction may in fact be the single most important difference between Aristotle's thought and Plato's. The *Ethics* ends, after all, not with the combination of the philosophic and the political that the philosopher-king represents, but with the two best lives: on the one hand, the philosophic life or the life of theoretical wisdom, and on the other, the political life, the life of practical wisdom.

There is, however, a promise of unity. Ethical virtue—our excellences of character—is finally based on *intellectual* virtue. Aristotle's distinction between political science and *phronesis*, one addressed toward universals and the other toward particulars, echoes his distinction made between justice as a universal virtue, that is "virtue simply" (*haplos arete*) and that directed "towards another" (*pros heteron*). The implication is not that *phronesis* constitutes all of human identity, but that *phronesis* covers as much of human identity as is political. Our *theoretical* reason is the part of us that is ourselves: *tou gar dianoetikou charin, hoper hekastos einai dokei* ["for the sake of the intellectual (*dianoetic*), just that which seems to be each person" (1166a15–16)]. Ethics, it seems, may imply a realm far beyond the merely political.

It is this realm that seems to render problematic the relation of the historical and the ethical. It is not at all clear that the solutions for modern problems such as deliberative democracy, multiculturalism, or the nature of liberal education lie in asking questions rather than seeking some sort of foundation. Aristotle seems acutely aware that the theoretical foundations that serve as the basis of a true ethical life cannot be set by the society by rule. Equally powerful is Aristotle's recognition that the exercise of practical reason—politics—cannot obviate the individual's requirement for theoretical foundations.

For Cicero, citizens who have the potential of reason, but with that potential not yet developed, may be able to follow persuasion, and in so doing to develop a sense of ethics that bridges the gap between the merely given and the merely received. Here Cicero seems to follow Aristotle, who at the beginning of the *Ethics* distinguishes between two senses in which the soul can be said to have *logos*. It can have it as a father has *logos*, in giving directions to a child, or it can have it as the child has *logos*, in the sense of being able to follow, although not to originate, reason. Thus in both Greek and Roman we perceive an ethics potentially capable of resolving the inherent tension.

With Cicero, the inherent tension in ethics takes the form of his theoretic belief in the equality of men and his practical support of an elitist Roman regime. Because of the distinction between the potential of human reason that exists in all people and its actual development, which depends on contingent accidents of time and place, all human beings have the potential for the individual reason that distinguishes them as ethical beings, even though few may be able to develop it. If so, a political system that provides a rigid and rule-based structure for some while leaving others—the "better sort" or Cicero's "optimates"—the ability to develop their own rational capacity freely makes perfect sense.

A second distinction goes further toward bringing together these two different senses of what it means to be "ethical." Cicero has not only a theoretical understanding of the political system and its implications for ethics, he also has a personal and practical one. If the first is based on his study of Greek philosophy and the Roman Constitution, the second is based on his own experience as an orator. There is a politics of rule, but there is also a politics of persuasion. It is in the latter, it seems, that the two senses of ethics, one based in individual reason and one based in a directed policy of the state, may come together.

It is here, as well, that history once more raises its hoary head. Despite Cicero's titling of the "Philippics," oratory had a very different meaning in Rome than it did in Greece, even in Demosthenean Athens. The *polis*, democratic or not, was based on the active participation of the citizens; the Roman Empire was based upon an agreed consent. The following of reason, or perhaps one should say "public discourse," means very different things in the two different situations. In Athens the people listen and then vote. In Rome the people listen and then obey. Oratory, or rhetoric, in the case of the latter can become far more than merely persuasive; it can become educational. If so it can be an education that brings together the potential and the actualization of human reason.

The potential of this reconciliation, however, as we have been throughout this book reminded, is not the actuality. As history did not end with Rome, the possible variations on the ways of viewing the basis of ethics did not end with Cicero.

And the question is not limited to the West. One of Confucius's Analects goes as follows: "He who learns but does not think is lost; he who thinks but does not learn is in great danger" (2.15). Or it may be that the first remark is a quotation, and the second Confucius's response to it: "'He who learns but does not think is lost.' He who thinks but does not learn is in great danger." Either way the Analect speaks directly to the subject at hand. We cannot be ethical human beings unless we can *both* learn and think.

Nor is the issue limited to ancient thought, as is well illustrated throughout the chapters of this book. In Mediaeval and Islamic thought, both versions of ethics appear: those who can be ethical only by following outside rules and those who can perfect their humanity by themselves supplying the reason that must be the basis of ethics. Reason again emerges as the crucial element of ethics in Immanuel Kant's opposition to an ethics based merely on rules. "Reason" for Kant may be the absolute basis of man's ethical nature, but it is a personal, innovative view of reason and not the rigid "foundational" view often associated with Kant.

But this understanding of ethics based on the human need to think for oneself is very much opposed to the sense of ethics that emerges from Niccolò Machiavelli, Jean-Jacques Rousseau, and Friedrich Nietzsche, where not reason but the state, society, or individual psychology begins to be seen as the essential element in ethics. The last stage of this argument emerges in a controversy very much alive in the modern world. On the one side, ethics emerges as imbedded in our genes and our memes; on the other, it appears to require a renewal of philosophy—that is, the basis of ethical life lies less in the answers than in the questions philosophy forces us to ask. We have come full circle. The question of what it means for us to be ethical turns out to be for the modern world as it was for Plato, a question of where we fit within the cosmos.

Afterword

Afterword

Chapter Fifteen

The Importance of "Instilling Ethics"

Walter Nicgorski

Much of the complexity and difficulty of activating and perpetuating ethical action is captured in the phrase "Instilling Ethics," the title of this volume. This is not to propose some settled or formulaic response to the generally perceived moral crisis and ethical neediness of the present time. Consider the phrase against other ways we tend to speak of our concern to foster ethics. We recoil at the concepts of "giving" or "imposing" ethics. The Western tradition, from at least its Socratic origins, has questioned and warned about the notion of "teaching" ethics. To speak of ethical or moral "formation" seems to give too much emphasis to the external agents in the process of becoming ethical, just as the more familiar phrase of moral or ethical "development" can be the cover for too little attention to those agents and accordingly for reliance on a nearly instinctive subjective dynamism to the fullness of humanity.

"Instilling ethics" seems to suggest at once a better balance between external factors and internal processes in becoming ethical. At the same time, "instilling" evokes a kind of distilling that seems to point at deep and complex internal processes leading to ethical living, processes not reducible to simply knowing the good or common ethical rules. Thus, "instilling" ethics seems especially reflective of the Aristotelian understanding that ethics is the actual doing of the good, not merely understanding or knowing the good, and that what is entailed in doing the good or being ethical might properly be called a stable pattern of performing good actions, not a chance hit upon one or another of such actions.

The potential richness of the titling phrase becomes apparent when we examine the question "Are we living in an ethical age?" and distinguish the widespread contemporary talk about and attention to ethics from the ethical action that might be "instilled" and come to hold the center of our attention. In the light of that enriched understanding of ethics, what follows is an attempt to elaborate the consensus or

223

agreement that emerges from the various contributions to this volume and the salient difficulties that suggest themselves for future attention and conversation.

There seems little doubt that we are living in an ethical age in that the presence of so much talk and press about ethics and morals is a fair reflection of a pervasive concern over the state of ethics in all phases of life, from the various professions to politics itself. This concern expresses itself in a proliferation of programs, conferences, centers, and courses on ethics. Ethical discourse in this vein seems much more present everywhere in American life than it was a generation or two ago. Though it would be cynical and harsh to dub as "idle talk" the many manifestations of this concern, caution seems appropriate about the degree to which it represents genuine rather than superficial, if not personally distancing and public relations inspired, efforts to satisfy the ethical dimension of human life. At its best, however, one might see the widespread interest in ethics as an alert to the absence of ethical practice in our society and even a felt sense of moral crisis that entails an apparent willingness and readiness to look to what must be done. We have heard often in recent years one form or another of James Q. Wilson's eloquent observation that "we live in a nation confident of its wealth and proud of its power, yet convinced that this wealth cannot prevent and this power cannot touch a profound corrosion of our cultural soul. We are materially better off than our parents but spiritually worse off" (Wilson, Boyer lecture, 1997).

We live then in an age of high ethical concern, awareness, and perplexity. So what then is to be done? This volume brings us to ask whether what must be done is to overcome the evident reluctance or inability to deal with the foundational questions entailed in self-understanding and providing or revivifying the basis for a moral life.

The structure of this volume draws attention to the possibility that some kind of intellectual or philosophical collapse or reorientation was a chief factor in the ethical inadequacies of the present. One case in point is the clarity and resolve with which Niccolò Machiavelli took aim at the very basis of the moral tradition that preceded him and for which Aristotle had been formative. Thus the significant level for concern and possible remediation of the crisis lies in the sources and foundations of the moral tradition. It appears from both healthy self-awareness and the multiple perspectives of this volume that self-understanding is bound up with an understanding of the larger whole in which the self is set, and when the understanding of that larger whole is troubled or problematic, the uncertainties and insecurities of any metaphysical or ontological perspective disrupt or at least destabilize self-understanding and the ethical life as generally understood.

Not surprisingly, then, there is much evidence in this volume that, contrary to the powerful conviction of many postmoderns, foundational concerns are not easily escaped or dismissed. Perhaps they are phoenixlike in their powers within the human mind, especially when ethical direction is a dominant consideration. At the same time, however, we remain aware throughout this volume that although foundational concerns are ineluctable, foundations are not easily asserted or claimed. This is much supported in the careful explorations of the classical sources most under attack in post-Machiavellian modernity. We are cautioned about readings of Aristotle that find him to be dogmatically systematic, and there seems to be broad agreement about the subtle and gingerly probing character of Plato's approach to the grounding of life. If we add to the Stoic Cicero the skeptical basis on which Cicero adopted that Stoicism, we can see Cicero in these respects as the student of the Socrates, Plato, and Aristotle he so loved.

Jean-Jacques Rousseau, among the sources of the moral tradition, is found to be an elusive thinker, one who helps us attend to so much that is significant about the human condition and the inadequacies of modernity. Yet we appear to be left by Rousseau with insufficient resources to overcome the problems of modernity he detected. Though Rousseau's "highly situational ethic" is extreme in its seemingly ad hoc and intuitive deference to context, it represents a dimension of ethics that the chapters in this volume on the other sources of the moral tradition are notably interested to bring forward. Thus, just as the traditional sources were not seen as providing comprehensive and dogmatic ontological foundations, so too their ethical or moral teaching was not to be one of a universally applicable code of conduct. Rather, ethics and the application of its principles were to incorporate sensitivity to the *endoxa* (ways and views) of particular contexts and to the specific concrete situation in which one acts. Even the apparent discordance between the commitments of Cicero's moral and political philosophy and the character of his practice might be largely explained with greater appreciation for the necessary prudential adaptation to circumstances that traditional ethics held as important. But nothing in the emphasis on sensitivity to context and concrete situation should be taken as an endorsement of the view that the highest imperative for ethics is to reflect and fit the historical and cultural context.

In returning to the foundational concerns that have especially marked the approach to ethics in this collection, more can be said about a wide agreement reflected in these chapters. Not only is the approach to foundations one that is consistent with a recognition that the intellectual and philosophical problems at foundations do not lend themselves to a formulaic solution of some dogma or another, to some quick and easy fix; but there are also a recognition and acceptance of the apparent truth that the dependence of self-understanding on a larger ontological or metaphysical understanding does not mean that such problems at the foundational level need to be decisively and absolutely settled for there to be positive development or gains in instilling ethics, in actually doing the good. This is so because not every difficulty at the foundational level critically impairs the foundation; even a Darwinian understanding of man is shown in this collection to be capable of mediation in various ways to the support of ethical action. Differences, challenges, and contestations at the fundamental level often allow, across party lines as it were, large areas of overlap from which one can sustain such common strategies for instilling ethics as habituation and stories of heroism. Our common moral ground seems often greater than the differences in the way we explain the basis of ethics.

Again, what is to be done? Now the question is asked with more awareness of the critical but ambiguous role of foundations in the project of instilling ethics. In the light of this, it seems that important conditions for instilling ethics are space and patience. It is, of course, a certain kind of space that we have in mind, space in three senses, two of which have not much directly entered into this volume and a third that accords well with the work of this volume on "Instilling Ethics." The three senses of space are (1) space for religious education, (2) space for liberal education, and finally (3) the personal space for inquiry and scholarship and the critical exchanges that contribute to greater understanding and greater proximity to the truth.

Space for religious education extends even to constitutional space, but first it must mean cultural space, the lack of which Stephen Carter highlighted a few years ago in his book *The Culture of Disbelief*. Like many others of late, we have thought that great cultural and other obstacles have been put in the way of a religious self-understanding, that kind of self-understanding that has nearly always played a critical part in ordinary morality. The obstacles put up to a religious self-understanding are part of, or closely related to, the difficulties of the modern family with respect to stability and effectiveness as a moral educator. The situation of the family has properly been widely seen as a critical element in the moral cultural crisis, an element to which Daniel Patrick Moynihan has been long and notably attentive. One need not be an Enlightenment "basher" to be concerned with the aggressive secularism to which it has often given rise and to notice the filter-down effect on sectors of modern society deeply suffering from moral disorder. Assessing Friedrich Nietzsche's role in the upheaval of moral foundations and his potential role in a renewal of at least aspects of the moral tradition is a matter of controversy. Is Nietzsche a help or a hindrance to any self-understanding consistent with the moral life as we have known it? One point seems clear: the paradox involving the morality we want and the religious understanding we tend to marginalize was grasped by Nietzsche. Later it was in the horizon of C. S. Lewis when he observed, "And all the time—such is the tragic comedy of our situation—we continue to clamor for those very qualities we are rendering impossible. We make men without chests and expect of them virtue and enterprise. We laugh at honor and are shocked to find traitors in our midst. We castrate and bid the geldings to be fruitful" (*The Abolition of Man*).

It is important to be clear that to associate religious education with ordinary morality, with what seems a condition for a decent society that might be the basis for higher education and the highest of personal inquiries, is not necessarily to limit the role of religious self-understanding to the most simple of citizens. Religious self-understanding might, of course, take a critical part in the highest or deepest personal inquiries, in the very grounding of the self. There, however, we might expect it to be more contested.

Besides providing the space for religious education, there is the continuing need to provide and defend the space for liberal education. This is the space in which the leadership elements, at the least, are to find the opportunity to attain the reflectiveness about prevalent opinions and the human condition toward which Aristotle is herein seen leading his readers. Another way to speak of this opportunity is to see it as providing space for a critical engagement with the fundamental alternatives for human living as they are cast in the modern condition. Without such space there is much more likelihood that whole societies will become victims of larger forces and lose the ability, by losing the very awareness, to deal with the challenges to the foundations of ethics. Awareness, understanding, and knowledge are not, as has been said, sufficient in themselves for ethical action, but they surely are the basis for the kinds of efforts and practices, collective and individual, that seem on the way to "instilling ethics." Space for liberal education and the quality of that education are then important objectives in higher education and the society at large. Much patience, judicious compromises, skillful adaptations to various contexts, and quite tireless efforts are necessary in pursuing those objectives.

Finally, there is the personal space for inquiry, scholarship, and discussion— space we use in the critical reading of this volume. With ourselves and the process of dialogue and contestation, there is room for patience in a focused persistence on our inquiry and exchanges, for problems do clarify and movements of mind and minds do occur. Just as sources and foundations were once attacked and perhaps reformed in some ways and harmed in others, so might our efforts in this time be fruitful in ways appropriate to the current problematic status of foundations. Such a focused persistence is not to be seen as digging in in defense of scholarship for scholarship's sake and the academic form of careerism that has often gone with that defense. Scholarship and critical inquiry, however, that take their bearings from and keep in view our ethical and foundational needs are wholly worthy of our patient care. This volume displays such scholarship and inquiry and is dedicated to it.

Index

The Abolition of Man, 226
American Bar Association, 180
American Medical Association, 180
amour de soi-même, 74–77
amour-propre, 74–75, 77
aporia, 6, 175. *See also* Aristotle, Plato, Socrates
architecture: and citizenship, 197, 202–204; civil aspect of, 198–202; and commodity, 196–198, 204; and *endoxa*, 197, 199, 203; and formal demands, 198–202; and Jefferson, Thomas, 200; and "Platonic" forms, 199; and Vitruvius, 196
Arendt, Hannah, 87
Aristotle: and *aporia*, 6; and contemplative life, 7, 47–50, 217; and deliberative democracy, 7–9; and divinity, 7; and *endoxa*, 3–11, 217; and *epieikeia*,7; and *eudaimonia*, 6, 99; and Hobbes, Thomas, 57, 98–99; and honor, 7; and human nature, 100; and intellectual virtue, 218; and justice, 7; and leisure, 47–49; and liberal education, 7, 9–11; and *logos*, 45, 218; and Machiavelli, Niccolò, 41–45, 47; and multiculturalism, 7, 9; and *Nicomachean Ethics*, 3–7, 31, 47–48, 57, 101, 217–218; and *nomos*, 7; and *phronesis*, 4–5, 218; and political life, 217; and *Politics*, 3–7, 45, 58, 57, 99; and *politike*, 4–5; and *politike*

episteme, 98, 100; and *praxis*, 3; and *prohairesis*, 4–9; and reason, 47–48, 217–218; and Rousseau, Jean-Jacques, 99–101; and soul, 100–101; and *Summum Bonum*, 99; and theoretical foundations, 218; and virtues, 6–7, 217–218; and *Wissenschaft*, 10
articulation, 142, 144–145, 149–157. *See also* Taylor, Charles
al-Ashari, 35–36
"Attempt at Self-Critique," 106

Bacon, Francis, 98
Baglioni, Giovampagolo, 52–53
Benhabib, Seyla, 87
Bentham, Jeremy, 148
Berlin, Isaiah, 142
Beyond Good and Evil, 97–98, 104–106, 109
Bickel, Alexander, 179
Birth of Tragedy, 106
Board of the American Society of Newspapers, 180
Boleyn, Ann, 91–92
Borgia, Cesare, 51
Boscovich, Ruggiero, 109
bourgeois, 66, 68–69, 73–76. *See also* Rousseau, Jean-Jacques
Burke, Edmund, 89

Cabell, James Branch, 192
Caddyshack, 169–171, 175

229

Camillus, 39–40, 56
Camus, 148, 158–159
Carter, Jimmy, 182, 192
Carter, Stephen, 226
Cartesian science, 109–111. *See also*
    Nietzsche, Friedrich
catastrophism, 124, 126. *See* Darwin,
    Charles
Catch 22, 169
categorical imperative, 86–88
Cato, 48
Cicero: and civic courage, 24; and *De
    legibus*, 20; and *De officiis*, 20, 23–24;
    and justice, 22, 24; and *otium*, 22–23,
    25; and peace 20–22; and *Pro Sestio*
    22; and reason 21–22, 218; and *De
    republica*, 27; and rule of law, 22, 27;
    and statesmanship 23–27; and virtue
    22, 25–27; and war, 20–22, 24
citizenship, 197, 202–204
civic courage, 24
Civil Service Reform Act, 180
Coffee, John, 182
comedy, 169–170
computer revolution, 207
Confucius, 219
Congress, 187–190
contemplative life, 7, 47–50, 217. *See*
    Aristotle
cosmos, 216–217, 219. *See* Plato
counter-Enlightenment, 63, 69–70. *See*
    Rousseau, Jean-Jacques
Crane, Peter, 186–187
creationism, 123–124
credibility crisis, domestic, 180–183, 191
critical ethics, 86, 88
critical philosophy, 90
critical theory, 89, 93
Critique of Practical Reason, 90–92. *See
    also* Kant
culture, 9
The Culture of Disbelief, 226

Darwin, Charles: and celibacy, 129–130;
    and Darwinian theory, 119–136; and
    Descent of Man, 127, 129; and natural
    selection, 123–124, 130–133; and

reversion, 124, 133; and
    Schauffhausen, 129; and social
    cooperation, 127–129; and species,
    122–125, 136; and sympathy, 129–131
Darwinism, social, 126, 134–135
Dawkins, Richard, 132; and *The Great
    Ape Project*, 125
democracy: and Aristotle, 7–9; and
    Rousseau, Jean-Jacques, 80
Derrida, Jacques, 153
Descartes, René, 98; and *Discourse on
    Method*, 110; and *Meditations
    Concerning First Philosophy*, 110
Descent of Man, 127, 129
Dewey, John, 157–159
Dionysius, 109
*Discourse on the Origin and Foundations
    of the Inequality among Men (Second
    Discourse)*, 71, 75, 99–100
*Discourse on the Sciences and Arts (First
    Discourse)*, 63, 69
*Discourses on the First Ten Books of Titus
    Livy*, 39–40, 42, 45, 47–48, 53–55
divinity, 7
Dowd, Maureen, 182–183

Ecce Homo, 97–98, 106
education: and Aristotle, 7, 9–11; and
    Rousseau, Jean-Jacques, 64–65, 69,
    72–75, 79
education, liberal, 226–227
education, religious, 226
Education of Cyrus, 49–50
Elshtain, Jean Bethke, 102
Emile, 66–78, 90
endoxa, 3–11, 197, 199, 203, 217
Enlightenment, 147–148, 154, 157–158, 161
epieikeia, 7
essentialist theory, 122–124
ethics: and appearance rules, 184–185,
    190; and Aristotle, 3–7, 31–32, 47–48,
    57, 101, 217–218; and bureaucrats,
    185–189; and Congress, 187–190; and
    consultants, 188–189; and criminal
    laws, 181–182; and domestic
    credibility crisis, 180–183, 191; and
    individual thought, 215–219; and

interest groups, 187–190; and Islam,
32–35; and "issue networks," 189; and
Judaism, 32–35; and liberal education,
226–227; and Maimonides, 31–34; and
Nietzsche, Friedrich, 170, 173; and
Plato, 170, 215–216; and politics,
179–192; and press, 184–185,
188–189; and reform measures,
179–184, 189; and religion, 32–36; and
religious education, 226–227; and
Vietnam War, 179–182
ethics bureaucrats, 185–189
ethics establishment, 180–191, 184–185,
188–189
Ethics in Government Act, 179–180, 187,
192
Ethics Reform Act, 186
eudaimonia, 6, 99
evolutionary progress, 119–123,
135–136
expressivism, 143, 148, 152–157

fact of reason, 91
al-Farabi, 31
First Discourse. See *Discourse on the
Sciences and Arts*
Florentine Histories, 49
Ford, Gerald, 182
Foreign Corrupt Practices Act, 180
Foucault, Michel, 153, 160
foundationalism, 85–90. *See also* Kant
foundations, 218. *See also* Aristotle
Freedom of Information Act, 180
functionalism, 196

Gadamer, Hans Georg, 149–150
Genealogy of Morals, 107–108
*Geschichte der Religion und Philosophie
in Deutschland*, 93
Gilmore, Grant, 179
God, 103–107, 112
Gosse, Philip, 135
Gould, Stephen Jay, 126
The Great Ape Project, 125
Grene, David, 216–217
Guide of the Perplexed, 33–35
Gutmann, Amy, 17

Habermas, Jürgen, 87
Hall, G. Stanley, 129
Hayy ibn Yaqzan, 34
Hegel, G.W.F.: and Heine, Heinrich, 89,
93; and historicism, 107; and Kant,
Immanuel, 91; and Nietzsche,
Friedrich, 106–107; and progress, 107;
and reason, 107; and Robespierre, 93;
and Taylor, Charles, 149, 152
Heraclitus, 109
Herman, Barbara, 87
Herzog, Don, 17
historicism: and Hegel, G.W.F., 107; and
Hobbes, Thomas, 101–103; and
Nietzsche, Friedrich, 106–108,
111–113; and Rousseau, Jean-Jacques,
101–103, 107–108, 110–111
Hobbes, Thomas 57–58; and Aristotle,
98–99; and hedonistic materialism,
101–102; and historicism, 101–103;
and idealism, 110; and *Leviathan*,
98–99, 103; and materialism, 101–102,
110; and Nietzsche, Friedrich, 108–109;
and progress, 101–102; and science of
politics, 109–110; and soul (rejection
of), 99–103, 110 and sovereignty, 99
Hofstadter, Richard, 183
honor, 7
human sociability, 21–22
Hume, David, 88–89
Huxley, T.H., 121, 127–128

Ibn Rushd (Averroës), 31
Ibn Tufayl, 34
"information age," 207
information objects, 207–210; and
cryptography, 211–214; and insecurity,
209, 211; and key recovery technology,
213–214; and privacy, 210–213; and
replication, 208–209, 211
Inspector General Act, 180
interest groups, 187, 189–190
irony, 169–170
Islam, 32–35

Jefferson, Thomas, 200
Judaism, 32–35

Julie, 66
Jurgen, 192
justice, 7, 22, 24

Kant, Immanuel: and Boleyn, Ann, 91–92; and categorical imperative, 86–88; and critical ethics, 86, 88; and critical philosophy, 90; and critical theory, 89, 93; and *Critique of Practical Reason*, 90–92; and *Emile*, 90; and emotivism, 88–89; and fact of reason, 91; and foundationalism, 85–90; and happiness, 90; and human experience, 89–90; and Hume, David, 88–89; and *Metaphysics of Morals*, 88, 91; and morality, 89–93; and Nietzsche, Friedrich, 104–108; on the distinction between "is" and "ought," 88–89, 94; and "On the Supposed Right to Lie from Altruistic Motives," 87–88; and reason, 219; and Rousseau, Jean-Jacques, 67–69, 72, 76, 80
Kitab al-Luma, 35–36
Kropotkin, Peter, 127–128

language, 21–22
Last and First Men, 125–126
law, 22, 27, 35–36, 32–36
Laws, 216
Leff, Art, 191–192
De legibus, 20
leisure, philosophic, 47–50, 56
Lewis, C.S., 226
liberal education, 226–227
Lives, 91
Livy, Titus, 45–46, 53
logos: and Aristotle, 45, 218; and Cicero, 218; and Plato, 216
Lycurgus, 41

Machiavelli, Niccolò 39; and acquisition, 54–56; and aristocratic republics, 43; and Aristotle, 41–45, 47; and Baglioni, Giovampagolo, 52–53; and Borgia, Cesare, 51; and Camillus, 39–40, 56; and Cyrus, 49–50, 53; and democratic republic, 42–47, 55–56; and

Discourses on the First Ten Books of Titus Livy, 39–40, 42, 45, 47–48, 53–55; and domestic tranquillity, 42–44; and education for rule, 55–56; and *Education of Cyrus*, 49–50; and extreme acts, 50–56; and *Florentine Histories,* 49; and foreign relations, 43–44; and Hobbes, Thomas, 57–58; and Livy, Titus, 45–46, 53; and Lycurgus, 41; and Moses, 52–53; and peoples, 46–47; and prince, 46–47, 54–55; and *The Prince*, 40, 49, 54; and reason, 45, 47; and Rome, 39, 42–44, 46–49; and Romulus, 52–54; and Scipio, 49–50; and Soderini, Piero, 51–53, 55–56; and Sparta, 41–44; and traditions, 39–41; and Venice, 42–44; and war, 41–49; and Xenophon, 49–50, 53
MacIntyre, Alasdair, 17–18
macroevolution, 125
Maimonides: and ethical virtue, 32; and ethics for the masses, 31–32, 34; and ethics for the philosophic individual, 31–32, 34; and *Guide of the Perplexed*, 33–35; and human perfection, 33–35; and moral virtue, 34; and rational virtue, 33–34
Malthusian theory, 119, 131, 133
McCarthy, Thomas, 87
Melzer, Arthur, 70
metaphysics, 57
microevolution, 124
militarism, 18–19
militaristic paradigm, 18–19, 22, 25–26
Milton, John, 189–190
modernity: and Nietzsche, Friedrich, 103–109; and Taylor, Charles, 147, 150–152, 157
moral certainty, 174–175
moral failure, 174–175
moral reflection, 167–168
moral sources, 146–161
morality, 129–139, 134, 179–180, 170–173
Moses, 52–53
multiculturalism, 7, 9

National Treasury Employees Union case, 186–187
natural selection, 123–124, 130–133
naturalism, 154, 158
nature, 66–75, 154, 158
necessity, 216
neo-Darwinism, 120, 124, 130, 134
Nicomachean Ethics, 3–7, 31, 101, 217–218
Nietzsche, Friedrich: and *The AntiChristian*, 171; and "Attempt at Self-Critique," 106; and *Beyond Good and Evil*, 97–98, 104–106, 109; and *Bildung*, 104; and *Birth of Tragedy*, 106; and Boscovich, Ruggiero 109; and Cartesian science 109–111; and Dionysius, 109; and *Ecce Homo*, 97–98, 106; and ethics, 170, 173; and *The Gay Science*, 103–104; and *The Genealogy of Morals*, 107–108; and German idealism, 105–108; and God, 103–107, 112; and Hegel, G.W.F., 106–107; and Heraclitus, 109; and Hobbes, Thomas, 108–109; and Kant, Immanuel, 104–108; and modern materialism, 109; and modernity, 103–109; and moral philosophy, 102–106; and morality, 170–173; and philosophical historicism, 106–108; 111–113; and Plato, 109; and progress, 107; and psychology, 97–98, 106–112, 175; and rhetoric of morality, 170–173; and Rousseau, Jean-Jacques, 70–71, 108; and Schopenhauer, Arthur, 106; and soul, 103, 106–113; and Taylor, Charles, 160–161; and *Thus Spake Zarathustra*, 104, 107; and *Twilight of the Idols*, 170; and *Übermensch*, 104, 107; and *Untimely Meditations*, 106; and Wagner, Richard, 106; and Zarathustra, 103–104, 107, 112
Nixon, Richard, 179
nomos, 7

Office of Government Ethics, 179–180, 186
Office of Independent Counsel, 180, 185
De officiis, 20

O'Neill, Onora, 87
"On the Supposed Right to Lie from Altruistic Motives," 87–88
otium, 23, 25
ozio, 48–50, 56

patriotism, 18–20, 25
peace, 20–22
Perrault, Claude, 197
philosophers, 33–36
philosophy: and Aristotle 7, 47–50, 217; and Plato, 216–217
phronesis, 4–5
The Plague, 148, 158–159
Plato: and *aporia*, 175; and cosmos, 216–217, 219; and ethics, 170, 215–216; and *Laws*, 216; and *logos*, 216; and moral failure, 174; and necessity, 216; and Nietzsche, Friedrich, 109; and philosophy, 215–216; and psychology, 175; and *The Republic*, 215–216; and soul, 175, 215–216; and state, 215–216; and thought, 216; and *Timaeus*, 215–217
Plutarch, 91
political life, 217
Politics, 3–7, 45, 48, 57
politike, Aristotle, 4–5
politike episteme, 98, 110
practical reason, 217–218
praxis, 3
press, 184–185, 188–189
The Prince, 40, 49, 54
progress: and Hegel, G.W.F., 107; and Hobbes, Thomas 101–102; and Nietzsche, Friedrich, 107; and Rousseau, Jean-Jacques, 102, 107
progress, evolutionary: and Darwin, Charles, 119–123, 135–136; *prohairesis*, 4–9, 195–199, 203
psychology: and Nietzsche, Friedrich, 97–98, 106–112, 175; and Plato, 175
Public Integrity Section (Department of Justice), 182

Ramsey, Paul, 167
rational discourse, 21–22

rationalism, 63, 66, 71 154
Rawls, John, 87
reason: and Aristotle, 217–218; and Cicero
    21–22, 218; and Hegel, G.W.F., 107;
    and Kant, Immanuel, 219
religion: and education, 226; and law,
    32–36; and Moral Majority, 36; and
    morality and ethics, 32–36
The Republic, 215–216
republic, acquisitive, 55–56
republic, democratic, 42–47, 55–56
De Republica, 27
Republicanism, civic, 17–18, 25
Reveries of the Solitary Walker, 67
reversion, 124, 133
romanticism, 148, 152–155
Rome: and Machiavelli, Niccolò 39,
    42–44, 46–49; and Rousseau, Jean-
    Jacques, 64; and tribunes, 42
Romulus, 52–54
Rorty, Richard, 158–159
Rousseau, Jean-Jacques: and *amour de
    soi-même*, 74–77; and *amour-propre*,
    74–75, 77; and Aristotle, 99–101; and
    bourgeois, 66, 68–69, 73–76; and civic
    education, 64–65, 68–69, 77; and
    compassion, 71–72; and conscience,
    70; and counter-Enlightenment, 63,
    69–70; and democracy, 80; and
    *Discourse on the Origin and
    Foundations of the Inequality among
    Men (Second Discourse)*, 71, 75,
    99–100, 102; and *Discourse on the
    Sciences and Arts (First Discourse)*,
    63, 69, 102; and domestic education,
    66; and *Emile*, 66–78; and historicism,
    101–103, 107–108, 110–111; and
    human nature, 100–103, 110; and *Julie*,
    66; and Kant, Immanuel, 67–69, 72,
    76, 80; and moral education, 64–65,
    69, 72–75, 79; and moral rationalism,
    63, 66, 71; and morality, 63–71, 77–80;
    and nature, 66–75; and Nietzsche,
    Friedrich 70–71, 108; and progress,
    102, 107; and rational self-interest, 63,
    67; and rational will, 67; and return to
    nature, 66–71; and *Reveries of the*

Solitary Walker, 67; and Rome, 64; and
    Schopenhauer, Arthur, 71; and self-
    legislation, 67; and sincerity, 70–71;
    and *Social Contract*, 67–68; and
    solitary walker, 78–79; and soul,
    100–103, 110; and Sparta, 64, 68; and
    virtue, 64, 68–69
Ruprecht, Louis, 179

Schindewolf, O.H., 124
Schopenhauer, Arthur: and Kant,
    Immanuel, 91; and Nietzsche,
    Friedrich, 106; and Rousseau, Jean-
    Jacques, 71; and Taylor, Charles, 155
Scipio, 49–50
Second Discourse. See *Discourse on the
    Origin and Foundations of the
    Inequality among Men*
Pro Sestio, 22
Skinner, Quentin, 142
Social Contract, 67–68
social Darwinism, 126, 134–135
Socrates, 174–175
Soderini, Piero, 51–53, 55–56
soul: and Aristotle, 100–101; and Hobbes,
    Thomas, 99–103, 110; and Nietzsche,
    Friedrich, 103, 106–113; and Plato
    175, 215–216; and Rousseau, Jean-
    Jacques, 100–103, 110
Sources of the Self, 143, 146–147, 149,
    153, 156–157, 159–160
Sparta, 41–44, 64, 68.
species, 122–125, 136. See also Darwin,
    Charles
speech, 21–22
Spencer, Herbert, 119, 122, 126–128
Stapledon, Olaf, 125–126
state, 215–216
statesmanship, 23–27
Stoics, 124
Stove, David, 131–135
Sturm und Drang, 154
Sullivan, Louis, 196

Taylor, Charles 17–18; and articulation,
    142, 144–145, 149–157; and
    constitutive goods, 147–148; and

Derrida, Jacques, 153; and Dewey,
John, 157–159; and Enlightenment,
147–148, 154, 157–158, 161; and
expressivism 143, 148, 152–157; and
Foucault, Michel, 153, 160; and
Gadamer, Hans Georg, 149–150; and
Hegel, G.W.F., 149, 152; and historical
embeddedness, 142; and immanent
counter-Enlightenment, 160; and
immanent transcendence, 160; and life
goods, 147, 159–160; and "lifeworld,"
150–151; and modern identity
(Western), 143–152; 157, 159; and
modernity (Western), 147, 150–152;
155, 157; and moral sources 146–161;
and Nietzsche, Friedrich, 160–161; and
Romanticism, 148, 152–155; and
Schopenhauer, Arthur, 155; and
Skinner, Quentin, 142; and *Sources of
the Self,* 143, 146–147, 149, 153,
156–157, 159–160; and strong
ontologies 141–144; 149; and *Sturm
und Drang* 154; and theism, 142–143;
146–149; 153–161; and utilitarianism,
146–148, 157–158; and weak
ontologies, 141–147, 152–153;
157–161
theism, 142–143; 146–149; 153–161
theologians, 35
theoretical foundations, 218
theoretical reason, 217–218
Timaeus, 215–217

Übermensch, 104, 107
Untimely Meditations, 106
utilitarianism, 146–148, 157–158

Venice, 42–44
Vico, Giambattista, 197
Vietnam War, 179–182
Viollet-le-Duc, Eugène-Emmanuel, 196
virtue: and Aristotle, 4; and Cicero, 22,
25–27; and Maimonides, 31–32; and
Rousseau, Jean-Jacques, 64, 68–69
virtue, ethical, 32; moral, 32; theoretical-
rational, 32
virtue, republican, 18–19, 22, 25
virtues, 6–7, 217–218
Vitruvius, 196

Wagner, Richard, 106
war: and Aristotle 41–42, 47, 49; and
Christian teaching, 41; and Cicero
20–22, 24; and Machiavelli, 41–49
Watergate, 179–182, 184, 187–188,
192
Wells, H.G., 129
Wilberforce, Samuel, 120–122
Wilson, E.O., 132
Wilson, James Q., 224
Wissenchaft, 10
Wright, Frank Lloyd, 196

Xenophon, 49–50, 53

About the Contributors

Dwight David Allman is assistant professor of political science at Baylor University. His research interests range from Greek political philosophy to contemporary constitutional theory. His most recent publication is "Ancient Friends, Modern Enemies: Plato and Nietzsche on the Life Most Worth Living." He is currently at work on a book that explores Nietzsche's social and political thought in the light of his radical historicism.

Stephen R. L. Clark, professor of philosophy, Liverpool University, is editor of the *Journal of Applied Philosophy*. His current interests include political philosophy, animals, metaphysics, and philosophy of religion. Among his books are *Animals and Their Moral Standing*; *God's World and the Great Awakening*; *Civil Peace and Sacred Order*; and *Aristotle's Man*.

Michael J. Fischer, professor of computer science, Yale University, has served as a member of several U.S. national committees on scientific research, including the Advisory Committee to the National Science Foundation and the Committee on Recommendations for U.S. Army Basic Scientific Research. Former editor in chief of the *Journal of the Association for Computing Machinery*, he is a frequent contributor to technical journals such as *Journal of Algorithms*, *Journal of Cryptology*, and *Theoretical Computer Science*.

Jeffrey Macy, senior lecturer in the political science department at the Hebrew University of Jerusalem, was the Jacob Perlow visiting professor in Judaic studies at Yale University. He has held visiting appointments in Jewish thought, political thought, philosophy, and religious studies at Yale University, Harvard University, Wesleyan University, and the University of Tulsa. He has written extensively on medieval Jewish and Islamic thought with an emphasis on the relationship between religion and politics.

Cary J. Nederman, associate professor of political science at the University of Arizona, writes on Aristotle, constitutionalism, and community in medieval political thought. His books include *Medieval Aristotelianism and Its Limits: Classical Traditions in Moral and Political Philosophy, 12th-15th Centuries* and *Difference and Dissent: Theories of Toleration in Medieval and Early Modern Europe*.

Susan Neiman, associate professor of philosophy, Tel Aviv University, has written on Rousseau and the problem of evil, Kant in the analytic tradition, the legacy of Rawls, and other topics in philosophy and literature. She is author of *The Unity of Reason: Rereading Kant* and *Slow Fire: Jewish Notes from Berlin*.

Stephanie A. Nelson is assistant professor in classics and the core curriculum at Boston University. Her book *God and the Land: The Metaphysics of Farming in Hesiod and Vergil* studies Hesiod's understanding of the interrelation of nature, the divine, and the human, and Vergil's use of that understanding as a contrast to his own more ambivalent vision of reality. She is currently working on a study of the ideas of Necessity and Intelligence, the tension between them, and the need for both in Greek philosophy and drama from Hesiod to Plato.

Walter Nicgorski, professor in the program of liberal studies and concurrent professor of government and international studies, University of Notre Dame, is chief editor of the *Review of Politics*. He has published essays on Cicero, liberal and character education, the American founding, and Leo Strauss. He is coeditor of *An Almost Chosen People: The Moral Aspirations of Americans* and *Leo Strauss: Political Philosopher and Jewish Thinker*.

Clifford Orwin is professor of political science at the University of Toronto. His research interests range from classical and early modern political thought to current issues of liberal democracy and the theory and practice of humanitarianism, human rights, and higher education. He is author of *The Humanity of Thucydides* and coeditor of *The Legacy of Rousseau*.

Glenn Harlan Reynolds is professor of law at the University of Tennessee. His work on space law, constitutional law, and international trade explores the issues raised by the juncture of new technology and society, with an emphasis on individual liberties and economic growth. He is author of *Outer Space: Problems of Law and Policy* and *The Appearance of Impropriety: How the Ethics Wars Have Undermined American Government, Business and Society*.

Louis A. Ruprecht Jr., adjunct professor of philosophy, Georgia State University, and adjunct professor, Mercer College, writes on the connections between ancient Greek and modern thought, examining ancient and modern attitudes on tragedy, decadence, and the power of the erotic. He is author of *Tragic Posture and Tragic Vision: Against the Modern Failure of Nerve*; *Afterwords: Hellenism, Modernism, and the Myth of Decadence*; and *Symposia: Plato, the Erotic, and Moral Value*.

Stephen G. Salkever, Mary Katharine Woodworth professor of political science, Bryn Mawr College, is chair of the department of political science. His writings include works on the problems of liberal democracy, citizenship, and the political philosophies of Aristotle, Plato, and Rousseau. He is author of *Finding the Mean: Theory and Practice in Aristotelian Political Philosophy*.

Vickie B. Sullivan, associate professor of political science, Tufts University, has written on religion, Machiavellian republicanism, and the connections between Shakespeare and Machiavelli. She is author of *Machiavelli's Three Romes: Religion, Human Liberty, and Politics Reformed* and coeditor of *Shakespeare's Political Pageant: Essays in Politics and Literature*.

Norma Thompson, associate professor of political science and special programs in the humanities, Yale University, is interested in reassessing contemporary issues in the thought of philosophers of ancient, modern, and democratic political community. She is author of *Herodotus and the Origins of the Political Community* and articles on classical philosophy and literature.

Carroll William Westfall is professor of architectural history, University of Virginia. His special interest is the history of the city and the connections between architecture and the political life of citizens. He is author of *In This Most Perfect Paradise: Alberti, Nicholas V, and the Invention of Conscious Urban Planning in Rome*, and coauthor of *Architectural Principles in the Age of Historicism*. His current research examines the career of classicism in architecture and the origins and development of the American city.

Stephen K. White is professor of political science, Virginia Polytechnic Institute and State University. His areas of interest include modern and contemporary political theory, philosophy of the social sciences, American political thought, and American constitutional law. He is author of *Edmund Burke: Modernity, Politics, and Aesthetics*; *Political Theory and Postmodernism*; and *The Recent Work of Jurgen Habermas: Reason, Justice, and Modernity*; and editor of *Cambridge Companion to Habermas* and *Lifeworld and Politics*.